# THE EFFECTIVE SPECIAL EDUCATION TEACHER

## A Practical Guide for Success

**Laurie U. deBettencourt**
Johns Hopkins University

**Lori A. Howard**
University of Virginia

PEARSON

Merrill
Prentice Hall

Upper Saddle River, New Jersey
Columbus, Ohio

**Library of Congress Cataloging-in-Publication Data**

deBettencourt, Laurie Ungerleider
  The effective special education teacher : a practical guide for success / Laurie U. deBettencourt & Lori Howard.
    p. cm.
  ISBN 0-13-196192-6
  1. Special education teachers.   2. First year teachers.   3. Effective teaching.   I. Howard, Lori   II. Title.
  LC4019.8.D43 2007
  371.9′043–dc22

2006040596

**Vice President and Executive Publisher:** Jeffery W. Johnston
**Executive Editor:** Ann Castel Davis
**Editorial Assistant:** Penny Burleson
**Production Editor:** Sheryl Glicker Langner
**Production Coordination:** Carol Singer, GGS Book Services
**Design Coordinator:** Diane C. Lorenzo
**Cover Designer:** Jeff Vanik
**Cover Image:** Getty One
**Production Manager:** Laura Messerly
**Director of Marketing:** David Gesell
**Marketing Manager:** Autumn Purdy
**Marketing Coordinator:** Brian Mounts

This book was set in Korinna by GGS Book Services. It was printed and bound by Bind-Rite/Command Web. The cover was printed by Coral Graphic Services, Inc.

Pearson Education Ltd.
Pearson Education Singapore Pte. Ltd.
Pearson Education Canada, Ltd.
Pearson Education—Japan

Pearson Education Australia Pty. Limited
Pearson Education North Asia Ltd.
Pearson Educación de Mexico, S.A. de C.V.
Pearson Education Malaysia Pte. Ltd.

10 9 8 7 6 5 4 3 2
ISBN: 0-13-196192-6

*To Dan, Justin, Megan, and Sandi (my first teacher)*

*To Craig*

# Teacher Preparation Classroom

**TEACHER PREP**

MERRILL
PRENTICE HALL

## Your Class. Their Careers. Our Future. Will your students be prepared?

We invite you to explore our new, innovative and engaging website and all that it has to offer you, your course, and tomorrow's educators! Organized around the major courses pre-service teachers take, the Teacher Preparation site provides media, student/teacher artifacts, strategies, research articles, and other resources to equip your students with the quality tools needed to excel in their courses and prepare them for their first classroom.

This ultimate on-line education resource is available at no cost, when packaged with a Merrill text, and will provide you and your students access to:

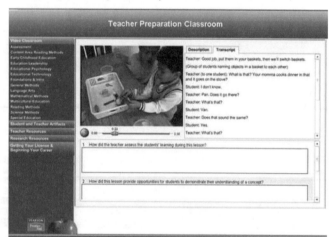

**Online Video Library.** More than 150 video clips—each tied to a course topic and framed by learning goals and Praxis-type questions—capture real teachers and students working in real classrooms, as well as in-depth interviews with both students and educators.

**Student and Teacher Artifacts.** More than 200 student and teacher classroom artifacts—each tied to a course topic and framed by learning goals and application questions—provide a wealth of materials and experiences to help make your study to become a professional teacher more concrete and hands-on.

**Research Articles.** Over 500 articles from ASCD's renowned journal *Educational Leadership*. The site also includes Research Navigator, a searchable database of additional educational journals.

**Teaching Strategies**. Over 500 strategies and lesson plans for you to use when you become a practicing professional.

**Licensure and Career Tools.** Resources devoted to helping you pass your licensure exam; learn standards, law, and public policies; plan a teaching portfolio; and succeed in your first year of teaching.

## How to ORDER *Teacher Prep* for you and your students:

For students to receive a *Teacher Prep* Access Code with this text, instructors *must* provide a special value pack ISBN number on their textbook order form. To receive this special ISBN, please email **Merrill.marketing@pearsoned.com** and provide the following information:
- Name and Affiliation
- Author/Title/Edition of Merrill text

Upon ordering *Teacher Prep* for their students, instructors will be given a lifetime Teacher Prep Access Code.

# PREFACE

Learning to teach is exciting and complex. The first few years of teaching are considered critical. During a teacher's initial steps in the education field, he or she is concerned about the "what" and the "how" of teaching. The fact that the day has only 24 hours in it often leaves many teachers asking for more time. Teachers' daily decisions concerning which instructional and behavioral methods to use in their classrooms are difficult ones. The responsibility to make the choice of any single method can seem awesome, particularly for beginning teachers, who will be exposed to hundreds of methods during their training. The methods they choose are critical.

The *Effective Special Education Teacher: A Practical Guide for Success* introduces not only the exciting field of teaching in the area of special education in public schools during the 21st century but also an overview of the current nature of public schools and the continuum of school placements used to serve students with special needs in these schools. This guide also discusses the professional and ethical standards of practice for special education teachers. The major focus of many of the chapters is on assisting new teachers with their decisions concerning planning units and lessons, writing individualized education programs (IEPs), managing classroom and individuals' behavior, and choosing instructional methods. Several areas of competencies for special educators are discussed, with practical suggestions and guides (e.g., templates, Websites, and resources) for each area based on current research. Thus, this guide, although written primarily for new teachers, will assist *all* teachers in developing their teaching competencies well beyond their first few months.

This guide is appropriate for college education courses usually titled Special Education Student Teaching or Student Practicum Experience. Most traditional special education training programs require such a course for state licensure. Most education schools also offer such a course as part of their graduate programs for career changers who are seeking "alternative licensure" or "initial licensure" in special education.

Both authors have spent many years in the field supervising new teachers. We incorporate into this guide suggestions based on the areas of concern brought to our attention by our teachers. Many of our teachers have commented that, as they begin their journey into teaching, they do not have the time or the energy to find the answers they need in their textbooks from the many courses they have taken. In *The Effective Special Education Teacher: A Practical Guide for Success*, we try to guide new teachers to success by discussing the issues of planning lessons, managing behavior, collaborating with others, working with diverse families, writing IEPs, and making instructional decisions. We include information for new teachers on how to have successful observations and evaluations as well as ideas on how to develop a professional teaching portfolio. We offer a great number of vignettes, guidelines, and templates that will allow for easy adaptation into a teacher's classroom.

We have been in the field for more than 30 years, and we would not have chosen any other field. It is exhilarating to be a teacher—especially a special educator. Welcome to all newly hired teachers—we hope this guide contributes to your success!

## *ACKNOWLEDGMENTS*

Preparation of a text is never accomplished by the authors alone. In this case, an idea was developed while supervising a grant-funded set of career changers who had chosen special education as their new field. We gathered many materials to try to assist them, and these materials mushroomed into this book. We work with many individuals every day who inspired, supported, and assisted us in this adventure. We gratefully acknowledge the support and encouragement we received from our editors at Merrill/Prentice Hall: Allyson Sharp and Ann Castel Davis, both of whom believed in this project and whose continued enthusiasm and persistent prodding helped get this book completed. Kathy Burk, Sheryl Langner, and Penny Burleson were instrumental in helping us with the details of production.

We also wish to thank the following reviewers for their valuable input and suggestions: Julia R. Bates, St. Mary's College of Maryland; Dawn J. Behan, Upper Iowa University; Kevin Callahan, University of North Texas; Doug Feldman, Northern Kentucky University; Ethel G. Jones, South Carolina State University; Deborah Metcalf, East Carolina University; Rhonda Collins Morton, Auburn University, Montgomery; Robert G. Simpson, Auburn University; and Lech Wisniewski, Metropolitan State College of Denver.

# Discover the Merrill Resources for Special Education Website

Technology is a constantly growing and changing aspect of our field that is creating a need for new content and resources. To address this emerging need, Merrill Education has developed an online learning environment for students, teachers, and professors alike to complement our products—the *Merrill Resources for Special Education* Website. This content-rich website provides additional resources specific to this book's topic and will help you—professors, classroom teachers, and students—augment your teaching, learning, and professional development.

Our goal with this initiative is to build on and enhance what our products already offer. For this reason, the content for our user-friendly website is organized by topic and provides teachers, professors, and students with a variety of meaningful resources all in one location. With this website, we bring together the best of what Merrill has to offer: text resources, video clips, web links, tutorials, and a wide variety of information on topics of interest to general and special educators alike. Rich content, applications, and competencies further enhance the learning process.

The *Merrill Resources for Special Education* Website includes:

- Video clips specific to each topic, with questions to help you evaluate the content and make crucial theory-to-practice connections.
- Thought-provoking critical analysis questions that students can answer and turn in for evaluation or that can serve as basis for class discussions and lectures.
- Access to a wide variety of resources related to classroom strategies and methods, including lesson planning and classroom management.
- Information on all the most current relevant topics related to special and general education, including CEC and Praxis™ standards, IEPs, portfolios, and professional development.
- Extensive web resources and overviews on each topic addressed on the website.
- A search feature to help access specific information quickly.

To take advantage of these and other resources, please visit the *Merrill Resources for Special Education* Website at

http://www.prenhall.com/debettencourt

# BRIEF CONTENTS

# CONTENTS

## PART II: DEVELOPING TEACHING COMPETENCIES

## PART III: EVALUATING INITIAL TEACHING EXPERIENCES

**CHAPTER EIGHT**    *Developing Your Teaching Portfolio*    **141**

**CHAPTER NINE**    *Evaluating Your Initial Teaching Experiences*    **153**

*Note*: Every effort has been made to provide accurate and current Internet information in this ook. However, the Internet and information posted on it are constantly changing, so it is inevitable that some of the Internet addresses listed in this textbook will change.

# PART 1

# Working in the Field of Special Education

# CHAPTER *One*

# *Being a Special Education Teacher*

## OBJECTIVES

After reading this chapter, the reader will be able to:

- describe the latest changes in and challenges of the role of the special educator in the 21st century;
- summarize the evolution of major federal laws that apply to serving students with disabilities in public schools today;
- identify the professional standards in the field of special education teaching;
- identify and discuss the ethics of teaching in the field of special education;
- identify strategies to prevent stress and burnout during a teacher's first years of teaching.

## INTRODUCTION

This chapter provides a brief introduction to the exciting field of teaching in the area of special education in public schools during the 21st century. It provides an overview of the current nature of public schools and the continuum of school placements used to serve students with special needs in these schools. The second section of the chapter discusses the professional and ethical standards of practice for special education teachers. The chapter concludes with a broad discussion of the profession in terms of what is happening nationally and how important it is to prepare special education teachers for their first years in the classroom so that they avoid stress and burnout. In each section, text boxes serve as guides for beginning special educators.

### *My Classroom*

Ms. Gonzales is finishing her training to be a special education teacher and excitedly looking forward to her own classroom of children. She is concerned about the possibility of needing more training now because of the newly implemented "highly qualified requirements." She also wonders whether the classes she has finished and the student teaching experiences she has had were enough preparation. Yet Ms. Gonzales is excited and optimistic. She can't wait to meet her children.

## FOCUS QUESTIONS

1. How do the roles and responsibilities of a special educator differ from those of a general educator?
2. What are several of the federal laws that apply to serving students with disabilities in public schools today?

3. What is meant by a continuum of placements in special education?
4. How can beginning special educators avoid stress and burnout during their first couple of years?

## TEACHING SPECIAL EDUCATION IN THE 21ST CENTURY

"Over the last several years, teacher education has become a front-burner political issue in Washington, DC, and in most statehouses" (McLeskey & Ross, 2004, p. 342). Many are asking if teachers are qualified in the disciplines they are teaching and, if not, how the situation should be remedied. Teaching in the field of special education is viewed differently depending on the political and social context of the viewer. Some have viewed teaching in the field of special education as a valued profession based on a set of programs with an empirically validated knowledge base of instructional techniques (e.g., Carnine, 1991). Others suggest that special education teachers should work only in general education classes as co-teachers so that students with special needs achieve with their peers while accessing the general education curriculum (Pugach & Warger, 1996).

It has long been believed that the preparedness and the quality of the teacher's training contribute more to student achievement than any other factor (Council for Exceptional Children [CEC], 2003; Darling-Hammond, 2000; Sanders & Horn, 1998). This belief has led to the inclusion of the highly qualified mandate in the No Child Left Behind Act (NCLB; Public Law [P.L.] 107–110) (Paige, 2002). Whether a teacher is "highly qualified" as defined by the NCLB is not an easy question to answer (Gelman, Pullen, & Kauffman, 2004). It depends on a variety of factors. In addition to the federal rules, each state has further clarified the meaning of several of these requirements, particularly the High Objective State Standard of Evaluation (HOUSSE). Therefore, it is important for teachers to check with their appropriate state agency to get the latest information on state requirements.

Currently, many states are in the process of setting guidelines for determining if a teacher is highly qualified (e.g., full certification, undergraduate course work in specific curriculum area, institutes of study in the area of teaching, and graduate classes for certification area). See Box 1-1 for more information on highly qualified guidelines.

---

**BOX 1-1**  *Highly Qualified Guidelines*

- As this book was put to press, many school districts were struggling to meet the No Child Left Behind Act (NCLB) requirements that suggest that teachers in Title I schools, hired before July 1, 2002, be "highly qualified" teachers by July 2006.
- The highly qualified teacher requirements apply only to special education teachers providing direct instruction in core academic subjects. Special educators who do not directly instruct students in core academic subjects, or who provide only consultation to highly qualified teachers in adapting curricula using behavioral supports and interventions, or selecting appropriate accommodations, do not need to demonstrate subject-matter competency in those subjects.

- Congress, at the time of this printing, is considering modifying how the highly-qualified teacher provisions of NCLB apply to special education teachers.
- The core academic subjects are English, reading or language arts, mathematics, science, foreign language, civics and government, economics, arts, history, and geography.
- The NCLB does not require current teachers to return to school or to get a degree in every subject they teach to demonstrate that they are highly qualified. The law allows them to provide an alternate method (HOUSSE) for experienced teachers to demonstrate subject-matter competency that recognizes, among other things, the experience, expertise, and professional training garnered over time in the profession.

**Certification Issues.** Currently, 47,532 special education teachers, or 11.4% of all those in the United States, lack full certification for their current teaching assignments. These teachers provide instruction for 800,000 students with disabilities (McLeskey, Tyler, & Flippin, 2004). Thus, the greatest shortage of highly qualified teachers with full certification is in the area where students have the greatest need for teachers with the most expertise: special education (McLeskey et al., 2004). In response to these shortages and the recent federal mandates (e.g., the NCLB), alternative preparations to traditional under-graduate certification programs are proliferating.

Alternative teacher licensing programs are usually programs that put individuals in the classroom quickly (see deBettencourt & Howard, 2004; Feistritzer, 2001; Zeichner & Schulte, 2001) with little course work or training behind them. Yet as Gelman and her colleagues (2004) suggest, no quick fixes in teacher preparation lead to greater student achievement. Rosenberg and Sindelar (2003) state that "at the same time that traditional teacher preparation pro-grams are subject to rigorous standards-based program reviews, local education agencies are permitted to hire less than fully qualified personnel and do so in large numbers" (p. 3). They also state, "There is a general recognition that valid and explicit professional standards are necessary for teacher preparation" (p. 3).

### Differences and Similarities Among General and Special Education Teachers and Their Classrooms.

All teachers need to be prepared across several competency areas. Many researchers believe that "special education instruction employs the same dimensions of instruction that all educators use, but it is more intensive, relentless, and goal-directed than general education is or can be. It is different instruction—not different in the essential acts that comprise teaching—but different in the degree to which they are used and the precision with which they are employed" (Kauffman & Hallahan, 2005, p. 53). "Pedagogy or teaching skill is at the heart of special education" (CEC, 2003, p. 7).

Where special education teaching actually takes place is often discussed and debated. Prior to P.L. 94–142, or the Education for All Handicapped Children's Act, later renamed the Individuals with Disabilities Education Act, most students with disabilities were taught in self-contained classrooms or in special separate schools by special educators. Many special educators were trained to "do their instructional magic" in their own rooms. Currently, after passage of more legislation dealing with special education, students with dis-abilities are provided instruction in their least restrictive environment (LRE), and many are mainstreamed in general education classrooms (Kauffman & Hallahan, 2005).

The LRE is defined as the educational setting where a child with disabilities can receive a free appropriate public education (FAPE) designed to meet his or her education needs while being educated with peers without disabilities in the general education environment to the maximum extent appropriate. A contin-uum of settings should be available for students with disabilities, although often they are placed full time in general education classrooms with or without con-sideration of other placements along the continuum. Such placements may or may not be accompanied by special educators consulting or co-teaching with general educators.

Such full-time mainstreaming or inclusion of students with disabilities in general education classrooms has placed increasing demands on the prepara-tion of both special and general education teachers. Teachers must provide instruction in a general education classroom, and some believe that the needed specialized instruction provided to students with disabilities served in general education is not individualized and does not produce achievement outcomes that are acceptable (Zigmond, 2003; Zigmond et al., 1995). See Table 1-1 for the continuum of placements available for students identified with disabilities.

**TABLE 1-1**   *Continuum of Placements for Students with Disabilities*

| | |
|---|---|
| **General education classroom** | The student's needs are met by the general education classroom teacher. No special education is required. |
| **General education classroom with consultation** | The student's needs are met by the general education classroom teacher with support from the special education teacher. The special education that is required is minimal. |
| **General education classroom with itinerant services** | The student's needs are met by the general education classroom teacher with support from an itinerant teacher. The level of special education is minimal. |
| **Resource room** | The student's needs are met primarily by the general education teacher with support from a resource teacher who may provide instruction outside the general education classroom. The special education required is not substantial. |
| **Self-contained classroom** | The student's needs are met by a special education teacher in a classroom with 15 or fewer students. The special education is substantial. |
| **Special day schools** | The student's needs are met by a special education teacher in a special all-day placement or center dedicated for students who need more specialization. The special education is substantial. |
| **Hospital or homebound instruction** | The student's needs are met by a special education teacher in his or her home or in a hospital setting. The special education is substantial, but may be time-limited. |
| **Residential school** | The student's needs are met by a special education teacher in a special 24-hour separate school setting. The special education is substantial. |

Beginning general education teachers are sometimes challenged by the needs of students served in inclusive classrooms and feel it is impractical in a classroom of 25 to 35 students to focus intensely on individual students (Zigmond, 2003). General educators' support for and willingness to implement appropriate instruction for special students appear to covary directly with the intensity of inclusion and the severity of the disability categories represented (Scruggs & Mastropieri, 1996). In addition, beginning special education teachers are challenged by their co-teaching and consultative placements, as they often are asked to serve as aides rather than as equal team decision-making teachers (Weiss & Lloyd, 2002; Zigmond & Matta, 2004).

Beginning general and special educators have many similar roles and responsibilities, yet some differences in responsibilities exist. Both need to understand the similarities and differences so that they learn to work together effectively to see that every student receives an appropriate education. To be effective, special education teachers need to understand their additional roles and responsibilities (Hallahan & Kauffman, 2006). See Box 1-2 for more information on roles and responsibilities.

**BOX 1-2**   *Roles and Responsibilities of Special and General Education Teachers*

| **General and Special Education Teachers** | **Special Education Teachers** |
|---|---|
| Work with students individually and in a group | Facilitate teachers' understanding of the laws applicable to students with special needs |
| Assess students' abilities | Provide instruction to students with special needs |
| Suggest students for more evaluation | Collaborate with other professionals to manage students with serious behavior problems |
| Participate in team conferences and meetings with parents | Facilitate use of specialized technology needed by students |
| Write portions of IEPs | Develop IEPs |
| Use technology | Serve as case managers for students with special needs |
| Collaborate with other professionals | |
| Deal with legal issues | |

Inexperienced teachers (those with fewer than 3 years of experience) are typically less effective than more senior teachers (Darling-Hammond, 2000). Effective teachers tend to be those who have a wide variety of teaching strategies. Doyle (1985) found that effective teachers adjusted their teaching to fit the needs of different students and the demands of different instructional goals, topics, and methods. No single instructional strategy has been found to be the most effective; rather, effective teachers use a broad array of approaches in the context of "active teaching" (see Lloyd, Forness, & Kavale, 1998). Several researchers have found that beginning teachers do not have all the knowledge of instructional approaches or the teaching skills that more experienced teachers do (Mumby, Russell, & Martin, 2001; Reynolds, 1995). Beginning teachers need more support to develop the skills necessary to determine the best instructional approaches to use.

New teachers are a "fragile and valuable resource" that require "care and support" (Rosenberg, Griffin, Kilgore, & Carpenter, 1997, p. 302). Support structures often provided to new teachers range from individual mentoring to collaboration and cohort instruction (Pugach, 1992). It is believed that beginning teachers need both psychological support and instructional support. Psychological support helps teachers build self confidence, become more self-reliant, develop a sense of efficacy, and better manage the stress of the classroom. Instructional support helps teachers develop the knowledge, skills, and strategies necessary for students' success (Brownell, Yeager, Sindelar, vanHover, & Riley, 2004). Teachers, particularly those who lack adequate certification, may need more psychological support to survive the challenges of the first year or two, whereas others may need only instructional support, as they are ready psychologically to focus on their instructional skills.

As part of their initial training, beginning teachers should be aware of their professional standards of practice. The next section discusses the current professional and ethical standards of practice in place for special educators.

## THE PROFESSIONAL AND ETHICAL STANDARDS OF PRACTICE FOR SPECIAL EDUCATORS

Central to any profession is its will to abide by a set of ethical standards and principles. Conducting oneself in an ethical and professional manner is an essential part of being a special educator. "Ethical issues lurk sometimes subtly behind and sometimes boldly in front of professional challenges in special education intervention, policies, research, and teacher education" (Paul, French, & Cranston-Gingras, 2001, p. 1). Although a code of ethics may not have played a significant role in teacher preparation programs in the past, professional ethical dispositions of teachers must now be addressed as part of the National Council for Accreditation of Teacher Education (NCATE) accreditation process. NCATE approved CEC's performance-based standards for the preparation and licensure of special education teachers (CEC, 2005). The CEC special education content standards are made up of 10 narrative standards. These standards parallel those of NCATE and the 10 Interstate New Teacher and Assessment Consortium (INTASC) principles. Standard 9 refers to a special education teacher's professional and ethical practice; that is, special education teachers should be guided by the profession's ethical and professional practice standards.

Beginning teachers may not know the specific ethical and legal requirements for special education. This section will help guide teachers in their understanding of the legislative requirements and ethical and professional standards for special educators.

**Legislation in Special Education.** It is important that all new special educators understand the major laws pertaining to services delivered to special education students. In 1975, the Education for All Handicapped Children Act (P.L. 94–142) passed, requiring that special education students have access to a FAPE and be educated in a LRE in the public schools. In 1990, the law was amended and renamed the Individuals with Disabilities Education Act (IDEA; P.L. 101–476). IDEA added several new requirements to the special education law passed in 1975, such as requiring transition components on the individualized education program (IEP), developing two additional categories (traumatic brain injury and autism), including more technology support, and clarifying the LRE. Again, the LRE is defined as the educational setting where a child with disabilities can receive a FAPE designed to meet his or her education needs while being educated with peers without disabilities in the general education environment to the maximum extent appropriate. It is important to remember that special education is not a "place" but rather a set of services. Similarly, the LRE provision of IDEA emphasizes services rather than placement.

In 1997, the law was amended again, but its name was not changed (Bateman & Linden, 1998). The 1997 amendments shifted the focus of IDEA to one of improving teaching and learning, with a specific focus on the IEP as the primary tool for enhancing the child's involvement and progress in the general curriculum. The law again was reauthorized in 2004 as the Individuals with Disabilities Education Improvement Act. This act aligns IDEA closely to the No Child Left Behind Act (NCLB), signed into law in the early 21st century, helping to ensure equity, accountability, and excellence in education for children with disabilities. While regulations implementing IDEA 2004 are being prepared, the regulations implementing IDEA 1997 remain in effect (U.S. Department of Education, 2005). See Figure 1-1 for the time line for laws pertaining to special education.

IDEA is a federal law that governs all special education services in the United States. In contrast, Section 504 of the Rehabilitation Act of 1973 is a civil rights statute. Yet Section 504 requires that schools, public or private, that receive federal financial assistance for educational purposes not discriminate against

**FIGURE 1-1**   *Special education legislation time line.*

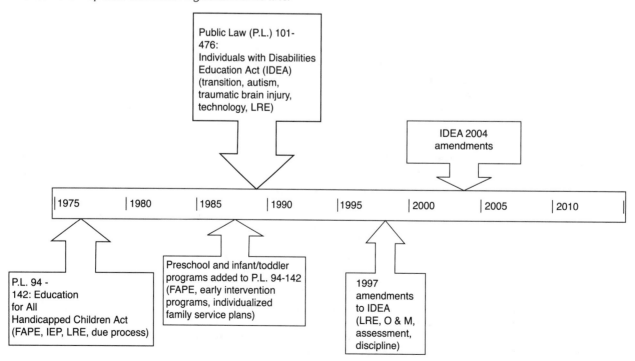

children with "handicaps." Schools must provide these students with reasonable accommodations comparable to those provided to their peers under the rulings of Section 504 (deBettencourt, 2002). Students who are handicapped but do not qualify for services under the regulations of IDEA may be served under Section 504 with an accommodation plan. Beginning teachers need to be aware of the similarities and differences between Section 504 and IDEA regulations so that they will know which law will guide them in providing the best services to students with disabilities. Figure 1-2 illustrates the questions to ask when determining whether a student should be served under IDEA or Section 504.

Another law that was passed in 1990 that also impacts students with special needs is the Americans with Disabilities Act (ADA), which ensures that individuals with disabilities are not discriminated against in areas outside the school, such as employment, public accommodations, state and local government, transportation, and telecommunications. The ADA's protection applies primarily but not exclusively to "disabled" individuals. An individual is "disabled" if he or she meets at least any one of the following tests: (a) he or she has a physical or mental impairment that substantially limits one or more of his or her major life activities; (b) he or she has a record of such an impairment; or (c) he or she is regarded as having such an impairment.

One other federal law that many beginning teachers may not be aware of is known as the Family Education Rights and Privacy Act (FERPA; 20 U.S.C.

**FIGURE 1-2**  *Questions to ask concerning the differences between IDEA and Section 504.*

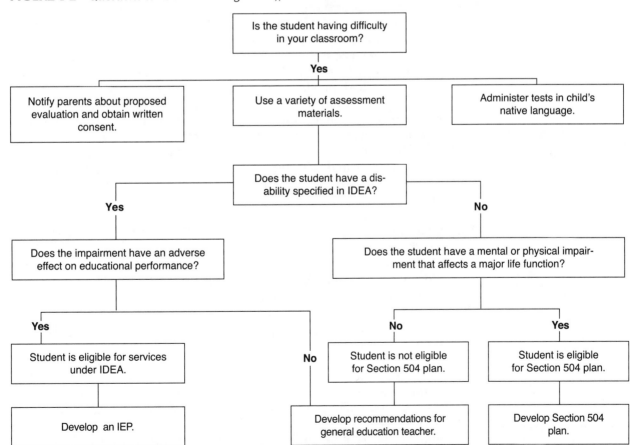

*Note:* IDEA = Individuals with Disabilities Education Act (amended 1997); IEP = individualized education program; Section 504 = Section 504 of the Rehabilitation Act pf 1973.
*Source:* From "Understanding the differences between IDEA and Section 504" by L.U. deBettencourt. *Teaching Exceptional Children, 34* (3), pp. 16–23. Copyright © 2002 by The Council for Exceptional Children. Reprinted with Permission.

§ 1232g; 34 CFR Part 99). The purpose of FERPA is to guarantee those with a right to know (such as parents and legal guardians) proper access to their students' educational records. In addition, school district personnel with a "legitimate educational interest," such as teachers, counselors, and principals may access and review student educational records. Beginning teachers need to know that all parental requests pertaining to access to the educational records of their children must be met within a reasonable time period. In addition, FERPA requires that school district employees maintain strict confidentiality of student educational records and other personally identifiable information in their custody and control. Release of such information to third parties should be done only with their written consent. Beginning teachers should be aware that they should not post lists of names of their students with special needs or chat about such students in a public forum (e.g., at McDonald's) (U.S. Department of Education, 2004).

New teachers also need to be familiar with two of the fundamental elements of special education laws in schools: child find and the IEP. Child find is the label attached to the requirement that school districts take an active approach toward identifying and serving students in need. Child find should be a continuous process of public awareness activities, screening, and evaluation designed to locate, identify, and refer as early as possible all young children with disabilities and their families who are in need of early intervention or preschool special education services. IDEA requires all states to have a "comprehensive child find system" in place and designate a lead agency to be responsible for planning and implementing the comprehensive system. In some states, the lead agency for these two programs (i.e., early intervention or preschool special education) is one and the same, while in others, different agencies oversee the two programs (see the following Web site for more details: http://www.childfindidea.org/overview.htm).

The IEP is the basic planning tool for the student's education and is developed collaboratively by school administrators, parents, and teachers (Bateman & Linden, 1988). Each public school child who receives special education and related services must have an IEP, each of which must be designed for one student and be a truly individualized document. The IEP creates an opportunity for teachers, parents, school administrators, related services personnel, and students (when appropriate) to work together to improve educational results for children with disabilities. The IEP is the cornerstone of a quality education for each child with a disability. (See Chapter 4 for more details on preparing IEPs.)

**Ethical and Professional Standards in the Field of Special Education.**
For over 75 years, the CEC has worked to develop and implement standards for beginning teachers. The premises of such developments are that "professional standards must come from the profession itself and that special education is an international profession, not limited to a single state, province or location" (CEC, 2003, p. ix). Beginning teachers should be made aware of the professional principles and standards approved by NCATE, INTASC, and CEC that guide their profession. See Table 1-2 for the outline of the CEC code of ethics and Table 1-3 for the outline of the standards for professional practice. "The code of ethics is made up of eight fundamental ethical principals to which all special educators are bound. The standards for professional practice describe the principles special educators should use in carrying out day-to-day responsibilities" (CEC, 2003, p. x).

Although few would argue that all teachers need to be aware of the ethics and standards for professional practice in education, few teachers take courses in ethics (Paul et al., 2001). As a beginning special educator, you should have received education and training in ethical issues so that you feel comfortable addressing the current dilemmas in assessment, instruction,

**TABLE 1-2** *Council for Exceptional Children's Code of Ethics*

"We declare the following principles to be the Code of Ethics for educators of persons with exceptionalities. Members of the special education profession are responsible for upholding and advancing these principles.

1. Special education professionals are committed to developing the highest educational and quality of life potential of individuals with exceptionalities.
2. Special education professionals promote and maintain a high level of competence and integrity in practicing their profession.
3. Special education professionals engage in professional activities which benefit individuals with exceptionalities, their families, other colleagues, students, or research subjects.
4. Special education professionals exercise objective professional judgment in the practice of their profession.
5. Special education professionals strive to advance their knowledge and skills regarding the education of individuals with exceptionalities.
6. Special education professionals work within the standards and policies of their profession.
7. Special education professionals seek to uphold and improve where necessary the laws, regulations, and policies governing the delivery of special education and related services and the practice of their profession.
8. Special education professionals do not condone or participate in unethical or illegal acts, nor violate professional standards adopted by the Delegate Assembly of CEC."

*Source:* From *What every special educator must know: Ethics, standards, and guidelines for special educators* (5th ed.) by The Council for Exceptional Children, p. 1. Copyright © 2003 by The Council for Exceptional Children. Reprinted with Permission.

**TABLE 1-3** *Council for Exceptional Children's Standards for Professional Practice*

**Instructional Responsibilities: Professionals strive to**

1. Identify and use instructional methods and curricula that are appropriate to their area of professional practice and effective in meeting the individual needs of persons with exceptionalities.
2. Participate in the selection and use of appropriate instructional materials, equipment, supplies, and other resources needed in the effective practice of their profession.
3. Create safe and effective learning environments which contribute to fulfillment of needs, stimulation of learning, and self-concept.
4. Maintain class size and caseloads which are conducive to meeting the individual instructional needs of individuals with exceptionalities.
5. Use assessment instruments and procedures that do not discriminate against persons with exceptionalities on the basis of race, color, creed, sex, national origin, age, political practices, family or social background, sexual orientation, or exceptionality.
6. Base grading, promotion, graduation, and/or movement out of the program on the individual goals and objectives for individuals with exceptionalities.
7. Provide accurate program data to administrators, colleagues, and parents, based on efficient and objective record keeping practices, for the purpose of decision making.
8. Maintain confidentiality of information except when information is released under specific conditions of written consent and statutory confidentiality requirements.

**Management of Behavior: Professionals**

1. Apply only those disciplinary methods and behavioral procedures which they have been instructed to use and which do not undermine the dignity of the individual or the basic human rights of persons with exceptionalities, such as corporal punishment.
2. Clearly specify the goals and objectives for behavior management practices in the persons' with exceptionalities Individualized Education Program.
3. Conform to policies, statutes, and rules established by state/provincial and local agencies relating to judicious application of disciplinary methods and behavioral procedures.
4. Take adequate measures to discourage, prevent, and intervene when a colleague's behavior is perceived as being detrimental to exceptional students.
5. Refrain from aversive techniques unless repeated trials of other methods have failed and only after consultation with parents and appropriate agency officials.

**Support Procedures: Professionals**

1. Seek adequate instruction and supervision before they are required to perform support services for which they have not been prepared previously.
2. May administer medication, where state/provincial policies do not preclude such action, if qualified to do so or if written instructions are on file which state the purpose of the medication, the conditions under which it may be

*(continued)*

**TABLE 1-3** *Continued*

administered, possible side effects, the physician's name and phone number, and the professional liability if a mistake is made. The professional will not be required to administer medication.

3. Note and report to those concerned whenever changes in behavior occur in conjunction with the administration of medication or at any other time.

**Parent Relationships: Professionals**

1. Develop effective communication with parents, avoiding technical terminology, using the primary language of the home, and other modes of communication when appropriate.
2. Seek and use parents' knowledge and expertise in planning, conducting, and evaluating special education and related services for persons with exceptionalities.
3. Maintain communications between parents and professionals with appropriate respect for privacy and confidentiality.
4. Extend opportunities for parent education utilizing accurate information and professional methods.
5. Inform parents of the educational rights of their children and of any proposed or actual practices which violate those rights.
6. Recognize and respect cultural diversities which exist in some families with persons with exceptionalities.
7. Recognize that the relationship of home and community environmental conditions affects the behavior and outlook of the exceptional person.

**Advocacy: Professionals**

1. Seek to improve government provisions for the education of persons with exceptionalities while insuring that public statements by professional as individuals are not construed to represent official policy statements of the agency that employs them.
2. Work cooperatively with and encourage other professionals to improve the provision of special education and related services to persons with exceptionalities.
3. Document and objectively report to one's supervisors or administrators inadequacies in resources and promote appropriate corrective action.
4. Monitor for inappropriate placements in special education and intervene at appropriate levels to correct the condition when such inappropriate placements exist.
5. Follow local, state/provincial, and federal laws and regulations which mandate a free appropriate public education to exceptional students and the protection of the rights of persons with exceptionalities to equal opportunities in our society.

*Source:* From *What every special educator must know: Ethics, standards, and guidelines for special educators* (5th ed.) by The Council for Exceptional Children, pp. 1–3. Copyright © 2003 by The Council for Exceptional Children. Reprinted with Permission.

philosophy of service delivery, and working with the families you face. The application and articulation of ethical theory needed to support special education practice are critical to the future of special education (Paul et al., 2001). For special education, the issue of ethics and professional practice is especially important because the students served make up a minority. The views that individual needs come before community needs and that "fair" does not mean the same as "equal" in terms of treatment are critical ethical issues. Educating students with disabilities in public schools today is a morally complex set of activities with many ethical challenges. As a beginning teacher, you need to be aware of your profession's code of ethics and set of professional standards. See Box 1-3 for guidelines on ethical behaviors.

## PREPARING SPECIAL EDUCATION TEACHERS FOR THE FIRST YEARS TO AVOID STRESS AND BURNOUT

Although many areas in education are experiencing teacher shortages (Boe, Bobbitt, Cook, Whitener, & Weber, 1997), the retention of special education teachers in particular is a critical concern for many school districts (Fore, Martin, & Bender, 2002). Some special educators are leaving to take other jobs in education (Brownwell, Smith, McNellis, & Miller, 1997), and others are

---

**BOX 1-3** *Ethical Behaviors*

As you begin teaching, remember to observe the highest ethical practices in relationships with other teachers, students, and the school administration in your building. Good judgment is important at all times, but the following rules are a minimum:

1. Promote growth in all your students. Apply your professional knowledge to promote student learning.
2. Consider confidential all data pertaining to student performances and conduct, such as scores on IQ tests. School walls have ears; be careful when you discuss students' behaviors with others.
3. Understand that culture and language can interact with exceptionalities, and become sensitive to the many aspects of diversity and individuals with exceptional learning needs and their families.
4. Avoid criticisms of the school or other school personnel. Encourage and support your colleagues to build and maintain high standards.
5. Keep abreast of the legal issues involved with the students with whom you are working.

---

leaving because of the stress of working with children with disabilities (Singh & Billingsley, 1996), in particular, students with behavioral disabilities.

Many stressors will be present as a first-year special education teacher, such as students with behavioral problems, lack of support from administrators, large student caseloads, co-teaching relationships, and paperwork responsibilities (Fore et al., 2002). Many of you began with great anticipation, excited to be taking your place in the classroom. Shortly, the reality of the skills and effort required to meet the needs of your children and the daily demands of your job may cause you to question your adequacy. The assault of reality early in your career may cause much stress.

The first step in stress management is to identify the sources and to re-examine your expectations. After you identify your sources, you must find and implement effective stress management strategies. Leaving your teaching at school, getting more exercise, networking with others to find solutions, keeping your humor, not scheduling all your leisure time, and so on have all been shown to help alleviate stress. You may need to make personal changes in the ways you accomplish your work or seek resources. The self-examination process can invigorate you. See Box 1-4 for signs of and solutions to stress in the field of special education.

Studies have shown that mentoring beginning teachers can help reduce the stress of the first year and elevate teachers' job satisfaction and retention (e.g., Whitaker, 2001). Many school districts provide first-year teachers with a mentor. If you do not have one, you should ask if one is available. Some school districts provide first-year teachers with special support programs. Take advantage of such programs. Other school district strategies have been recommended to reduce the first-year teacher's burnout (see Fore et al., 2002). At an individual level it is best to find a friend to keep you laughing, and be sure to celebrate the small successes of your students, try to work smarter (not harder) by networking, find time for the support programs your system has in place, and do not feel you must do everything perfectly your first year of teaching.

The decision to leave teaching in the field of special education is often complex and may be the result of many factors. Brownell et al. (1997) found that stress, certification status, and frustrations with workload manageability significantly predict a teacher's decision to leave. For some teachers, improving the working conditions of classrooms and schools by working with administrators may work. Other options include seeking professional support through attending graduate classes, participating in related workshops, or joining your professional organizations.

---

**BOX 1-4** *Signs of and Solutions to Teacher Stress and Burnout*

**Potential Signs: Do you**

Feel like not going to work or actually miss days?

Have difficulty concentrating on your teaching tasks?

Feel overwhelmed by your caseload?

Find yourself withdrawing from colleagues or engaging in conflict with co-teachers?

Have a general feeling of irritation regarding school?

Experience insomnia, digestive disorders, headaches, and heart palpitations?

**Potential Solutions: Try to**

Set realistic and flexible professional goals and objectives.

Establish priorities.

Network with colleagues.

Leave your work at school.

Pace yourself.

Use available professional opportunities.

Look for the "silver lining."

Keep your humor.

---

Most of us were drawn to teaching by our passion for our students and because we believe that by connecting our students to potent ideas, we will make a difference in their lives. We also believe strongly that we are engaging in meaningful work. It is hoped that the remaining chapters will help you prepare for your first years of teaching in special education so that you will be successful and choose to stay in the field. In the authors' view, no job is more demanding or more rewarding.

## SUMMARY

This book provides many suggestions to help special educators prepare to be successful during their first years of teaching. Sections are devoted to developing collaborative relationships, preparing individualized educational programs, writing lesson plans, selecting instructional and behavioral techniques, and understanding the teacher evaluation methods currently used in your classroom and school. Guidance is also provided in developing a teaching portfolio of evidence of highly qualified teaching, including the development of a reflection journal. Numerous reproducible templates and rubrics are available in each chapter to assist you. Welcome to the exciting world of teaching.

## ACTIVITY QUESTIONS

1. Discuss with your mentor how you see your role and your responsibilities in relation to your general education peers.

2. What are some of the challenges of your first years of teaching? How have you addressed them?

3. What aspects of the federal laws mentioned in this chapter do you deal with on a regular basis?

Who serves as your contact for guidance in following legal policies?

4. Meet with your peers and discuss ways for all of you to avoid stress and burnout. Did anyone have any ideas you had not thought of yet in your career?

## SELECTED WEBSITES

http://www.ed.gov/policy/speced/guid/idea/idea2004.html
*U.S. Department of Education—News and Information on the Individuals with Disabilities Education Act of 2004, the nation's law that works to improve results for infants, toddlers, children, and youth with disabilities.*

http://www.cec.sped.org
*The Council for Exceptional Children (CEC) is the largest international professional organization dedicated to improving educational outcomes for individuals with exceptionalities, students with disabilities, and/or the gifted.*

http://www.naset.org

*The National Association of Special Education Teachers (NASET) is a national membership organization dedicated to rendering all possible support and assistance to those preparing for or teaching in the field of special education. NASET was founded to promote the profession of special education teachers and to provide a national forum for their ideas*

http://www.nichcy.org

*The National Dissemination Center for Children with Disabilities is the national information and referral center that provides information on disabilities and disability-related issues for families, educators, and other professionals. Their special focus is children and youth (birth to age 22).*

http://www.eeoc.gov/facts/fs-ada.html

*The U.S. Equal Employment Opportunity Commission provides facts about the Americans with Disabilities Act on this Website.*

## REFLECTION JOURNAL ACTIVITIES

As you begin your first years of teaching, it is a good idea to keep a daily journal reflecting on how your days progress. The reflection journal can be an important component of your teaching portfolio. It is an opportunity to address your career development. In many districts, teachers are asked to provide self-assessment information as part of the performance review process. This journal provides the opportunity to develop your self-assessment skills while reflecting on your teaching experiences. These skills are important for future success in the profession. We have developed several reflection journal activities relevant to each chapter to help you get started.

1.  Discuss the laws relevant to special education with your special education supervisor. Does your school provide a written summary of these laws for new teachers?

2.  Talk to other teachers at your school and determine what they felt were stressors during their first two years of teaching. Do they have any suggestions for you on how to avoid the stress?

3.  What are your thoughts on the CEC organization or your colleagues' perspectives of the organization? Do you belong to any professional organizations that support teachers?

4.  Discuss the CEC's code of ethics and the standards of professional practices in reference to your current employment.

## REFERENCES

Bateman, B. D., & Linden, M. A. (1998). *Better IEPS: How to develop legally correct and educationally useful programs* (3rd ed.). Longmont, CO: Sopris West.

Boe, E. E., Bobbitt, S. A., Cook, L. H., Whitener, S. D., & Weber, A. L. (1997). Why didst thou go? Predictors of retention, transfer, and attrition of special and general education teachers from a national perspective. *Journal of Special Education, 30,* 390–411.

Brownell, M. T., & Smith, S. W., McNellis, J. R., & Miller, M. D. (1997). Attrition in special education: Why teachers leave the classroom and where they go. *Exceptionality, 7*(3), 143–155.

Brownell, M. T., Yeager, E. A., Sindelar, P. T., vanHover, S., & Riley, T. (2004). Teacher learning cohorts: A vehicle for supporting beginning teachers. *Teacher Education and Special Education, 27,* 174–189.

Carnine, D. (1991). Direct instruction applied to mathematics for the general education classroom. In J. W. Lloyd, N. N. Singh, & A. C. Repp (Eds.), *The regular education initiative: Alternative perspectives on concepts, issues, and models* (pp. 163–176). Sycamore, IL: Sycamore.

Council for Exceptional Children. (2003). *What every special educator must know: Ethics, standards, and guidelines for special educators* (5th ed.). Arlington, VA: Author.

Council for Exceptional Children. (2005). *CEC performance-based standards.* Retrieved January 11, 2006, from http://www.cec.sped.org/ps/perf_based_stds/standards.html#standards

Darling-Hammond, L. (2000). Teacher quality and student achievement: A review of state policy evidence. *Educational Policy Analysis Archives, 8*(1). Retrieved May 30, 2005, from http://epaa.asu.edu/eppaa/v8n1

deBettencourt, L. U. (2002). Understanding the differences between IDEA and Section 504. *Teaching Exceptional Children, 34*(3), 16–23.

deBettencourt, L. U., & Howard, L. (2004). Alternatively licensing career changers to be teachers in the field of special education: Their first-year reflections. *Exceptionality, 12,* 225–238.

Doyle, W. (1985). Recent research on classroom management: Implications for teacher preparation. *Journal of Teacher Education, 36*(3), 31–35.

Feistritzer, E. (2001). *Alternative teacher certification: An overview 2001.* Washington, DC: National Center for Education Information. Retrieved May 13, 2005, from www.ncei.com/2001_alt_ Teacher_cert.htm

Fore, C., III, Martin, C., & Bender, W. N. (2002). Teacher burnout in special education: The causes and the recommended solutions. *High School Journal, 86*(1), 36–44.

Gelman, J. A., Pullen, P. L., & Kauffman, J. M. (2004). The meaning of highly qualified and a clear roadmap to accomplishment. *Exceptionality, 12*, 195–207.

Hallahan, D. P., & Kauffman, J. M. (2006). *Exceptional learners: An introduction to special education* (10th ed.). Boston: Allyn & Bacon.

Kauffman, J. M., & Hallahan, D. P. (2005). *Special education: What it is and why we need it.* Boston: Allyn & Bacon.

Lloyd, J. W., Forness, S. R., & Kavale, K. A. (1998). Some methods are more effective. *Intervention in School and Clinic, 33*(1), 195–200.

McLeskey, J., & Ross, D. D. (2004). The politics of teacher education in the new millennium: Implications for special education teacher educators. *Teacher Education and Special Education, 27*, 342–349.

McLeskey, J., Tyler, N. C., & Flippin, S. S. (2004). The supply of and demand for special education teachers: A review of research regarding the chronic shortage of special education teachers. *Journal of Special Education, 38*, 5–21.

Mumby, H., Russell, T., & Martin, A. K. (2001). Teachers' knowledge and how it develops. In V. Richardson (Ed.), *Handbook of research on teaching* (pp. 877–904). Washington, DC: American Educational Research Association.

Paige, R. (2002). *Meeting the highly qualified teacher's challenge: The secretary's annual report on teacher quality.* Washington, DC: U.S. Department of Education, Office of Postsecondary Education. Retrieved May 13, 2005, from http://www.ed.voe/offices/OPE/Mews/teacherprep? index.html

Paul, J., French, P., & Cranston-Gingras, A. (2001). Ethics and special education. *Focus on Exceptional Children, 34*(1), 1–16.

Pugach, M. C. (1992). Uncharted territory: Research on the socialization of special education teachers. *Teacher Education and Special Education, 15*, 133–147.

Pugach, M. C., & Warger, C. L. (1996). (Eds.). *Curriculum trends, special education, and reform.* New York: Teachers College Press.

Reynolds, A. (1995). The knowledge base for beginning teachers: Education professional expectations versus research findings on learning to teach. *The Elementary School Journal, 95*, 199–221.

Rosenberg, M. S., Griffin, C. C., Kilgore, K. L., & Carpenter, S. L. (1997). Beginning teachers in special education: A model for providing individualized support. *Teacher Education and Special Education, 20*, 301–321.

Rosenberg, M. S., & Sindelar, P. T. (2003). *The proliferation of alternative routes to certification in special education: A critical review of the literature* (COPPSSE Document No. RS-10E). Gainesville: University of Florida, Center on Personnel Studies in Special Education.

Sanders, W., & Horn, S. (1998). Research findings from the Tennessee Value-Added Assessment System (TVAAS) database: Implications for educational evaluation and research. *Journal of Personnel Evaluation in Education, 12*, 247–256.

Scruggs, T. E., & Mastropieri, M. A. (1996). Teacher perceptions of mainstreaming/inclusion, 1958–1995: A research synthesis. *Exceptional Children, 63*, 59–74.

Singh, K., & Billingsley, B. S. (1996). Intent to stay in teaching: Teachers of students with emotional disorders versus other special educators. *Remedial and Special Education, 17*(1), 37–47.

U.S. Department of Education. (2004). *Family Educational Rights and Privacy Act (FERPA).* Retrieved June 6, 2005, from http://www.ed.gov/ policy/gen/guid/fpco/ferpa/index.html

U.S. Department of Education. (2005). *Special education and rehabilitative services: IDEA 2004 resources.* Retrieved June 4, 2005, from http:// www.ed.gov/policy/speced/guid/idea/idea2004.html

Weiss, M. P., & Lloyd, J. W. (2002). Congruence between roles and actions of secondary special educators in co-taught and special education settings. *The Journal of Special Education, 36*, 58–68.

Whitaker, S. D. (2001). Supporting beginning special education teachers. *Focus on Exceptional Children, 34*(4), 1–18.

Zeichner, K., & Schulte, A. (2001). What we know and don't know from peer-reviewed research about alternative teacher certification programs. *Journal of Teacher Education, 52*, 266–282.

Zigmond, N. (2003). Where should students with disabilities receive special education services? Is one place better than another? *The Journal of Special Education, 37*, 193–199.

Zigmond, N., Jenkins, J., Fuchs, L. S., Deno, S., Fuchs, D., Baker, J. N., et al. (1995). Special education in restructured schools: Findings from three multi-year studies. *Phi Delta Kappan, 76*, 531–540.

Zigmond, N., & Matta, D. W. (2004). Value added of the special education teacher in secondary school co-taught classes. In T. E. Scruggs & M. A. Mastropieri (Eds.), *Secondary interventions: Advances in learning and behavioral disabilities* (Vol. 17, pp. 57–78). Oxford, UK: Elsevier Science/JAI.

# CHAPTER *Two*

## *Collaborating with Others*

### OBJECTIVES

After reading this chapter, the reader will be able to:

- describe the role and function of a clinical supervisor during the first year of teaching;
- identify the characteristics of a successful relationship with a supervisor;
- identify and describe the necessary prerequisites for establishing a successful mentoring relationship;
- identify and implement successful communication strategies with a variety of school personnel;
- demonstrate an understanding of the importance of documenting all communication and establishing ongoing methods of documentation;
- develop a portfolio of materials that will facilitate communication and collaborative activities in a school environment.

### INTRODUCTION

This chapter provides an introduction for special educators working with others in school settings, including clinical supervisors and mentors, school professionals, and paraeducators. The first part of the chapter addresses the importance of communication between a new teacher and his or her clinical supervisor or mentor. The second part of the chapter addresses collaboration among school professionals, such as administrators, specialists, and paraeducators. In both sections, templates and suggestions are included to guide the teacher in developing his or her own communication systems and materials.

In the previous chapter, the laws pertaining to special education were discussed. A consistent thread among the laws has been the required involvement of parents, the recognition that other professionals are needed to help ameliorate the educational implications of a disability, and the emphasis on placement in the general education classroom (U.S. Department of Education, 2004). All these individuals (specialists and general educators) must work together to ensure that the student's educational needs are met. Thus, a fundamental principle of special education is the need for collaboration. This chapter includes suggestions on how to easily document communication among professionals, and several examples are provided.

## My Classroom

Finally! After all the courses, papers, and classroom observations, Miss Gellar is ready for her first day as a special education teacher. She arrives early and introduces herself to the school secretary, and her clinical supervisor provides a brief tour of the school. "Here's the teacher's lounge, here's a key to the ladies room, and you'll find the copier over there. By the way, we have an IEP meeting scheduled in 3 days." Miss Gellar, her head spinning, enters the classroom to prepare to meet the students she will be teaching.

### FOCUS QUESTIONS

1. What is the role of a clinical supervisor or mentor?
2. How can effective communication be established between school professionals and a new special education teacher?
3. How can a new special education teacher ensure collaborative working relationships with different school professionals?

## COLLABORATION

In the field of special education, the term *collaboration* is used extensively. It often seems that the first rule of special education is, "Thou shalt collaborate." The term *collaboration* is defined as "to work jointly with others or together especially in an intellectual endeavor" (Merriam-Webster, 2006). According to Friend and Cook (2003), for collaboration to be successful, the following must be acknowledged:

- Collaboration is voluntary—While this is the ideal, in reality special education teachers must collaborate to ensure that individual student needs are met.
- Collaboration requires mutual goals—Again, this is the ideal, but remember that all professionals working with a student should be committed to the student's success. The special education teacher may also function as the student's case manager and should maintain regular communication with all the team members to elicit their support for shared goals.
- Collaboration requires shared responsibility and accountability— Everyone working with a student should be responsible for implementing and monitoring the student's achievement. This should also include shared decision making among the team members.
- Collaboration requires parity among team members and sharing of resources—Every team member's contribution should have equal value, and the individual members should share ideas, strategies, methods, and other resources that will ensure the student's achievement.

Collaboration can be a frustrating or exhilarating experience for a new special education teacher, depending on the school culture, the individuals involved, and time constraints. Time management is one of the biggest challenges for new teachers (Pelletier, 2000). The challenge is complicated for new special education teachers by the paperwork needed for individualized education programs (IEPs). Documentation of communication among all the players (co-teachers and specialists) can be critical for the success of an IEP meeting and to support the student's educational achievement.

**Working with a Clinical Supervisor.** While the first few weeks of teaching can be exhilarating as theory becomes daily practice, it can also be overwhelming with daily lessons to plan and new people to meet. Simply learning a school's physical layout can be a challenge (e.g., "Where do I find the laminator?"). Schools have many different people to meet: principals, secretaries, custodial staff, instructional assistants, volunteers, other teachers, parents, and students. Among all the people to know, the clinical supervisor or mentor is critical to the success of first-year teachers.

During the first year or two of employment, the school district may assign new teachers a clinical supervisor or a mentor. The clinical supervisor is often another educator or professional employed by the school district who is given the responsibility of providing feedback to new teachers on their teaching performance. In some cases, this information is held in confidence between the new teacher and the clinical supervisor. In other cases, the information may be shared with the principal or another professional who is responsible for evaluating the new teacher's performance.

The clinical supervisor may be a professional within a school who has supervisory responsibilities, such as those of a special education department chair, or it may be another professional outside the teacher's school who is responsible for many new teachers. A new teacher should determine the professional status of the clinical supervisor or mentor assigned to work with him or her. In addition, school district policies and procedures should outline the responsibilities of both parties. These procedures should address areas of communication, paperwork, required in-service training, procedures in case of performance concerns, and procedures for conflict resolution between the clinical supervisor and new teacher (see Table 2-1).

**Working with a Mentor.** In some school districts, a new teacher may be assigned a mentor who does not have supervisory responsibilities and is not someone who will evaluate the new teacher. A critical difference exists between a clinical supervisor and mentor. A clinical supervisor may provide information for the new teacher's performance evaluation or be the person responsible for completing the evaluation. A mentor may provide guidance on

*TABLE 2-1*   *Template for Meeting with Clinical Supervisor*

| Name/Title: | E-mail: |
|---|---|
| Location: | Home Telephone: |
| Address: | Cell Phone: |
| Initial meeting date: | Schedule next meeting date: |

(Begin with listening! What does your clinical supervisor want to know about you and your teaching skills? What does your clinical supervisor want you to know about his or her supervision?)

**Questions to Ask:**

- How often will I be observed?
- How often and how long will our meetings be?
- What do you think is the most important thing for me to know about this school and class?
- What are your expectations for me?
- Do I need to complete paperwork for the school or district regarding supervision?
- What else do I need to know?
- How often and what type of feedback will I get?

- What is the best way to communicate with you (e-mail or telephone)?
- What paperwork (IEPs or lesson plans) do you need from me?
- Do you have any suggestions for professional development or training I should attend?
- Who at the school or district will the clinical supervisor's observations or reports be shared with?
- If a problem arises, what are the school's or district's policies and procedures to resolve the situation?

---

**BOX 2-1** *Professionalism*

Teachers are expected to maintain professionalism throughout their teaching careers. Consider the following:

- Confidentiality—Information on students, their parents, their disability, and their IEPs is considered confidential. New teachers should be careful about sharing information with others and in the places where they talk about students. Any concerns should be discussed with your clinical supervisor or mentor. Because of confidentiality, IEP documents should not be shared via e-mail, though e-mail can be used for scheduling meetings and sharing progress notes. Review your school's policies on the use of e-mail.
- Discretion and language—Teachers are role models to their students; therefore, it would be inappropriate to use profane language or to make a joke about a student. Teachers should also be cautious when using slang or sarcasm in the classroom.
- Attire and grooming—Most schools have dress codes, and the rules may be provided in the new employee packet provided by district. It is a good

rule of thumb to dress in a similar fashion to other teachers at the school. Teachers should also consider their responsibilities. For example, if you must supervise recess on the playground, stiletto heels may not be appropriate attire. Again, new teachers are encouraged to discuss any attire concerns with their clinical supervisor or mentor.
- Sick days—The district provides written procedures on whom to call and by what time when a teacher needs to take a sick day. It is helpful to be familiar with these procedures before a sick day is needed. Remember, this is another reason to regularly and consistently write lesson plans.
- Professional development and training—An important responsibility of all teachers is to stay current on new methods, strategies, and research. Every new teacher should join a professional organization (e.g., Council for Exceptional Children) and take advantage of training opportunities offered by the school district. The district's training offerings are a good way to continue growing in the profession and to network with other teachers.

---

instruction, classroom management, school culture, or any other related concerns without an evaluative component. The mentor may or may not be located in the same physical setting or school building. See Box 2-1 for information on professionalism.

An ideal mentoring relationship is based on confidentiality and trust, which often is inhibited if the mentor is asked to judge the new teacher's performance (Portner, 1998). In some school districts, a mentor is an experienced teacher who provides feedback and guidance but does not judge. A good mentoring relationship is established through the following four functions:

1. Relating—The new teacher and mentor need to establish good communication, build trust, and develop mutual respect. The new teacher should be encouraged to build on his or her existing teaching strengths and to develop skills in weak areas.
2. Assessing—The new teacher and mentor should collect data on teaching behaviors. Such data might include observations by the mentor, or the new teacher might share data he or she collected while teaching.
3. Coaching—The new teacher and mentor need to discuss experiences, ideas for enhancing professional skills, new strategies for instruction, and how to increase the new teacher's confidence. The mentor may also provide insight into how the school or school district functions.
4. Guiding—The new teacher and mentor should recognize that as the new teacher develops skills and confidence, dependence on the mentor will be decreased (Portner, 1998).

The mentor should help the new teacher develop a sense of independence and competence, not foster a sense of dependency (Palmer, 1998). Sometimes a mentoring relationship can last for many years, while other relationships terminate after a few months. This variability is normal, though more positive benefits are seen when the relationship lasts for at least a year (Portner, 1998).

As new teachers continue their professional development, they may want to become a mentor to other new teachers (Palmer, 1998). This can be a rewarding accomplishment and provide a way for a mentored teacher to provide guidance to others.

**Working with School Professionals.** All school communities have many people who serve various roles. Teacher education programs often provide information on titles and areas of responsibilities. While this is helpful information, it nonetheless can be overwhelming for a new teacher to put faces with names, and titles with areas of responsibility, especially when preparing an IEP. In addition, each school professional often has his or her own language or "jargon" that a new teacher must learn. Of course, every school professional must be prepared to complete multiple tasks within a limited amount of time (Friend & Cook, 2003).

Every new teacher must be prepared to work with the school administrator (principal) and other school professionals (Zutter, 2004). Recognizing that the principal, general education teachers, instructional assistants, and discipline-specific professionals each have different roles and perspectives can make this complex situation easier to navigate (Friend & Cook, 2003). Just like you, other school professionals are busy and have many responsibilities. Take time to introduce yourself and ask if the professional has any classroom strategies that they would like to incorporate into your instruction. A speech clinician may have suggestions for working with oral language goals, or an occupational therapist may encourage you to include activities using scissors. Try to follow through on these suggestions. In addition, a new teacher must establish regular and ongoing communication with all these professionals (see Tables 2-2 and 2-3).

**TABLE 2-2**  *Template for School Professionals Contact Information*

| | |
|---|---|
| School principal<br>Telephone:<br>E-mail: | Assistant principal<br>Telephone:<br>E-mail: |
| School psychologist<br>Telephone:<br>E-mail:<br>Students in common (initials) | Guidance counselor<br>Telephone:<br>E-mail:<br>Students in common (initials) |
| Special education chairperson<br>Telephone:<br>E-mail:<br>Students in common (initials) | Itinerant teacher<br>Telephone:<br>E-mail:<br>Students in common (initials) |
| Speech and language clinician<br>Telephone:<br>E-mail:<br>Students in common (initials) | 504 compliance officer<br>Telephone:<br>E-mail:<br>Students in common (initials) |
| Occupational therapist<br>Telephone:<br>E-mail:<br>Students in common (initials) | Physical therapist<br>Telephone:<br>E-mail:<br>Students in common (initials) |
| Reading specialist<br>Telephone:<br>E-mail:<br>Students in common (initials) | General education teacher<br>Telephone:<br>E-mail:<br>Students in common (initials) |
| Other professionals<br>Telephone:<br>E-mail: | Other professionals<br>Telephone:<br>E-mail: |

***TABLE 2-3***   *Template for Meeting Notes*

Date/time: _____
Purpose of Meeting: _____
Attendees: _____

**Agenda items:**                                    **Discussion:**

1.
2.
3.
4.
5.

**Resolution/follow-up:**                            **Responsible person:**
**Due date:**

1.
2.
3.
4.

Next meeting: _____

A special education teacher prepares lesson plans for students, provides the accommodations or modifications listed on a student's IEP, provides general education teachers a list of the accommodations or modifications for each student with special needs served in general education classrooms, and establishes ongoing communication so that any problems or changes can be addressed in a timely manner. In many cases, the special education teacher is also the person responsible for maintaining records of all the IEPs for all children served in a school (see Table 2-4).

**Working with Co-Teachers.** In many schools, special education teachers co-teach with general education teachers in inclusive classrooms. This practice has been fostered because the Individuals with Disabilities Education Act (and its reauthorization of 1997) requires that special education students have access to the general education curriculum, and often the general education classroom is the preferred least restrictive setting for students with IEPs (U.S. Department of Education, 2004). Research suggests that co-taught classrooms provide a smaller student-to-teacher ratio, reduce the stigma for special education students, increase individualized instructional support for students, and increase professional support for the teachers (Friend & Cook, 2003).

While some research has been conducted on the overall efficacy (i.e., increased achievement for special education students) of co-teaching, it is very limited (Magiera & Zigmond, 2005). However, as the No Child Left Behind Act has increased administrators' concern over the "highly qualified" and "content certification" designations for special education teachers, the use of co-teaching to serve special education students is likely to continue. Special education teachers should be prepared to co-teach.

Friend and Cook (2003, pp. 177–184) describe the following six models of co-teaching:

- One teacher, one observer—One teacher provides the instruction, while the other teacher observes a student, a group of students, or the entire class.

**TABLE 2-4** *Template for Accommodations or Modifications Checklist*

Dear *Name of General Education Teacher,*

*Name of Student* has an IEP with the following accommodations or modifications listed. The IEP requires that the listed accommodations or modifications be provided to help facilitate learning. Please contact me at *e-mail/telephone* if you have any questions.

Thank you,

*Name of Special Education Teacher*
Special Education Teacher/Case Manager

**Setting**
- ❏ Preferential seating
- ❏ Small group
- ❏ Individual study carrel

**Assignments**
- ❏ Shorter assignments
- ❏ Extended time
- ❏ Reduced level of difficulty
- ❏ Oral response
- ❏ Reduced paper-and-pencil tasks
- ❏ Use of computers

**Instruction**
- ❏ Planner or assignment book
- ❏ Taped lectures
- ❏ Reduced language or reading levels
- ❏ Shorter instructions
- ❏ Advanced organizers or note taking

**Testing**
- ❏ Oral exams
- ❏ Exams read to student
- ❏ Extended time
- ❏ Individual or small group

**Materials**
- ❏ Taped text or material
- ❏ Highlighted text or materials
- ❏ Braille
- ❏ Large-type text or materials
- ❏ Modified textbooks
- ❏ Calculator
- ❏ Assistive technology
- ❏ Keyboard modifications (touch screen or alternative input devices)

**Behavior**
- ❏ Frequent breaks
- ❏ Positive reinforcement
- ❏ Quiet time
- ❏ Behavior management plan (see plan)
- ❏ Excused to counselor's office

**Other**
- ❏ Use of FM system
- ❏ Health paraprofessional
- ❏ Other: _____
- ❏ Other: _____

Comments:

- One teacher, one drifter—One teacher provides the instruction, while the other teacher moves around the classroom, providing individual assistance as needed.
- Station teaching—Both teachers provide instruction, while students move around the classroom to stations. In some cases, one station is set aside for peer tutoring, homework, or independent work.
- Parallel teaching—Both teachers plan the instruction, while each teacher then teaches half the class at the same time.
- Alternative teaching—One teacher may provide small-group instruction, while the other teacher provides instruction to the whole class.
- Team teaching—Both teachers are responsible for planning and instruction for all the students in the class.

Every special education teacher should be prepared to use any of these co-teaching models with a general education teacher. Co-teaching has been described as a "professional marriage," and communication is critical between the two teachers (Friend & Cook, 2003). When beginning a new position as a co-teacher, plan to spend time getting to know your partner. Successful co-teaching is a partnership. It is also helpful to explore your and your co-teacher's likes and dislikes in the classroom. See Box 2-2 for some questions to consider about your teaching beliefs.

Successful co-teaching requires administrative support, ongoing professional development for the teachers, parity between the teachers, and joint planning time (Friend & Cook, 2003). Special education teachers are not curriculum specialists; however, they do have special expertise in strategies to help individual learners. Lesson planning for co-taught (inclusion) classes should address both the curriculum and the needs of individual learners (See Table 2-5).

**Working with Paraeducators.** Special education teachers must be prepared to train and oversee the work of paraeducators. Paraeducators may also be known as instructional assistants, teacher's aides, educational assistants, or paraprofessionals (French, 2003). Paraeducators are individuals who work in the special education classroom to provide assistance to the teacher. They may provide support services in a variety of classrooms: self-contained, inclusive, or general education.

---

**BOX 2-2**    *Teaching Beliefs*

The following are some questions to ask yourself when entering a co-teaching environment:

- What are your feelings and thoughts about the classroom environment? (Consider noise issues, placement of teacher and student desks, layout of classroom, your personal teaching space or desk, use of computers, blackboard, bulletin boards, and so on.)
- What are your feelings and thoughts about classroom management? (Consider discipline issues, what types of things will and will not be tolerated in the class, the levels of infractions of classroom rules, and whether students can eat or drink in class.)

- What are your preferences for instructional strategies? (How do you teach? Small groups, individual attention, lecture, or reading assignments? What types of methods do you find work best for you?)
- What is your philosophy of teaching? (Go beyond the common belief that all children should be successful and achieve in the classroom. How can you make a difference? How do children learn best?)
- What do you feel and think about co-teaching and working in team situations? (What aspects do you like or dislike? What works well for you? What difficulties have you had? Consider any other issues related to collaboration or co-teaching.)

---

**TABLE 2-5**    *Co-Teaching Lesson Plan Organizer*

General education teacher: _____
Special education teacher: _____

| | |
|---|---|
| Class (subject, number of students, time) | Homework assignments?<br>Who will collect and grade? |
| Topic of unit | |
| Lesson objectives | How will you evaluate progress on these objectives? |
| Relevant IEP goals | How will you document progress? |
| Materials needed | Who is responsible? (What needs to be prepared before the lesson?) |
| Sequence of instruction | Who does which instructional task? |
| What co-teaching techniques/strategies will you use? | Who is responsible for each technique or strategy? |
| How will you evaluate progress for the unit (tests, papers, or projects)? | Who is responsible for monitoring or grading each assessment (tests, quizzes, papers, or projects)? |

The paraeducator can work with small groups or individual students under the direction of the special education teacher. They may also work in a general education classroom providing support for a small group or for individual special education students. While their work will be overseen by a special education teacher, they must work closely with the general education teacher as well.

The teacher must provide the lesson plan and modify the curriculum; however, in some classrooms, the paraeducator is responsible for ensuring that the accommodations or modifications are implemented (Dover, 2000). Special education teachers may find it helpful to have the paraeducator gather documentation (work samples, homework, and grading) for progress toward an individual student's IEP goals. Often the school district or the school principal designates the responsibilities (or tasks) the paraeducator may be given.

The training and experience of paraeducators vary. In some cases, the paraeducator may have no experience or training in special education but exhibits a desire to work with children. In other cases, the paraeductor may be a retired teacher with many years of experience (French, 2003). In some schools, the paraeducator may have language skills that may be useful when working with students who are English speakers of other languages. The special education teacher should take the time to discern the unique abilities of any paraeductor assigned to them.

Many special education teachers enter classrooms without any training on how to work with or supervise paraeducators (French, 2003). It is always a good idea to first review the school's personnel policies and, if necessary, ask for further clarification from your department chair or principal. It is always best to prevent any potential problems by checking with your supervisors as to the roles and responsibilities allowed and then communicating clearly the responsibilities you delegate to the paraeducators working in your classroom. See Box 2-3 for tips on working with paraeducators.

---

**BOX 2-3** *Tips for Working with Paraeductors*

- Paraeducators are to provide support services for special needs students. They can provide accommodations (e.g., extra time or one-on-one), but the teacher should decide what is appropriate. Sometimes in the interest of helping the student a paraeducator may provide too much assistance, and a teacher will need to tactfully reinforce how important it is for the student to become an independent learner.
- Paraeducators may work with any student in a classroom. The needs of the special education students are to have priority, but any student requesting help can be assisted by the paraeducator. This is particularly helpful to teachers when a paraeducator is assigned to students in inclusive classrooms.
- Paraeducators may need training and guidance in working with special needs students. While a new special education teacher can be overwhelmed with teaching, it is his or her responsibility to ensure that a paraeducator can provide the support services needed. This may require that

the teacher provide on-the-job training for the paraeducator. Allow time for this in your planning. Paraeducators may be more knowledgeable about the school and students than the new special education teacher. In some cases, a paraeducator may have been employed for several years by the school before the new teacher begins working at the school. Welcome the paraeducator's insights and perspectives. Strive to develop a collaborative working relationship based on trust and respect.
- Paraeducators should be treated with respect. Take time to learn their names and personal interests. Find a place in the classroom for the paraeducator's personal belongings (e.g., coat, handbag, and lunch) (Riggs, 2004).
- Paraeducators need clearly defined responsibilities and expectations (Riggs, 2004). You should provide a daily list of responsibilities or tasks for paraeducators. Always find time to meet and plan with your paraeducators on a regular basis.

**TABLE 2-6**  *Template for Paraeducator Planning*

| Class/period/teacher: | Date: |
|---|---|
| Student(s):<br>❑ Individual<br>❑ Small group | Materials needed: |
| Accommodations/modifications | Lesson topic and objective(s): needed: |
| Student expectations: | IEP objectives: |
| Paraeducator tasks: | Documentation:<br>❑ Worksheets<br>❑ Quizzes<br>❑ Homework<br>❑ Other |

Comments/follow-up:

You can establish ongoing and regular communication with paraeducators through the use of notebooks, e-mail, or regular meetings. Pick a method that works best for both of you. A spiral notebook in which the paraeducator keeps notes during the day and one that you take home to review may make it easy for you to keep abreast of any issues the paraeducator may have (see Table 2-6).

## SUMMARY

This chapter provided templates and resources to help new special education teachers document their successful collaborations with the many individuals encountered in a school setting. Clinical supervisors/mentors provide important support in the professional development of new teachers and provide much-needed guidance during the first years of teaching. See the note for new teachers in Box 2-4.

Collaborating with school professionals to plan and conduct IEP meetings or co-teaching lesson plans can be challenging; however, through respect and communication, these relationships can be successful. New teachers can use the templates provided to guide their consistent documentation (e.g., student progress notes or weekly progress reports). Paperwork and documentation

---

**BOX 2-4**  *Note to New Teachers*

The foundation of good collaboration can be simplified to "develop good people skills." During your first few years of teaching, consider the following:

- Treat people with compassion and respect. Try to understand other perspectives. Develop your listening and questioning skills.
- Fulfill your commitments. If you agree to create, produce, or oversee something, make sure that you do it within the time frame when it is needed. (Be careful of over committing yourself, but do volunteer for some responsibilities or jobs that come up in faculty meetings.)
- Keep a positive attitude. Everyone has the occasional bad day, but do not become the

person who is seen as always negative or complaining. Try to find the positives.
- Clean up after yourself. Throw out your trash or wash your dishes in the teacher's lounge. Fix a copier jam or let someone know that it needs to be fixed.
- Attend school social functions. This might be a parent–teacher night, holiday party, or school carnival. This is a good way to get to know people on a personal level.
- Recognize that some conflict is inherent in any school. Differences in opinion can be resolved respectfully and without becoming personally negative.

**TABLE 2-7**　*Evidence Checklist: Collaboration*

To provide evidence of competency in the area of collaboration, a special education teacher might include the following in a teaching portfolio:

**Working with School Professionals**

❑ Copies of notes from meetings

❑ Copies of telephone calls and e-mails

❑ Copies of IEP team meetings

❑ Copies of accommodations or modifications for student(s) shared with others

**Working with Co-Teachers**

❑ Copies of joint unit or lesson plans

❑ Copies of telephone calls and e-mail

❑ Copies of trainings attended jointly

**Working with Paraeducators**

❑ Copies of assignment sheets given to paraeducators

❑ Copies of e-mail and written notes

❑ Copies of paraeducators planning documents

*Note.* Student confidentiality should be maintained. Please block out any identifying information.

management are ongoing processes, but every new teacher should adopt a system that can be easily employed. See Table 2-7 for evidence that could be provided to demonstrate teaching competency in the area of collaboration.

## ACTIVITY QUESTIONS

1. Discuss your expectations and goals for your first year of teaching with your clinical supervisor or mentor.

2. Introduce yourself to other school professionals at your school. Make an effort to "put faces with professions."

3. Discuss your expectations and teaching beliefs with your co-teacher (see Box 2.2).

4. Develop a portfolio or binder of materials that you can use for parent communication.

## SELECTED WEBSITES

www.naspweb.org
*National Association of School Psychologists—Includes information for parents, teachers, and psychologists. Many of their forms can be downloaded in PDF format.*

www.ncld.org
*National Center for Learning Disabilities—Has information for both teachers and parents.*

## REFLECTION JOURNAL ACTIVITIES

1. Reflect on what you would like to gain from your mentoring experience. Consider writing personal goals. What areas of teaching would you like to focus on? What skills would you like to focus on developing? What would you like for your mentor to help you accomplish?

2. Reflect on all the school professionals you have met and/or worked with and consider how you think you collaborate best. How does your perspective as a special education teacher influence your relationships with others in the school?

3. Reflect on how you manage the paperwork and documentation for your students. Consider your organization of paperwork. Consider how often you update student progress. Do you regularly collect work samples, homework, and quizzes? Have you developed a system that works for you?

4. Reflect on what evidence you can use in your teaching portfolio to demonstrate competency in collaborating with other school professionals. Consider making a list of all the documents you could include.

## REFERENCES

Dover, W. (2000). *The classroom teacher's guide for working with paraeducators*. Manhattan, KS: Leadership Lane.

French, N. K. (2003). *Managing paraeducators in your school: How to hire, train, and supervise non-certified staff*. Thousand Oaks, CA: Corwin Press.

Friend, M., & Cook, L. (2003). *Interactions: Collaboration skills for school professionals* (4th ed.). New York: Allyn & Bacon.

Magiera, K., & Zigmond, N. (2005). Co-teaching in middle school classrooms under routine conditions: Does the instructional experiences differ for students with disabilities in co-taught and solo-taught classes? *Learning Disabilities Research & Practice, 20*(2), 79–85.

Merriam-Webster. (2006). *Dictionary*. Retrieved January 4, 2006, from http://www.m-w.com

Palmer, P. J. (1998). *The courage to teach*. San Francisco: Jossey-Bass.

Pelletier, C. M. (2004). *Strategies for successful student teching: A comprehensive guide* (2nd ed.). Boston: Allyn & Bacon.

Portner, H. (1998). *Mentoring new teachers*. Thousand Oaks, CA: Corwin Press.

Riggs, C. (2004). To teachers: What paraeductors want you to know. *Teaching Exceptional Children, 36*(5), 8–13.

U.S. Department of Education. (2004). *Individuals with Disabilities Education Act*. Retrieved August 14, 2005, from http://ideadata.org

Zutter, T. (2004). Working with principals and administrators: Developing skills in politics and negotiation. In J. Burnette & C. Peters-Johnson (Eds.), *Thriving as a special educators: Balancing your practices and ideals* (pp.15–28). Arlington, VA: Council for Exceptional Children.

# CHAPTER *Three*

## *Working with Diverse Families*

### OBJECTIVES

After reading this chapter, the reader will be able to:

- identify and implement successful communication strategies for working with parents;
- develop strategies for conducting successful parent conferences;
- demonstrate understanding of the myriad influences and stresses on families with a special needs child;
- demonstrate sensitivity to the needs of diverse families;
- initiate a resource list of helpful organizations to be given to parents as appropriate;
- develop a portfolio of materials to be used for documenting communication with parents.

### INTRODUCTION

This chapter provides an introduction for special educators working with parents of special needs students. The first part of the chapter addresses the importance of sensitivity to the needs of parents and families while establishing communication between a new special education teacher and the parents of children on his or her caseload. The second part of the chapter addresses special circumstances that may affect the families of special needs children. In both sections, templates and suggestions are included to guide the teacher in developing his or her own communication system and materials.

In the previous chapter, the importance of collaboration among school professionals was discussed. In addition, a consistent emphasis has been made on the laws related to special education on parental involvement (U.S. Department of Education, 2004). Parents are to be included in all decisions regarding their child's individualized education program (IEP). The Individuals with Disabilities Education Act (IDEA) ensures that parents have the right to request or decline special services or, if not satisfied with an IEP, to request a due process hearing (Association of Service Providers Implementing IDEA Reforms in Education Partnership & IDEA Local Implementation by Local Administrators Partnerships, 2003).

While IDEA mandates parental involvement, establishing rapport with parents is vital to aiding student success. Documentation of communication with parents can be critical for the success of an IEP meeting and to support the student's educational achievement. This chapter includes suggestions on how to easily document communication and conduct conferences, and includes templates for the new teacher.

*My Classroom*

During his planning time, Mr. Balboa is writing notes home to the parents of students on his caseload. Mr. Balboa checks his voice mail and hears a frantic call from Mrs. Deere about her son. She is worried because her son forgot to bring his assignment book to school, and would have trouble remembering his homework. Mr. Balboa pulls out his student folder and dials Mrs. Deere's work number. He knows that a quick telephone call of reassurance, which he will follow up with the student, will alleviate Mrs. Deere's concerns.

**FOCUS QUESTIONS**

1. How should a special education teacher establish good rapport and communication with parents of children on his or her caseload?
2. How can informal parent meetings support student achievement?
3. How can a special education teacher effectively establish rapport with parents while respecting diversity?

## SENSITIVITY TO FAMILY NEEDS

The identification of a child as a special needs child can be a difficult, stressful event for parents. Some children are identified at birth or shortly thereafter, while other children may not be identified until years later when academic progress is slow. In all these situations, parents must realign their expectations for their child, adapt to a special education process that includes new concepts and language, and continue to parent all their children. This can be overwhelming.

Emily Perl Kingsley (1987) has described this experience as arriving in Holland when you prepared for a trip to Italy. Holland is a different land from Italy, and you must learn to speak a different language. Kingsley describes the confusion parents feel with the new terminology and different ways of doing things. She also discusses how the parents must meet new people and establish trust with them. Finally, she describes how parents come to understand and appreciate being in Holland while still mourning the lost trip to Italy. Many parents of special needs children appreciate this metaphor for the changes their families have experienced and recognition of their personal pain.

Many parents describe feelings of grief when their child is identified as a special needs student. These feelings are powerful, and parents can feel helpless in navigating a complex system of special education services. Teachers should be empathetic and strive to help parents understand the complexities while respecting their feelings.

While controversy has arisen regarding the theory of stages of grief, it may be helpful to consider the stages as described by Kubler-Ross (1969). It is important to note that Kubler-Ross was describing a process that ends in death, while the grief a parent may feel for a special needs child is not an actual death but more a loss of an idealized version of the child. Nevertheless, teachers should consider that parents will navigate certain stages as they accept their child's disability:

- Denial—In Kubler-Ross's description, this is the initial stage when a person does not believe that he or she is dying (Kubler-Ross, 1969). For a parent of a special needs child, this may be denial of a learning problem or the unrealistic hope of a cure.

- Anger—In Kubler-Ross's description, this is when the dying person becomes angry at his or her diminishing time in life and may lash out at family members (Kübler-Ross, 1969). For a parent of a special needs child, this anger may be directed at teachers, specialists, or other school personnel. It may be related to parents asking, "Why is this happening to my child?"

- Bargaining—In Kübler-Ross's description, this is when the dying patient tries to gain more time by offering a deal to God, doctors, or family members (Kübler-Ross, 1969). For a parent of a special needs child, it may take different forms, such as bargaining for a cure, searching for the ultimate accommodation/modification, or increased religious activity (Doka, 2000).
- Depression—In Kübler-Ross's description, this is sadness, helplessness, and feelings of loss (Kübler-Ross, 1969). For a parent of a special needs child, the feelings of sadness, helplessness, and loss may be very similar. Parents may need to be referred for therapeutic intervention if these feelings persist.
- Acceptance—In Kübler-Ross's description, this is when patients accept the finality of death and appear ready to die (Kübler-Ross, 1969). For a parent of a special needs child, the feeling of acceptance may signal when the parent has accepted the child's disability.

It should be noted that these stages are not rigidly defined and that parents may move through them at differing paces. A child's milestones (e.g., learning to read or high school graduation) may trigger parents to revisit earlier stages that may have been previously resolved.

Teachers should be sensitive to the parents' feelings and recognize that the stages may influence how parents interact with them. Specifically, parents may be angry about their child's disability, and this anger may be directed at the teacher. While it is very difficult to maintain equanimity in the face of parental anger, try to understand how the stages of grief may be a factor in the parents' reactions.

---

**BOX 3-1** *When a Student Dies*

One of the most devastating experiences for both parents and teachers is when a student dies. This is a profoundly sad time and teachers should consider how to assist the following people:

- The student's parents—Consider gestures of support, such as writing a letter to the parents sharing special memories of their child, attending the child's funeral/memorial service, packing up the child's belongings and work that are in your classroom, offering to listen as they share stories about their child, and offering to help them in other ways. Recognize and respect any cultural differences in how death is handled.
- The student's classmates—Consider how you will support grieving students. The school principal or counselor may provide support and guidance. Recognize that routine is important in helping students process their feelings. It may be useful to help students with their grief by drawing about their feelings, writing poetry, or finding a way to share a special memory of the deceased student (Doka, 2000). These activities should be developmentally

appropriate. Parents of the students should be kept informed of events and encouraged to help their child grieve.

- The student's teachers—Consider your own sadness and grief. What do you need to do to honor this child? Teachers will need to help their students through the sadness while maintaining professional demeanor in the classroom. This may be very difficult, but it is important to focus on helping the student's classmates express their feelings. Recognize that you may need to take some time for yourself, share your feelings with others in the school, attend a memorial service, and seek spiritual solace.
- Resources on death and dying can be found at the Web site for the Hospice Foundation of America at http://www.hospicefoundation.org. This includes age-appropriate material and bibliographies that may be useful to both parents and teachers. Leo Buscaglia's (2002) *The Fall of Freddie the Leaf* is a short book appropriate to all age levels that may help children understand life and death.

---

*BOX 3-2*   *Child Abuse Reporting*

---

If you suspect child abuse or neglect, you must report this suspicion to the proper authorities. Teachers should review school policies and procedures for reporting suspected child abuse or neglect at the beginning of the year. In some schools, the teacher should report the suspected abuse or neglect to an administrator who then notifies the appropriate agencies. Child abuse is a very difficult situation for new teachers, and it may be helpful to discuss any feelings or concerns with a mentor or department chair at the beginning of the year. Teachers are mandated to report suspected child abuse or neglect and by reporting provide a "safety net" for students.

---

On occasion, parents and teachers experience the actual death of a student. See Box 3-1 for guidelines on what to do if one of your students dies.

The presence of a special needs child in a family may increase feelings of stress for the parents. Consider how tired you feel at the end of a day or week working with students. Often, parents are employed outside the home while parenting on nights, weekends, and holidays. They may have more than one child to parent. Parenting is a full-time responsibility and is difficult.

Often teachers ask parents to supervise homework, check worksheets, or read to their child. All these are important foundations for school success, but consider the busy life of a parent. On returning home from work, a parent may need to prepare a family meal, give showers or baths to children, read mail, pay bills, follow up on work-related matters, listen to family members share the events of their day, and ensure clean clothes for the next day. These are the typical routines and stresses of most families that can be compounded for special needs families (Dyson, 1997).

An effective strategy for many special needs parents is to seek support from other special needs families (Hallahan & Kauffman, 2006). In some schools, the Parent-Teacher Organization has a subgroup for special needs families that provides social support and workshops on topics of interest to parents of special needs children. Other parents have found it beneficial to connect with other parents who have children with similar disabilities. Support groups also exist for siblings of special needs children. Special education teachers should begin to collect a list of parent organizations (e.g., contact information or Web sites) that they can provide as a resource to parents.

Unfortunately, some families are so fractured, stressed, or dysfunctional that students may be neglected or harmed. See Box 3-2 for guidelines on what to do if you suspect child abuse or neglect with one of your students. See Box 3-3 for guidelines on dealing with a school-wide traumatic event.

Finally, because of these complexities of life with a special needs child, special education teachers should strive to establish supportive and trusting relationships with parents of students on their caseloads. An important strategy for accomplishing effective parent–teacher relationships is ongoing communication.

## COMMUNICATION STRATEGIES

For a special education teacher, working with parents is one of the most complex, difficult, and rewarding aspects of the profession. IDEA requires that parents be an integral part of the IEP team; however, parents often feel overwhelmed with the IEP process (Patterson, 2000). The role of the special education teacher is to help parents understand their child's disability and the services provided. A special education teacher needs to establish excellent rapport, good communication, and a sense of common purpose with parents.

---

**BOX 3-3** *Trauma or Disaster Aftermath*

Every school has a prepared disaster plan, and this will be reviewed at the beginning of each school year. Teachers should be familiar with their school policies of what to do in a disaster, evacuation, or emergency. When a disaster or traumatic event does occur, teachers should consider how they will discuss the events with their students on returning to regular class schedules. Consider the following:

- The principal or school counselor may provide specific instructions on how to discuss events with your students.
- Keep parents informed regarding scheduled activities and available resources, and

communicate with them about any anxieties their child may express in class. Respect their wishes as to what and how much should be shared with their child. Recognize that you may need to increase the amount of communication with parents during these times.

- Know the resources that are available for helping teachers discuss traumatic events with students. The American Red Cross (http://www.redcross.org) and the National Association of School Psychologists (http://www.nasponline.org) have a variety of materials that teachers can use.

---

Typically, teachers send letters home to parents at the beginning of a new school year. This letter to the parent serves as an introduction to the teacher and provides information on how your class will be conducted. You should plan to send a letter home to all the parents of students on your caseload. Remember, a special education teacher may have a self-contained class or an inclusion class with another general education teacher or may provide case management services for any special needs students. See Tables 3-1 and 3-2 for examples of letters that can be sent to parents at the beginning of the school year.

Most schools plan a back-to-school night or an open house for parents and teachers to meet. These events are often near the beginning of the school year and provide informal face-to-face meeting time. Teachers should prepare a handout briefly describing class expectations and providing teacher contact information. This is also a great opportunity to ask parents to share information about their child. What would they like me to know about their child?

The general open-house meeting is not the appropriate time for an in-depth conversation about a child's problems. Should these types of concerns be raised, teachers should ask parents to call them to schedule a private meeting to discuss the issues more comprehensively.

---

**TABLE 3-1** *Introductory Letter to Parents*

Date

Dear Parents,

I am your child's new special education teacher. I am looking forward to getting to know your child and meeting with you. This year we will be working on *Insert subject matter, IEP goals, and special projects*. Please feel free to contact me when you have questions about your child's performance or just want to check in. My e-mail is *Insert email address*, and my school voice mail number is *Insert telephone number*. I can be reached at my home from 6 to 9 p.m. at this number: *Insert home or cell phone number*.

The school's open house (or back-to-school night) is scheduled for (*Insert date and time*). I look forward to meeting you and hearing about your child. Please bring with you a short note telling me about your son or daughter. I'd like to know about their strengths, areas you feel they need help on, and how you think they learn best.

Thank you.

Name

School

Your school telephone number/Your e-mail

**TABLE 3-2** *Introductory Letter to Parents (Co-teachers)*

Dear Parents,

We are the teachers for your child's *Insert grade or subject* class. We are looking forward to getting to know your child and meeting with you. This year we will be working on *Insert subject matter, IEP goals, and special projects*. Please feel free to contact either of us when you have questions about your child's performance or just want to check in. Our e-mail addresses are *Insert email address*, and our school voice mail number is *Insert telephone number*. We can be reached at home from 6 to 9 p.m. at these numbers: *Insert home or cell phone numbers*.

The school's open house (or back-to-school night) is scheduled for *Insert date and time*. We look forward to meeting you and hearing about your child. Please bring with you a short note telling us about your son or daughter. We'd like to know about their strengths, areas you feel they need help on, and how you think they learn best.

Thank you.

| | |
|---|---|
| Special Education Teacher | General Education Teacher |
| School | School |
| *School telephone/e-mail* | *School telephone/e-mail* |

Special education teachers should have a plan to establish ongoing and regular communication with parents. It is critical that such communication is documented and that a record of contacts with parents, the list of concerns, and the follow-up and resolution are detailed. With the use of e-mails and cell phones, communication is easier and often more frequent. Therefore, it is even more critical that the system you adopt allow for multiple means of communication to be documented. Telephone, e-mail, and notes home are all ways in which information about a student's progress, lack of progress, and any concerns can be communicated with parents. An example of a contact log can be seen in Table 3-3.

Remember to keep the documentation individualized for reasons of confidentiality. It is also helpful to keep the student's schedule on the contact log sheet as well as any other current teacher names and contacts in case a parent is calling and wants to know what class their child is in at the time of the call. It is critical to also have a column that is designated for follow-up. It is in this column that any resolution to any issue that occurs is documented. Tables 3-4 and 3-5 provide other templates that can be used to communicate with parents.

Special education teachers should recognize that parent conferences provide opportunities for communication with parents. While IDEA provides details on who should be present at IEP meetings and what role each participant must play, parent conferences may not be as scripted. New teachers may conduct several parent conferences prior to the first day of school. It is critical that new teachers know how to conduct parent conferences successfully.

A parent conference can occur as you wait to put a child on a bus or when a parent comes to collect his or her child for a dentist visit. Most meetings with parents may occur informally, but you always need to maintain a professional attitude and use good communication skills. Parent conferences may include unscheduled meetings, scheduled conferences, and home visits.

**Unscheduled Meetings.** Impromptu meetings can be disconcerting for teachers. It is always good to have each student's IEP (with documented progress for each goal) along with contact information and schedules at your fingertips. An example of a pocket folder that can serve this purpose is shown in Figure 3-1. When parents show up at your door, it is helpful to quickly determine what the parent wants to accomplish: Do they want to give you information? Are they angry or displeased, or do they want to get some information from you?

***TABLE 3-3*** *Parent or Guardian Contact Log*

Student Name _____     Telephone (H) _____
Parents' or Guardian's _____     Telephone (W) _____
Address _____     Telephone (W) _____
_____     E-mail _____

Student Schedule:

| Time/Block | Subject | Teacher/Room |
|---|---|---|
|  |  |  |
|  |  |  |
|  |  |  |
|  |  |  |
|  |  |  |
|  |  |  |

| Date | Who Initiated Contact? | How Was Contact Initiated? (Phone, Note, or Conference) | Reason | Follow-Up | Resolution |
|---|---|---|---|---|---|
|  |  |  |  |  |  |
|  |  |  |  |  |  |
|  |  |  |  |  |  |
|  |  |  |  |  |  |
|  |  |  |  |  |  |
|  |  |  |  |  |  |

If it appears that it may take time to respond fully to their request, answer briefly and ask the parents to schedule a more formal conference at a later time when you can give them your undivided attention and a more detailed response. In some cases, you should attempt to address the parents' concerns by listening and responding at the time they arrive at your door. Remember, if you have been called out of your class, you need to ensure that an appropriate adult is covering the activities in your classroom.

**Scheduled Conferences.** When scheduling a formal meeting with parents such as a parent conference, you should plan prior to the meeting, make an agenda for the meeting, and review your notes after the meeting. A complete discussion of IEP meetings is provided in the next chapter.

When planning for the conference, collect and review student work samples. Try to provide specific details and evidence or data to support your observations. For example, it may be most helpful to have a list of strategies that have been tried or suggestions for other strategies that you would like to attempt.

During the conference, listen to the parents' concerns and suggestions without becoming defensive. Demonstrate respect for parents through eye contact, tone of voice, and professional demeanor. Following the conference, it may be helpful to send home a summary of the meeting and to clarify any discussion of specific responsibilities between the parent and teacher. Table 3-6 provides a template for a handout for parents concerning parent conferences.

**TABLE 3-4**  *Template for Weekly Progress Note*

Student Name _____     Date _____

| Subject | Behavior | Study/Work Habits |
|---|---|---|
| Reading<br>1    2<br>3    4<br>Comments: | 1    2<br>3    4<br>Comments: | Missing homework assignments?<br><br>Comments: |
| Writing<br>1    2<br>3    4<br>Comments: | 1    2<br>3    4<br>Comments: | Missing homework assignments?<br><br>Comments: |
| Social Studies<br>1    2<br>3    4<br>Comments: | 1    2<br>3    4<br>Comments: | Missing homework assignments?<br><br>Comments: |
| Math<br>1    2<br>3    4<br>Comments: | 1    2<br>3    4<br>Comments: | Missing homework assignments?<br><br>Comments: |
| Other<br>1    2<br>3    4<br>Comments: | 1    2<br>3    4<br>Comments: | Missing homework assignments?<br><br>Comments: |

Parent Signature _____                    Please return this the next day.
Parent Comments

Any questions or concerns, please contact me.
1 = Unsatisfactory       2 = Needs Improvement       3 = Good       4 = Outstanding ☺

**TABLE 3-5**  *Weekly Progress Note to Parents (Middle or High School)*

Student Name _____     Date _____

| Subject | Behavior | Study/Work Habits |
|---|---|---|
| 1    2<br>3    4<br>Comments: | 1    2<br>3    4<br>Comments: | Missing homework assignments?<br>Comments: |
| 1    2<br>3    4<br>Comments: | 1    2<br>3    4<br>Comments: | Missing homework assignments?<br>Comments: |
| 1    2<br>3    4<br>Comments: | 1    2<br>3    4<br>Comments: | Missing homework assignments?<br>Comments: |
| 1    2<br>3    4<br>Comments: | 1    2<br>3    4<br>Comments: | Missing homework assignments?<br>Comments: |
| 1    2<br>3    4<br>Comments: | 1    2<br>3    4<br>Comments: | Missing homework assignments?<br>Comments: |

Parent Signature _____                    Please return this signed form the next day.
Parent Comments

Please contact me if you have any questions or concerns.
1 = Unsatisfactory       2 = Needs Improvement       3 = Good       4 = Outstanding ☺

**TABLE 3-6** *Template for Handout for Parents Concerning Parent Conferences*

I want our conferences to be helpful to you and supportive of your child's learning. The following are some ideas that might help ensure that our meetings are successful:

- I want to hear your observations and feelings about your child's learning. Your insights may help me to better work with your child.
- I want to make sure that I answer your questions. Please feel free to write your questions down before coming to the meeting so that they are not forgotten during our discussion.
- I want to be effective in my communication with you. Please feel free to take notes during our discussion and ask me to clarify if anything doesn't make sense to you. If you have suggestions for ongoing communication, please share these with me.
- I know that you are interested in what your child is doing in my classroom. Please ask me to show you samples of his or her work.
- I want to know about your child's past educational experiences. Please review or bring past records with you to the meeting.
- I know conferences can be hard to schedule. Please let me know how I can make this easier for you. Are there any special circumstances I should know about?

Please contact me if you have any questions. *Insert e-mail address and telephone number*

**Home Visits.** Visiting parents in their homes can provide a unique opportunity to establish rapport and gain insight into the student's functioning outside the classroom. Review your school's policies on home visits before conducting one. Recognize that some parents may be uncomfortable with a home visit and respect their needs. In some preschool and elementary education programs, home visits are conducted to provide parents with intervention strategies for their child (Hallahan & Kauffman, 2006). In some situations, it is appropriate to have a pair of professionals conduct the visit. Following a home visit, thank the parents for their hospitality. It is also a good idea to follow up with a written summary to the parents that highlights key points that were discussed.

FIGURE 3-1 *Use of pocket folder.*

**Dissatisfied Parents.** Sometimes, despite our best efforts, parents can become angry or unhappy about their child's services or progress. When parents get upset, teachers should demonstrate empathy, listening, and patience (McEwan, 2005). It is difficult to express empathy when someone is confronting you with anger, but attempting to stay calm helps the situation. The teacher may want to ask for assistance from a principal or department chair.

In some cases, parents are unhappy with the entire IEP team or with what the team has recommended for their child. Recognize that if parents disagree with the IEP team's goals or recommendations for services, IDEA provides a mechanism (e.g., a due process hearing) for these concerns to be resolved (U.S. Department of Education, 2004). Members of the IEP team should work together to minimize the need for hearings by ensuring that parents' concerns are heard and addressed.

## SPECIAL CONSIDERATIONS FOR WORKING WITH DIVERSE POPULATIONS

Schools in the United States are becoming more ethnically diverse, and this diversity may present unique challenges to special educators (Johnson, 2003). At the same time, individual family circumstances are becoming more varied. While sensitivity and respect are needed in all interactions with parents, some special situations may occur in schools, such as differing cultures and nontraditional families.

Many special education teachers work with students who come from other countries or cultures. These students may be known as ESOL-SWD (English speakers of other languages–student with disability). ESOL is preferred in some school districts over ESL (English as a second language) because often the student speaks more than just one language other than English. Of course, parents may also be ESOL, and communication in English creates a barrier to full participation in their child's education.

Some school districts may have multilingual secretaries or interpreters (for both oral and written communication) who provide support for families from other countries (e.g., Fairfax County Public Schools, 2003). If you use an oral interpreter, keep eye contact with the parent, not the interpreter. IDEA also requires that handouts on parental rights and responsibilities be provided to the parents in their native language (U.S. Department of Education, 2004).

In addition to language issues, special education teachers should be aware of and sensitive to other cultural issues. It is impossible to detail all cultural taboos, preferences, and differences; however, resources are available to assist the teacher. One readily accessible set of resources consists of the secretaries in your school. Often they know the families and the language. The paraeducators serving in your school may also be from the community and can function as informal cultural liaisons for a teacher (Patterson, 2000). Other resources may be available from the ESOL department in the school district.

While it is expected that some ESOL parents will have low levels of literacy in English, 13% of the adult population of the United States in 2003 was described as being below basic literacy (White, 2005). This represents over 30 million people who may not have the basic literacy skills necessary to read a newspaper (White, 2005) or notes from teachers. Schools are required to provide handouts on parental rights; however, many parents may not have the skills necessary to read or understand them. Consider how this may affect parents' ability to support their child's education or understand the language of an IEP.

Many special education teachers work with students from nontraditional families. Such families may include grandparents, same-sex parents, divorced parents, homeless families, and/or foster parents (Gorman, 2004). Each of these situations provides unique challenges and opportunities for communication. It is helpful for the teacher to remember that students' lives outside the classroom may affect their performance in class.

The prevalence of poverty and the impact of a lack of resources on a family with a special needs child can be devastating. In 2004, the poverty rate for children under the age of 18 was 17.8%, representing 13 million children (Denavas-Walt, Proctor, Lee, & U.S. Census Bureau 2005). While several different programs (Aid to Families with Dependent Children and free and reduced lunch) can ameliorate the effects of poverty, do not underestimate the consequences for families who must struggle to afford food, heat, rent, and clothing. Parents may have difficulty getting time off from a job to attend an IEP meeting, they may be unable to afford child care for siblings while they attend parent conferences, or they may send an ill child to school because they cannot take time off to care for the child.

Teachers should know the community resources available to low-income families and identify discreet ways in which help can be offered to families. Misconceptions exist about what community resources (food banks or clothing stores) and poverty programs (welfare or heating assistance) can provide. For example, food stamps can be used to purchase only food, not sundry items such as paper towels, toilet paper, soap, shampoo, or deodorant. Consider the social consequences for a child who does not have shampoo or deodorant at

**TABLE 3-7**   *Evidence Checklist: Working with Parents*

To provide evidence of competency in the area of working with parents, a special education teacher might include the following in a teaching portfolio:

- ❏ Parent contact log
- ❏ Copies of progress notes sent home
- ❏ Copies of telephone calls and e-mails with parents
- ❏ Copies of class newsletters and/or back-to-school letters
- ❏ Copies of IEP and documentation of progress
- ❏ Photos of parent conferences at back-to-school night

*Note.* Student confidentiality should be maintained. Please block out any identifying information.

home. Or consider the family who cannot afford to purchase a winter coat for their child. Families who have daily struggles for basic needs may not have the time or energy to supervise homework, communicate regularly with a teacher, or follow up on educational goals.

In all these cases, the special education teacher must remain professional and committed to establishing trust with the parents and other professionals who work with families. You should recognize how individual circumstances may affect the entire special education process for the student. For example, a grandparent may be too tired or lacking in knowledge to adequately help with a student's homework. A homeless family may not have the resources to provide for special class projects. A family going through a divorce may have difficulty communicating with each other so that IEP meetings may become fractious. In each of these cases, an understanding teacher can bring a positive influence to the situation. Remember, the student's learning and individual needs should be the focus of any communication or meeting.

## SUMMARY

This chapter provided a discussion of how special education teachers can be both sensitive and effective as they work with parents of students on their caseloads. Working with parents can be challenging, and teachers were reminded of how individual family circumstances may affect their working relationships with family members. The chapter included examples and templates that teachers can incorporate into their own practice. See Table 3-7 for evidence that could be included in your teaching portfolio for working with parents.

## ACTIVITY QUESTIONS

1. Discuss parental communication with more experienced teachers. What has worked for them? How have they established good relationships with parents?

2. Develop a list of Websites and resources that you can share with parents.

3. Reflect on a parent meeting or conference. What went well? What could have been done differently?

## SELECTED WEBSITES

http://www.air.org/cecp/schools_special.htm
*Center for Effective Collaboration and Practice—
Provides helpful information on behavior plans and
working with students who have emotional or
behavioral disabilities.*

http://www.familiestogetherinc.org
*Families Together provides helpful information to
families of children with disabilities.*

http://www.ed.gov/parents/academic/involve/
nclbguide/parents guide.html
*Provides a parent's guide with information for
parents on the No Child Left Behind Act.*

http://www.pacer.org
*Parent Advocacy Coalition for Educational Rights—
Provides information to parents about their legal
rights under IDEA.*

http://www.peatc.org
*Parent Educational Advocacy Training Center—
Provides training and information to parents on
how to become advocates for their child.*

## REFLECTION JOURNAL ACTIVITIES

1. Reflect upon all the stresses that every family
   experiences. Consider how this is complicated
   with the addition of a special needs child. How
   can you help simplify the life of a parent?

2. Reflect on how you document communication
   with parents. Consider your listening skills.
   Consider how often you communicate with them
   about their student. Do you contact them only
   when a problem arises? Or do you share
   positives too?

3. Reflect on your knowledge of community
   resources that can help families with specific
   difficulties (food banks or ESL classes).

Consider creating a portfolio or folder of these
resources to assist families as needed. Consider
how you can discreetly offer this help. What do
you need to know about your local resources?

4. Reflect on what types of evidence you can
   provide in your teaching portfolio that will
   demonstrate your competency in working with
   parents. Consider making a list of the
   documents you can include. Reflect on all the
   issues that arise when working with parents and
   how you can demonstrate your effectiveness in
   assisting parents.

## REFERENCES

Association of Service Providers Implementing IDEA
    Reforms in Education Partnership & IDEA Local
    Implementation by Local Administrators
    Partnerships. (2003). *Discover IDEA: Supporting
    achievement for children with disabilities—An
    IDEA practices resource guide.* Arlington, VA:
    Council for Exceptional Children.

Buscaglia, L. (2002). *The fall of Freddie the Leaf.* New
    York: Henry Holt.

Denavas-Walt, C., Proctor, B. D., Lee, C. H., & U.S.
    Census Bureau. (2005). *Current population reports,
    P60-229, income, poverty, and health insurance
    coverage in the United States: 2004.* Washington,
    DC: U.S. Government Printing Office.

Doka, K. (2000). *Living with grief: Children,
    adolescents, and loss.* Washington, DC: Hospice
    Foundation of America.

Dyson, L. L. (1997). Fathers and mothers of school-
    age children with developmental disabilities:
    Parental stress, family functioning, and social
    support. *American Journal of Mental Retardation,
    102,* 267–279.

Fairfax County Public Schools. (2003). *Culturally and
    linguistically diverse exceptional students.* Fairfax,
    VA: School Board of Fairfax County.

Gorman, J. C. (2004). *Working with challenging
    parents of students with special needs.* Thousand
    Oaks, CA: Corwin Press.

Hallahan, D., & Kauffman, J. (2006). *Exceptional
    learners: Introduction to special education*
    (10th ed.). Boston: Allyn & Bacon.

Johnson, L. M. (2003). *What we know about: Culture
    and learning.* Arlington, VA: Educational Research
    Service.

Kingsley, E. P. (1987). *Welcome to Holland.* Retrieved
    December 20, 2005, from http://www.nas.com/
    downsyn/holland.html

Kubler-Ross, E. (1969). *On death and dying.* New
    York: Macmillan.

McEwan, E., K. (2005). *How to deal with parents
    who are angry, troubled, afraid, or just plain crazy*
    (2nd ed.). Thousand Oaks, CA: Corwin Press.

Patterson, J. (2000). *Essentials for principals:
    School leader's guide to special education.*

Arlington, VA: Educational Resource Service and National Association of Elementary School Principals.

U.S. Department of Education. (2004). *Individuals with Disabilities Education Act.* Retrieved August 14, 2005, from http://ideadata.org

White, S., & Dillow, S. (2005). *Key concepts and features of the 2003 national assessment of adult literacy (NCES 2006-471) U.S. Department of Education.* Washington, DC: National Center for Education Statistics.

# PART 2

## Developing Teaching Competencies

# CHAPTER *Four*

## *Writing Individualized Education Programs (IEPs)*

### OBJECTIVES

After reading this chapter, the reader will be able to:

- identify and describe the required components of an IEP;
- describe and write appropriate IEP goals and objectives;
- demonstrate an understanding of the importance of documenting progress toward IEP goals and objectives for each student;
- develop a system for organizing IEP paperwork.

### INTRODUCTION

This chapter provides an introduction for special educators developing, implementing, and monitoring individualized education programs (IEPs). The first section of the chapter addresses the required components of IEPs. The second section addresses the importance of writing measurable goals and objectives as well as documenting progress toward these goals and objectives. The final section addresses conducting IEP meetings as well as initial eligibility meetings and transition planning. In all the sections, examples and suggestions are included to guide the teacher in developing his or her own documentation systems and materials.

IEPs make up the essential element that characterizes the profession of special education. In 1975, when Congress passed the Education for All Handicapped Act (Public Law 94–142), the IEP was mandated for all students identified as in need of special education (Association of Service Providers Implementing IDEA Reforms in Education Partnership & IDEA Local Implementation by Local Administrators Partnerships, 2003). Subsequent reauthorizations of this legislation (the Individuals with Disabilities Education Act [IDEA] of 1990, 1997, and 2004) have continued to focus on providing individualized education programs for students with disabilities (U.S. Department of Education, 2004b).

For many new special education teachers, managing the paperwork requirements of IEPs for all the students on their caseloads is difficult. Special education teachers must document progress toward IEP goals, manage time lines so that IEP requirements are met within required time frames, and develop ongoing assessment and instructional procedures so that the individual student's needs are met. These responsibilities are complex, and each teacher should strive for organization with paperwork. As IEPs are a fundamental responsibility of a special educator, IEP paperwork should be organized to ensure timely compliance with IDEA requirements. In addition, individual schools may have established deadlines or additional requirements (e.g., special education department chair notification or input from a school counselor).

When preparing a teaching portfolio, a special education teacher should provide documentation and evidence of his or her ability to successfully manage

IEP paperwork requirements. This evidence could include but should not be limited to samples of completed IEPs, student work samples documenting progress toward individual IEP goals and objectives, systems or templates used to ensure that required time lines are met, and samples of communication with other IEP team members. The following discussion should provide the new special education teacher with a review of IEP requirements and suggestions on documentation that can be included in a teaching portfolio.

## My Classroom

Ms. Wong is reviewing her calendar and weekly lesson planner to gain a sense of what is upcoming in the next few weeks. In addition to her teaching and staff meetings, she notes three annual IEP meetings. Ms. Wong has established good rapport with all the parents of students on her caseload, but she will have to make contact with all of them prior to the scheduled meeting. She'll also have to send e-mail reminders to all the IEP team members and solicit their input on students' progress. Ms. Wong makes notes on her calendar: "I'll have to pull my files with work samples on each student to check on their progress, too." "Which goals and objectives will need to be updated or changed?"

## FOCUS QUESTIONS

1. What are the essential requirements and components of IEPs that a special education teacher must be prepared to manage?
2. How can a special education teacher write IEP goals and objectives that are individualized, observable, and measurable?
3. Why is it important for a special education teacher to regularly and consistently document progress toward IEP goals and objectives?
4. How can a special education teacher establish and organize a system to ensure that all IEP paperwork requirements are met in a timely manner?
5. How can a special education teacher manage special circumstances relating to IEP meetings, such as an initial eligibility meeting or transition planning?

## INDIVIDUALIZED EDUCATION PROGRAMS

**Definition.** IDEA of 1997 (hereafter IDEA 97) defines an individualized education program (IEP) as "a written statement for a child with a disability that is developed, reviewed, and revised in a meeting" (U.S. Department of Education, 2004b). IDEA further requires that an IEP be in effect before services are provided to a child with a disability, that it describe the services and accommodations and modifications to be provided, and that parents and school district personnel agree on the IEP and detail responsibility for implementing the IEP (Association of Service Providers Implementing IDEA Reforms in Education Partnership & IDEA Local Implementation by Local Administrators Partnerships, 2003).

A focus of the IDEA 97 requirements for IEPs is to help ensure that students with disabilities have access to the general education curriculum (Patterson, 2000). While it may seem simplistic to emphasize that an IEP must be individualized for the student with a disability, a special education teacher must consider what specific modifications and/or accommodations each student needs to access the general education curriculum. These modifications

---

**BOX 4-1**   *IEP Components*

IDEA requires that IEPs contain the following components:

- A description of the student's present level of performance (PLOP). IDEA 2005 has changed this to "present levels of academic achievement and functional performance" (PLAAFP) (U.S. Department of Education, 2004b).
- A description of how the student's disability affects his or her participation and progress in the general education curriculum.
- A description of measurable annual goals/objectives and how they will be assessed.
- A description of the special education services provided to the student, including any school supports, personnel, and/or accommodations or modifications needed to ensure progress in the general education curriculum. This should include type of service, frequency, location, and amount of service.

- A description of how progress will be measured and reported. This also includes how the parents will be informed regularly of their student's progress.
- A description of any needed accommodations or modifications for the student to participate in district- or statewide assessments. If the IEP team determines that it is not appropriate for the student to participate in these assessments, they should include a description of why the assessment is inappropriate and how the student will be assessed.
- A description of other services or accommodations as needed, such as transition planning, assistive technology, behavior plans, and participation with English speakers of other languages.

---

*Source:* Adapted from Association of Service Providers Implementing IDEA Reforms in Education Partnership & IDEA Local Implementation by Local Administrators Partnerships (2003).

may vary significantly, depending on the student's disability and the content of the curriculum. An IEP should reflect these considerations. See Box 4-1 on IEP components.

An IEP should also contain a statement about whether the student will participate in state- or districtwide assessments and whether the student will participate in the state or district assessment with or without accommodations (Wright & Wright, 2005). The IEP team may determine that the student will not participate in the state or district assessment and that an alternative assessment will be used. The IEP will then contain a statement about why the student cannot participate in the assessment and why the alternative assessment is appropriate for this student (U.S. Department of Education, 2004).

**Managing IEPs.** Many new special education teachers find the IEP process overwhelming because the paperwork is so detailed and legally defined. Depending on the disability and the needed accommodations, IEPs can contain in excess of 30 pages. Finding the time to read through such a detailed IEP may be difficult, not to mention gaining a comprehensive understanding of the individual student's needs. Nevertheless, one of the first tasks for a new special education teacher should be to review the IEPs for students on their caseloads.

The IEP provides a comprehensive plan for how the student will participate in the general education curriculum and what services, accommodations, or modifications the student needs to be successful (U.S. Department of Education Office of Special Education Programs, 2000). The new special education teacher may also want to review the student's personal data file to gain further knowledge of assessments, grades, extracurricular activities, and other issues. While it may seem time consuming to read through all these documents, this is time well spent in getting to know the student and his or her IEP. After reviewing the student's file and IEP, a special education teacher should develop a system for ensuring that annual goals and objectives are monitored for progress, that parents are regularly informed of such progress, and that

*TABLE 4-1* IEP Overview and Signature Page

**Xperts School District**
502 NE 4th St
YourDistrict, WA

Student ID:
FTE Number:
Date of Birth:

## IEP Cover Page

Student's Name: _____ Date: _____

Student ID Number: _____ Grade: _____

DOB: _____ Age*: _____

Disability(ies) (if identified): _____

_____

Parent/Guardian Name: _____

Home Address: _____ Phone # (H): _____

_____ Phone # (W): _____

Most recent Eligibility date _____

Most recent re-evaluation date _____

Next re-evaluation must occur before this date _____

Date of Plan meeting _____

This IEP will be reviewed no later than this date _____

Date parent notified of Plan meeting _____

Date student notified of Plan meeting (if transition will be discussed) _____

Copy of Plan given to parent/student by (Name): _____ Date: _____

IEP Teacher/Manager: _____ Phone Number: _____

---

The list below indicates that the individual participated in the development of this Plan and the placement decision; it does not authorize consent. Parent or student (age 18 or older) consent is indicated on the "Prior Notice/Consent" page.

| **Excused** | **Name of Participant** | **Title** |
|---|---|---|
| ☐ | _____ | _____ |
| ☐ | _____ | _____ |
| ☐ | _____ | _____ |
| ☐ | _____ | _____ |

**\* The student must be informed at least one year prior to turning 18 that the IDEA procedural safeguards (rights) transfer to him/her at age 18 and be provided with an explanation of those procedural safeguards.**

**Date informed:** _____

If the parent did not attend, what method was used to ensure their participation:

**DEIDRE A. ZALE**

Student ID: 0000002058
FTE Number: F0000002058
Date of Birth: 03/01/1996

## IEP Cover Page

Student's Name: DEIDRE A. ZALE                                              Date: 01/19/2006

Student ID Number: 0000002058                                              Grade: 05

DOB: 03/01/1996          Age*: 10

Disability(ies) (if identified): Specific Learning Disablities

Parent/Guardian Name: CHRIS ZALE/ EMILY ZALE

Home Address: 5631 GERMAIN                                    Phone # (H): 9998765/ 9998765

RICHMOND, WA  23224                                          Phone # (W): 999-1010 / 999-1010

| | |
|---|---|
| Most recent Eligibility date | 01/17/2006 |
| Most recent re-evaluation date | 01/10/2006 |
| Next re-evaluation must occur before this date | 01/10/2009 |
| Date of Plan meeting | 01/19/2006 |
| This IEP will be reviewed no later than this date | 01/22/2007 |
| Date parent notified of Plan meeting | 10/17/2005 |
| Date student notified of Plan meeting (if transition will be discussed) | |

Copy of Plan given to parent/student by (Name): Beth Holland                    Date: 01/23/2006

IEP Teacher/Manager: Beth Holland                              Phone Number: (804) 967-0700

---

The list below indicates that the individual participated in the development of this Plan and the placement decision; it does not authorize consent. Parent or student (age 18 or older) consent is indicated on the "Prior Notice/Consent" page.

| Excused | Name of Participant | Title |
|---|---|---|
| ☐ | | Student |
| ☐ | | Parent |
| ☐ | | Principal/Designee |
| ☐ | | Psychologist |
| ☐ | | Speech Language Pathologist |

**\* The student must be informed at least one year prior to turning 18 that the IDEA procedural safeguards (rights) transfer to him/her at age 18 and be provided with an explanation of those procedural safeguards.**

**Date informed:** _____

If the parent did not attend, what method was used to ensure their participation:

---

*Source:* © Xperts, Inc. 2006.

any accommodations, modifications, or services needed by the student are in place. See Table 4-1 for IEP overview and signature page.[1]

A calendar can be a vital tool in developing a system for managing the IEP paperwork. Special education teachers should review when annual IEP meetings should be scheduled and make notes on a calendar. The teacher can then plan when to contact the IEP team to set up the meeting, coordinate obtaining work samples to document progress, and decide when new IEP goals and objectives should be drafted. It is recommended that teachers review their calendars during the first few weeks of school and begin to regularly update or modify important IEP dates as parents and other professionals add their input. A school or 9-month planning calendar may be helpful. Some teachers use a wall-size calendar that is made of erasable material so that they can see the entire school year at the same time. Remember that all names should be confidential.

Special education teachers have responsibility for drafting IEPs prior to IEP meetings. The student's case manager usually coordinates the IEP meetings and is responsible for ensuring that all forms are completed. In many cases (though not all), this will be a special education teacher. Since many IEPs may have multiple forms or pages, many teachers find this time consuming. Recently, school districts have begun providing blank IEP forms in electronic versions that are easily completed and then printed, thus reducing the time needed for drafting an IEP. (Caution: The actual IEP must be developed by the entire IEP team [including parents]; therefore, until agreement about the student's needs and services has been reached by the team, these documents are drafts. Parents should be provided these documents for review prior to the IEP meeting (e.g., Fairfax County Public Schools, 2001.) See Box 4-2 for Section 504 and Box 4-3 for family privacy information.

## GOALS AND OBJECTIVES

The IEP details the overall educational plan for a student, including accommodations and modifications, special services, and goals. These goals are critical to the success of the IEP because "the purposes of annual goals and benchmarks or objectives are to assess the appropriateness of the special services and to monitor the child's progress" (Bateman & Linden, 1998, p.43). New special education teachers must be prepared to write annual goals and objectives that can address these purposes.

The importance of writing clearly defined, measurable goals is vital to the success of the IEP for special education students. IDEA 97 emphasizes that special education students should make progress and that this progress should be accurately assessed and monitored (Bateman & Herr, 2003). Thus, goals and objectives must be written so that accurate and objective information on

---

[1]IEP forms shown in Tables 4-1 through 4-6 are provided courtesy of Xperts, Inc.

"Xperts, Inc. is a software development firm dedicated to delivering pragmatic and technological solutions. Our educational products division is a proven leader in the field and is passionate in our pursuit to deliver outstanding applications to the K-12 education marketplace. Our web-based special education management solution, **IEP.Online**, is designed to streamline the every-day process of special educators and allow them to reduce manual filling, track student data, manage administrative functions and most importantly, focus on children - not paperwork. Our development process not only involves intelligent thinking from within our organization, but we involve teachers, educators, IT directors, administrators and superintendents to help shape our products into effective educational tools. We strive for the ultimate customer experience, and our dedicated implementation, training and support teams exemplify our goals. To learn more about Xperts, Inc. and our educational products, please visit our websites, www.xperts.com and www.ieponline.net."

---

*BOX 4-2*  *Section 504: What You Need to Know*

Special education teachers are familiar with the IDEA. However, they should also be conversant with Section 504 of the Rehabilitation Act of 1974. While IDEA ensures that individuals with disabilities receive an appropriate education (Hallahan & Kauffman, 2006), Section 504 is a civil rights statute that ensures that students with disabilities have "equal access" to educational services (deBettencourt, 2002).

New special education teachers should identify the school's Section 504 compliance officer and familiarize themselves with the school's procedures for providing accommodations to students under Section 504. The following table provides some general guidance for special education teachers.

| | |
|---|---|
| Awareness of personnel | Teachers should know who serves as the School Based Chairperson for IDEA and who serves as the Section 504 Complaince Officer. |
| Awareness of forms | Teachers should know what school district forms are used to document the process of identifying and serving students under IDEA and Section 504. |
| Teacher documentation | Examples of students' inability to stay on task, emotional outbursts, and completed work should be kept on a daily basis. Copies of individualized education programs (IEPs) and completed forms should be available for review by the teacher on a regular basis. A record of all telephone calls and meetings with parents should be kept in a secure place. |
| Awareness of school policies | Teachers should keep a copy of school district requirements for Section 504 and IDEA. |
| Confidentiality | Teachers should keep all materials confidential, including names of children. |

*Note:* IDEA = Individuals with Disabilities Education Act (amended 1997); Section 504 = Section 504 of the Rehabilitation Act of 1973.

*Source:* From "Understanding the differences between IDEA and Section 504" by L.U. deBettencourt. *Teaching Exceptional Children, 34* (3), pp. 16–23. Copyright © 2002 by The Council for Exceptional Children. Reprinted with Permission.

---

*BOX 4-3*  *Family Educational Rights and Privacy Act: What You Need to Know*

Special education teachers need to be familiar with the Family Educational Rights and Privacy Act (FERPA), which is a federal law that protects the privacy of student records. In most cases, teachers and school officials cannot release information from

the student records without the written permission of the parent. In addition, parents have the right to review these records and to request changes if they think a document is inaccurate or misleading (U.S. Department of Education, 2004a).

---

progress can be ascertained. They should incorporate the special education teacher's knowledge about the individual student's needs, abilities, and achievement levels. After all, it is called an *individualized* education program.

Most special education teachers have had training in the writing of annual goals and objectives, and the purpose of this discussion is to provide a brief review, not a comprehensive text. Readers are referred to the IEP sources at the end of this chapter for texts and resources that can provide a more thorough review. The following four elements are important for successful IEPs: present level of performance (PLOP) goals, benchmarks and short-term objectives, and documenting progress.

**Present Level of Performance.** Many special education teachers provide this in a descriptive narrative. While this narrative may convey important information, it should also contain measurable descriptions of the student's current level of functioning. These descriptions should be able to serve as initial points in time against which future progress can be measured. A well-written

PLOP "must be specific, objective, and measurable" (Bateman & Herr, 2003) as well as an accurate portrayal of the student's current level of performance. In IDEA 2004, the definition of a PLOP was changed to PLAAFP, defined as "present levels of academic achievement and functional performance" (U.S. Department of Education, 2004b). Note that academic achievement and functional performance must be determined through objective data or assessment.

A well-considered PLOP or PLAAFP is important because progress on annual goals and benchmarks (short-term objectives) will be judged by the measures used in the PLAAFP (see Table 4-2). Consider the following example: "Currently, student is able to instantly and correctly recognize 20 words on the ABC sight word list" (Bateman & Herr, 2003, p. 45). This PLOP or PLAAFP provides a measurable (20-word) description of the student's performance. An annual goal that measures an increase in sight word recognition (by the end of the school year, the student instantly and correctly recognizes 120 sight words) can be formulated, and the PLOP provides a stating point for the measure (20 words) (Bateman & Herr, 2003).

**Annual Goals.** Once measurable PLOP or PLAAFPs have been established, the IEP team creates annual goals. A special education teacher may present drafts of these goals for review, but it is the IEP team's responsibility to agree on these goals and how their progress will be measured (U.S. Department of Education Office of Special Education Programs, 2000). Annual goals should reflect your professional assessment of how much progress a student can make on his or her individual goals for the year. While these should be observable, specific, measurable, and an estimation of the student's projected progress, they can be adjusted to reflect individual ability (Bateman & Linden, 1998). In other words, if your estimation of the student's rate of progress is inaccurate, the IEP goals can be modified.

A well-written annual goal reflects the measures stated in the PLOP or PLAAFP. Consider the previous example: The student could instantly and correctly recognize 20 ABC sight words (PLOP) (Bateman & Herr, 2003). The annual goal stated was that the student could instantly and correctly recognize 120 ABC sight words. Note how the annual goal is stated in the same measures (words) as the PLOP/PLAAFP (see Table 4-3).

**Benchmarks or Short-Term Objectives.** Once the annual goal has been formulated, the interim goals (short-term objectives or benchmarks) need to be determined. The annual goal is broken into smaller units, known as short-term objectives or benchmarks, that are the measuring points to monitor student progress. Thus, a measure or assessment of progress will be conducted on a regular basis (quarterly or monthly) to note the student's current progress toward an individual goal. Each annual goal should have two or more short-term objectives or benchmarks. (see Table 4-4).

Just as a well-written PLOP or PLAAFP is needed to formulate annual goals, well-considered benchmarks depend on well-written annual goals. Consider the previous example: The student will instantly and correctly recognize 120 ABC sight words (annual goal). PLOP states that the student's current level of performance is instantly and correctly recognizing 20 ABC sight words (Bateman & Herr, 2003). Benchmarks might be considered for the student to recognize 60 ABC sight words and then 90 ABC sight words.

At regular times throughout the year, the student's progress toward these benchmarks should be assessed. Once the student had achieved the 60-word benchmark, the new benchmark of 90 words would become the instructional focus. Finally, the student's progress toward the 120 words should be assessed prior to the following year's annual IEP meeting.

*TABLE 4-2*  *Present Level of Performance PLOP or PLAAFP*

**Xperts School District**
502 NE 4th St
YourDistrict, WA

Student ID:
FTE Number:
Date of Birth:

## Present Level of Educational Performance

Student's Name: _____  Date: _____

Student's Number: _____

The Present Level of Educational Performance describes the effects of the student's disability upon the student's involvement and progress in the general curriculum and area(s) of need. This includes the student's performance in academic achievement (reading, math, communications, etc.) and functional performance (behavior, social skills, daily life activities, mobility, extra-curricular activities, etc.) in objective terms. Test scores, if appropriate, should be self-explanatory or an explanation should be included. For preschool students this section should include how the student's disability affects the student's participation in appropriate activities. **There should be a direct relationship between the present level of educational performance and the other components of the IEP.**

**Medical-Physical**

**General Education**

**Social/Emotional/Adaptive**

**Cognitive**

**Academic**

**Communication**

**Fine Motor**

**Gross Motor**

*(continued)*

53

*TABLE 4-2* *Continued*

Student ID:
FTE Number:
Date of Birth:

**Xperts School District**
502 NE 4th St
YourDistrict, WA

**Present Level of Educational Performance**

**Vision and Mobility**

**Observation**

**Other**

**DEIDRE A. ZALE**

Student ID: 0000002058
FTE Number: F0000002058
Date of Birth: 03/01/1996

**Xperts School District**
502 NE 4th St
YourDistrict, WA

## Present Level of Educational Performance

Student's Name:  DEIDRE A. ZALE                                                    Date:  01/19/2006

Student's Number:  0000002058

The Present Level of Educational Performance describes the effects of the student's disability upon the student's involvement and progress in the general curriculum and area(s) of need. This includes the student's performance in academic achievement (reading, math, communications, etc.) and functional performance (behavior, social skills, daily life activities, mobility, extra-curricular activities, etc.) in objective terms. Test scores, if appropriate, should be self-explanatory or an explanation should be included. For preschool students this section should include how the student's disability affects the student's participation in appropriate activities. **There should be a direct relationship between the present level of educational performance and the other components of the IEP.**

### Medical-Physical

Deidre's medical screening revealed hearing and vision within normal limits.  Her mother reports she has had all of the "usual" childhood illnesses.  Her school attendance history is good.

### Social/Emotional/Adaptive

Qualitative observations and test results suggest that Deidre experiences high levels of stress, anxiety and low self esteem.  Concerns voiced by Deidre's mother include the possibility that Deidre is developing a failure identity and is finding hope and enthusiasm for school increasingly difficult.

### Cognitive

Deidre's psychoeducational profile is consistent with a student who has specific learning disabilities based on her language processing, psychomotor, clerical motor and memory processing impairments.  These impairments are manifested by difficulty in decoding words, reading for comprehension, solving mathematical equations and writing for understanding and communication.

### Academic

An assessment of Deidre's current academic skills was obtained by Ms. Ann Clark on 1/7/06, using the Woodcock-Johnson:III.  The results of the assessment are as follows:
Basic Reading is very low fer her age (2.8 grade equivalent)
Reading comprehension skills are very low for her age: (2.0 grade equivalent)
Math Calculations skills are low for her age (3.0 grade equivalent)

### Communication

Deidre's receptive and expressive language skills place her in the low average range, as compared with peers of her same age.  Her receptive language scores are 2 deviations below the mean.  Based on academic testing, Deidre's speech deficits in receptive and expressive language have an adverse educational impact in the areas of reading comprehension, math problem solving and written language.

### Fine Motor

Fine motor skills are developmentally appropriate.  There is no indication that her academic concerns are connected to fine motor concerns.

*(continued)*

55

*TABLE 4-2* Continued

**DEIDRE A. ZALE**

Student ID: 0000002058
FTE Number: F0000002058
Date of Birth: 03/01/1996

**Xperts School District**
502 NE 4th St
YourDistrict, WA

### Present Level of Educational Performance

**Gross Motor**

Gross motor skills are age and developmentally appropriate as well. Deidre enjoys all physical and recreational activities and takes an active participation role.

**Vision and Mobility**

Vision and mobility are within normal functioning parameters.

**Observation**

The IEP team concurs with Mrs. Zale's assessment of Deidre's enthusiasm for school and the learning environment. Deidre is a cooperative student. She does seek to quietly avoid tasks where she is not strong academically.

*Source:* © Xperts, Inc. 2006.

*TABLE 4-3* Annual Goals

Student ID:
FTE Number:
Date of Birth:

**Xperts School District**
502 NE 4th St
YourDistrict, WA

## Annual Goals and Objectives

Student's Name: _____   Date: _____

Student ID Number: _____   Disability: _____

**Annual Goal:** _____
By _____ ,

**Report of Student Progress:** ☐ Monthly   ☐ Quarterly   ☐ Yearly   ☐ Other

| Progress of Goals: | 1 | 2 | 3 | 4 | 5 | 6 | 7 | 8 |
|---|---|---|---|---|---|---|---|---|
| Date of Review: | | | | | | | | |
| Progress toward goal: | | | | | | | | |

Progress on this goal will be reported using the following codes.
ES - Emerging Skill demonstrated but may not achieve annual goal within duration of IEP.
IP - Insufficient Progress demonstrated to meet this annual goal and may not achieve annual goal within duration of IEP.
M - Mastered this annual goal.
NI - Not been provided Instruction on this goal.

## Short Term Objectives or Benchmarks

**Objective:**
By _____ , _____ will


**Comments:**                                                                 Last Updated: _____

**Mastery Criteria:**

**Evaluation method:**          _____

**Other evaluation method:**    _____


**Objective:**
By _____ , _____ will


**Comments:**                                                                 Last Updated: _____

**Mastery Criteria:**

**Evaluation method:**          _____

**Other evaluation method:**    _____

*(continued)*

*TABLE 4-3* *Continued*

**DEIDRE A. ZALE**

Student ID: 0000002058
FTE Number: F0000002058
Date of Birth: 03/01/1996

**Xperts School District**
502 NE 4th St
YourDistrict, WA

## Annual Goals and Objectives

Student's Name: DEIDRE A. ZALE                     Date: 01/19/2006

Student ID Number: 0000002058                     Disability: Specific Learning Disablities

**Annual Goal: Math Goals-Calculation**

By 01/22/2007, when given a collection of objects/equation DEIDRE will calculate the sum or difference improving calculation skills from using manipuatives with 50% accuracy to using symbols only with 80% accuracy as measured by teacher data collection.

**Report of Student Progress:**  ☐ Monthly  ☒ Quarterly  ☐ Yearly  ☐ Other

| Progress of Goals: | 1 | 2 | 3 | 4 | 5 | 6 | 7 | 8 |
|---|---|---|---|---|---|---|---|---|
| Date of Review: | | | | | | | | |
| Progress toward goal: | | | | | | | | |

Progress on this goal will be reported using the following codes.

ES - Emerging Skill demonstrated but may not achieve annual goal within duration of IEP.

IP - Insufficient Progress demonstrated to meet this annual goal and may not achieve annual goal within duration of IEP.

M - Mastered this annual goal.

NI - Not been provided Instruction on this goal.

SP - Sufficient Progress being made to achieve annual goal within duration of IEP.

### Short Term Objectives or Benchmarks

**Objective: Math**

By 10/19/2006, DEIDRE will Write the numeral that precedes given numerals

**Comments:**                                                     Last Updated:

**Mastery Criteria:**

**Evaluation method:**

**Other evaluation method:**

**Objective: Math**

By 10/19/2006, DEIDRE will Write the numeral that follows given numerals

**Comments:**                                                     Last Updated:

**Mastery Criteria:**

**Evaluation method:**

**Other evaluation method:**

**DEIDRE A. ZALE**
Student ID: 0000002058
FTE Number: F0000002058
Date of Birth: 03/01/1996

**Xperts School District**
502 NE 4th St
YourDistrict, WA

## Annual Goals and Objectives

**Objective: Math**
By 10/19/2006, DEIDRE will Write the numeral that precedes given numerals

**Comments:**                                                          Last Updated: _____

**Mastery Criteria:**

**Evaluation method:**

**Other evaluation method:**

*Source:* © Xperts, Inc. 2006.

*TABLE 4-4* *Short-Term Objectives*

**DEIDRE A. ZALE**
Student ID: 0000002058
FTE Number: F0000002058
Date of Birth: 03/01/1996

**Xperts School District**
502 NE 4th St
YourDistrict, WA

## Annual Goals and Objectives

**Annual Goal: Math Goals-math Readiness**

By 01/22/2007, when given a collection of objects DEIDRE will identify the attributes (I.e., color, shape, size) improving geometric sense from 50% accuracy to 80% accuracy as measured by teacher data collection

**Report of Student Progress:** ☐ Monthly ☒ Quarterly ☐ Yearly ☐ Other

| Progress of Goals: | 1 | 2 | 3 | 4 | 5 | 6 | 7 | 8 |
|---|---|---|---|---|---|---|---|---|
| Date of Review: | | | | | | | | |
| Progress toward goal: | | | | | | | | |

Progress on this goal will be reported using the following codes.

ES - Emerging Skill demonstrated but may not achieve annual goal within duration of IEP.

IP - Insufficient Progress demonstrated to meet this annual goal and may not achieve annual goal within duration of IEP.

M - Mastered this annual goal.

NI - Not been provided Instruction on this goal.

SP - Sufficient Progress being made to achieve annual goal within duration of IEP.

## Short Term Objectives or Benchmarks

**Objective:**

By _____ , DEIDRE will

**Comments:**                                                                      Last Updated: _____

**Mastery Criteria:**

**Evaluation method:** _____

**Other evaluation method:** _____

**DEIDRE A. ZALE**

Student ID: 0000002058
FTE Number: F0000002058
Date of Birth: 03/01/1996

## Annual Goals and Objectives

**Annual Goal: Reading Goals-Fluency Rate**

By 01/22/2007, when given a 4th grade level passage to read DEIDRE will orally read the passage to the teacher improving fluency rate from 20 correct words per minute to 60 correct words per minute as measured by CBM

**Report of Student Progress:** ☐ Monthly ☒ Quarterly ☐ Yearly ☐ Other

| Progress of Goals: | 1 | 2 | 3 | 4 | 5 | 6 | 7 | 8 |
|---|---|---|---|---|---|---|---|---|
| Date of Review: | | | | | | | | |
| Progress toward goal: | | | | | | | | |

Progress on this goal will be reported using the following codes.

ES - Emerging Skill demonstrated but may not achieve annual goal within duration of IEP.

IP - Insufficient Progress demonstrated to meet this annual goal and may not achieve annual goal within duration of IEP.

M - Mastered this annual goal.

NI - Not been provided Instruction on this goal.

SP - Sufficient Progress being made to achieve annual goal within duration of IEP.

## Short Term Objectives or Benchmarks

**Objective: Reading Readiness Skills**

By 10/19/2006, DEIDRE will Read common sign words (stop, men, women, ladies, exit)

**Comments:**                                                                 Last Updated: _____

**Mastery Criteria:**

**Evaluation method:** _____

**Other evaluation method:** _____

**Objective: Reading Readiness Skills**

By 10/19/2006, DEIDRE will Read common sign words (stop, men, women, ladies, exit)

**Comments:**                                                                 Last Updated: _____

**Mastery Criteria:**

**Evaluation method:** _____

**Other evaluation method:** _____

Special education teachers should recognize how interdependent the PLOP or PLAAFP, annual goals, and benchmarks are and how they must be written in terms that are specific and measurable. The IEP is the student's overall educational program; the PLOP or PLAAFP, annual goals, and benchmarks are the measures of how successful this program is for the student. See Box 4-4 for an example of how these are related.

**Documenting Progress.** As previously discussed, progress toward annual goals should be monitored and measured. The need for ongoing monitoring and assessment of individual student progress is one of the defining characteristics of special education (Kauffman & Hallahan, 2005); therefore, it becomes a responsibility of the special education teacher to ensure that this monitoring is regular and documented.

IDEA 97 requires that special education teachers regularly inform parents of the student's progress (U.S. Department of Education Office of Special Education Programs, 2000), which is enhanced when specific examples can be provided. Documentation of progress can include work samples, quizzes, homework, unit tests, reports, essays, informal teacher notes, and other ways of judging an individual student's achievement. These examples should be collected regularly for each student. A pocket folder for each student provides a place to store the work samples. Each teacher should develop his or her own personal system for regularly communicating with parents, collecting work samples, and assessing student progress. See Box 4-5 for information on incorporating IEPs into lesson planning.

---

**BOX 4-4**  *Example of PLOP, Goal, and Objectives*

PLOP: Tanika can recognize and add single-digit numbers but cannot subtract or multiply them.

Goal: When given a page of 30 single-digit mixed addition, subtraction, and multiplication problems, Tanika will complete the page in 1 minute with no more than two errors.

Objectives:

1. When given a page of 30 single-digit subtraction problems, Tanika will complete the page in 1 minute with no more than two errors.

2. When given a page of 30 mixed single-digit addition and subtraction problems, Tanika will complete the page in 1 minute with no more than two errors.

3. When given a page of 30 single-digit multiplication problems, Tanika will complete the page in 1 minute with no more than two errors.

*Source:* Bateman and Herr (2003).

---

**BOX 4-5**  *IEPs and Lesson Planning*

When possible, it is helpful to integrate individual IEP goals or objectives into unit planning. The integration of IEP goals and objectives into unit or lesson planning may be most productive in co-taught inclusion classes. Integrating IEPs while planning can be time consuming; however, a significant benefit exists for both the teacher and the student. The teacher can benefit by maintaining focus on individual student needs while addressing the curriculum. Remember that IDEA 97 emphasizes individual students participation in the general education curriculum (U.S. Department of Education, 2004b). The student can benefit because the teacher addresses any needed accommodations or modifications in the planning of the unit. Finally, the teacher can use unit assessments as documentation for progress toward individual goals without having to conduct a separate assessment.

## IDEA 2004

At the time of this writing, IDEA 2004 was being implemented. IDEA 2004 contains substantive changes to writing IEPs and conducting IEP meetings. It is a professional obligation for special education teachers to keep abreast of new regulations in the field. The list of Web sites at the end of this chapter can help new teachers review changes to IDEA and how to incorporate these into their individual teaching practice. While the changes have not been administratively finalized, the following are some areas where changes are anticipated.

**IEPs.** The language about PLOPs was changed to PLAAFP (U.S. Department of Education, 2004b). IDEA 2004 also focused annual goals on "measurable academic and functional goals" (U.S. Department of Education, 2004b). A focus also exists on reporting about the student's progress toward meeting these goals (Wright & Wright, 2005). An IEP can be revised or modified without a formal IEP meeting as long as the revisions are done in writing and the entire team agrees to the changes. IEP meetings and due process hearings can be conducted via conference call or videoconference (Wright & Wright, 2005).

**IEP Team Members.** The language of IDEA 2004 stresses that parental concern for enhancing their child's educational achievement must be addressed by the IEP team. The team should consider special factors for children who have behavior problems, impaired levels of English literacy, visual impairments (or blindness), or hearing impairments (or deafness) (Wright & Wright, 2005). An IEP team member may be excused from an IEP meeting if one's area of expertise will not be discussed and the parent agrees to one's absence (Wright & Wright, 2005). A team member may also submit a written report to the parents and other team members in advance, and the parents should provide written consent for the team member's absence (U.S. Department of Education, 2004b).

## CONDUCTING IEP MEETINGS

IDEA requires that at a minimum the following people must be present at an IEP meeting: parents, general education teacher, special education teacher, administrator or administrator's designee, someone who can discuss testing and evaluation (may be the special education teacher or school psychologist), anyone the parents would like to include, and the student when appropriate (U.S. Department of Education, 2004b). While IDEA describes the roles and responsibilities of IEP participants, good meeting etiquette can establish a cooperative atmosphere among the team members.

The case manager (often the special education teacher) should arrange for a comfortable room with a conference table. Parents should be offered seating that indicates they are team members (e.g., similar chairs to the school people or seating on the same level). It is often helpful to have a pitcher of water and glasses available as well as a box of tissues. Remember that some parents may have difficulty arranging child care for younger siblings. In these cases, it is often helpful to have a space where the younger siblings can engage in quiet activities (e.g., coloring, drawing, or small manipulatives). These actions can help establish a positive atmosphere for the IEP meeting.

Each school has policies and procedures regarding notification of IEP meetings, attendance at the meeting, and related issues that ensure compliance with IDEA requirements. New special education teachers should review these guidelines prior to scheduling their IEP meetings. Teachers can also benefit by using a three-stage approach to meetings. These three stages are premeeting planning, IEP meeting, and postmeeting follow-up:

### Premeeting Planning

- Notify parents about the IEP meeting by a written note. Provide a reminder by either e-mail or phone.
- Provide the purpose of the meeting (agenda), the date, the time, the expected length, and the location.
- Send materials home well ahead of time to allow parents time to read and prepare. Send a draft of proposed goals and objectives and ask parents for input.
- Review the student's record and progress, and note areas of concern.
- Gather specific examples of the student's work and any other materials that might help.
- Prepare an outline for the meeting, including items to be discussed and a list of other professionals who may need to be invited.
- Notify other professionals who need to attend the conference.

### IEP Meeting

- Ensure seating arrangements that promote the sharing of information.
- Establish an atmosphere that enhances communication among the parents and the educators. The meeting might begin with a preview of the agenda, clarifying the purpose and the role of each participant. The teacher might acknowledge appreciation to the parents and staff for their attendance.
- Begin the meeting on a positive note, raise issues of concern, listen attentively to parent input, and end on a positive note.
- Review present levels of academic achievement and performance. Have each team member report on his or her observations, work samples, and assessments. Be aware of and responsive to the effect of what is being said to the parents.
- Discuss goals and objectives for the next year. The IEP team should strive to reach consensus on measurable goals and objectives. This discussion may also include accommodations or modifications.
- Ensure that parents are given the written statement of their rights.
- Conclude the meeting on a positive note. Remember that parents have the right not to sign the IEP and to request a due process hearing.

### Postmeeting Follow-Up

- Summarize the notes of the meeting and provide a written copy of the IEP (and notes) to all participants.
- Make a follow-up phone call or send an e-mail to the parents.
- Follow up with other team members.
- Review the meeting with the student if he or she was not present.
- Document all communication.

**Student Advocacy Skills.** It is critical that students with disabilities learn self-advocacy skills. One of the best ways to foster these skills is to have the student attend IEP or other parent conferences (Van Dycke & Peterson, 2003). Students should be welcomed into the meetings and encouraged to actively participate. They might be asked to discuss their work samples, how they feel they have progressed on their IEP goals, and what goals they would like to make for the next year. Special education teachers might spend time with the student prior to the meeting explaining process and procedures. Another option is to incorporate IEP instruction into the student's curriculum (Van Dycke,

Martin, & Lovett, 2006). Students should have a clear understanding of what is going to occur and their role in the meeting.

According to IDEA, when the student becomes 14 years of age, transition planning and student involvement should be integrated into IEP meetings (U.S. Department of Education, 2004b). This is a natural time to begin including students in their IEP meetings; however, some students may be ready to attend at much younger ages. This is a decision that parents should be encouraged to consider.

**Transition Planning.** Previously, for students age 14 and older, IDEA required a transition plan detailing the services and goals needed to help support the student's goals for adult life (Association of Service Providers Implementing IDEA Reforms in Education Partnership & IDEA Local Implementation by Local Administrators Partnerships, 2003). IDEA 2004 eliminated the need for a statement of transition services at age 14 but requires "appropriate measurable postsecondary goals" that are to be based on "age appropriate transition assessments" at age 16 (Wright & Wright, 2005). This transition plan must be included in the IEP and should include a statement regarding the student's needs for transition services that focus on classes that are being taken (U.S. Department of Education, 2004b).

The IEP must include with the transition plan a description of services, including coordination with other agencies (rehabilitation or job placement) for helping the student transition from school to postschool (military, college, or vocational training) (Association of Service Providers Implementing IDEA Reforms in Education Partnership & IDEA Local Implementation by Local Administrators Partnerships, 2003). The IEP team must address these requirements.

Special education teachers at the middle and high school levels should be prepared to facilitate discussions of transition services with parents and students (Sabornie & deBettencourt, 2004). Teachers should be knowledgeable of options, local service agencies, and requirements for placement and be sensitive, as some parents and students find these issues emotionally laden. Transition from school to early adulthood is complex, and teachers should consider special training on working with adolescents. In addition, the school guidance counselor can be a valuable resource for the new special education teacher (Sabornie & deBettencourt, 2004). Documentation and record keeping for transition planning should be done as well (see Table 4-5).

**Eligibility Meetings.** IDEA also provides for how determinations of a student's eligibility for special education services are managed. Special education teachers must be prepared to serve on the school's IEP team for determining eligibility, sometimes referred to as "child find." The purpose of this IEP team is to review, assess, and analyze information on students who are referred to determine if they need special education services (U.S. Department of Education, 2004b).

Parents, teachers, physicians, or specialists can refer students to the IEP team for an eligibility determination. The team may request additional assessments. A student is determined eligible for services when the student's disability fits within one of the categories specified in the legislation and the child needs special education services because of the disability (Patterson, 2000). Documentation and record keeping for initial eligibility determination should be done as well.

This can be an emotionally difficult time for parents of newly identified special needs students and overwhelming, as they must learn the language of special education, understand the services to be provided, and navigate their first IEP meetings. Special educators should provide resources and explanations as needed by the parents. Review chapter 3 for information on working with parents.

*TABLE 4-5* *Transition Plan*

## SASHA T. ACEY
Student ID: 0000001160
FTE Number: F0000001160
Date of Birth: 03/01/1986

**Xperts School District**
502 NE 4th St
YourDistrict, WA

---

### Secondary Transition

---

Student's Name: SASHA T. ACEY                                      Date: 06/16/2005

Student ID Number: 0000001160

**Present Levels:**

**Vocational**

Sasha's vocational assessment is in line with her state career goals.  She has volunteered in the lower grades as a tutor during high school and shows a marked aptitude for working with her peers.

### Transition - Course of Study
(Beginning at age 14 or younger )

Describe the focus of the student's course of study ( i.e., specify the educational courses and experiences in school and the community that will assist the student in achieving his/her post-school goals). For students pursuing a modified standard diploma, consider the student's need for occupational readiness, including courses to prepare the student as a career and technical educational program completer.

Sasha is enrolled in a college preparatory course of study

### Transition Services
(Beginning at age 16 or younger )

IEP teams may assign an expected graduation year beyond four years for students in special education. Changes to the expected graduation year for special education students must be made by the Individualized Education Program (IEP) team on a case-by-case basis no later than when the student becomes age 16. Such a change must be reflected in each student's IEP.

1. Desired Outcomes - **Postsecondary Employment** (including integrated or supported employment)

Sasha career goal is to be a high school English teacher

Is specially designed instruction needed?     ☐ Yes  ☒ No
If yes, describe (make sure the IEP addresses this need through goals, services, etc.):

2. Desired Outcomes - **Career and Technical Education**

English teacher

Is specially designed instruction needed?     ☐ Yes  ☒ No
If yes, describe (make sure the IEP addresses this need through goals, services, etc.):

3. Desired Outcomes - **Postsecondary Education**     (including continuing and adult education)

English teacher

Is specially designed instruction needed?     ☐ Yes  ☒ No
If yes, describe (make sure the IEP addresses this need through goals,services, etc.):

*(continued)*

**66**

*TABLE 4-5* *Continued*

**SASHA T. ACEY**

Student ID:  0000001160
FTE Number:  F0000001160
Date of Birth:  03/01/1986

**Xperts School District**

502 NE 4th St
YourDistrict, WA

**Secondary Transition**

4. Desired Outcomes - **Independent Living**

apartment

Is specially designed instruction needed?          ☐ Yes   ☒ No
If yes, describe (make sure the IEP addresses this need through goals, services, etc.):

5. Desired Outcomes - **Community Participation**

independence

Is specially designed instruction needed?          ☒ Yes   ☐ No
If yes, describe (make sure the IEP addresses this need through goals, services, etc.):

**Student Exit Summary**

For a child whose eligibility terminates due to graduation or exceeding the age of eligibility, provide a summary of the child's academic achievement and functional performance, which shall include recommendations on how to assist the child in meeting the child's postsecondary goals.

After graduation, Sasha intends to tutor at the local community center.  In the fall following graduation she has applied to the local university to enroll in a teacher preparation program.

**SASHA T. ACEY**

Student ID: 0000001160
FTE Number: F0000001160
Date of Birth: 03/01/1986

**Xperts School District**
502 NE 4th St
YourDistrict, WA

---

### Secondary Transition Interagency Responsibilities and Needed Linkages

---

Student's Name: SASHA T. ACEY                                    Date: 06/16/2005

Student ID Number: 0000001160

1. To assist in achieving post-secondary employment outcomes or goals, the student will be referred to the following agency(ies) or organization(s):

Agency/Organization:                              Person Responsible for Referral:
job placement agency                              Chris Martin

Reason for Referral Including Requested Service(s):

Sasha has expressed interest in voluteering as a tutor at the local high school after graduation.

2. To assist in achieving career and technical education outcomes or goals, the student will be referred to the following agency(ies) or organization(s):

Agency/Organization:                              Person Responsible for Referral:

Reason for Referral Including Requested Service(s):

no agency linkages are required

3. To assist in achieving post-secondary education outcomes or goals, the student will be referred to the following agency(ies) or organization(s):

Agency/Organization:                              Person Responsible for Referral:
college placement agency                          Mary Smith

Reason for Referral Including Requested Service(s):

assistance is course selection

4. To assist in achieving independent living outcomes or goals, the student will be referred to the following agency(ies) or organization(s):

Agency/Organization:                              Person Responsible for Referral:

Reason for Referral Including Requested Service(s):

no agency linkages required

*(continued)*

*TABLE 4-5*  *Continued*

**SASHA T. ACEY**

Student ID:  0000001160
FTE Number:  F0000001160
Date of Birth:  03/01/1986

**Xperts School District**

502 NE 4th St
YourDistrict, WA

### Secondary Transition Interagency Responsibilities and Needed Linkages

5. To assist in achieving community participation outcomes or goals, the student will be referred to the following agency(ies) or organization(s):

Agency/Organization:                                    Person Responsible for Referral:

Reason for Referral Including Requested Service(s):

no agency linkages

*Source:* © Xperts, Inc., 2006.

## SUMMARY

This chapter provided a review of required elements in an IEP and a discussion of PLOP, annual goals, and objectives. Special education teachers were reminded of the importance of providing specific measurable descriptions for PLOPs, annual goals, and benchmarks as well as consistently documenting progress toward these. In addition, an overview of conducting IEP meetings, transition planning, and eligibility meeting requirements for special education teachers was conducted. See Table 4-6 for list of documents relating to all these IEP requirements that can be used as evidence of competency in a teaching portfolio. See Table 4-7 for an example of a complete IEP.

## ACTIVITY QUESTIONS

1. Review the IEPs and files for the students on your caseload. Plan to speak with other teachers who have worked with these students to gain insight about the individual needs of these students.

2. Review the actual IEP forms that your school uses prior to writing your first IEP. Notice how the forms are presented, where signatures are required, and how the forms are individualized for each student.

3. Prepare for your first IEP meeting by drafting an IEP. Have your mentor or another experienced special education teacher review your draft and make suggestions for revisions.

4. Develop a record-keeping system for IEP paperwork. Discuss record keeping with your mentor or another experienced special education teacher. Are there ideas that you can incorporate into you own system? How do they manage all the IEP paperwork requirements?

## SELECTED WEBSITES

http://www.ed.gov/policy/gen/guid/fpco/index.html
*Family Policy Compliance Office / U.S. Department of Education / 400 Maryland Avenue SW / Washington, DC 20202-5920. This department and its Website can provide resources on confidentiality, privacy, and family rights.*

http://www.ideadata.org
*This Website provides resources and explanations on IDEA regulations.*

http://www.childfindidea.org
*This Website provides information on rules and regulations for eligibility determinations under IDEA.*

http://www.ncset.org
*This Website from the National Center on Secondary Education and Transition provides information and resources to assist with transition planning.*

http://www.wrightslaw.com
*This Website from Wright's Law provides information, interpretation of legal terms, and resources for compliance with IDEA rules.*

## REFLECTION JOURNAL ACTIVITIES

1. Review an IEP for one of your students. Think about how each component affects the education of the student for whom it was written. Is this a good educational plan? Would you make any changes? Does it reflect what you know about the child's strengths as well as his or her disability?

2. Review the annual goals and objectives for several students on your caseload. Are these well written? How are they being measured or monitored? Do they accurately reflect what you know about the student? Would you revise or rewrite any of them?

3. How can you manage the paperwork? Are you regularly and consistently documenting student progress on IEP goals?

4. IEPs are an important professional responsibility for the special education teacher. Reflect on what evidence you will provide to demonstrate your competence with IEPs. What evidence are you going to include in your teaching portfolio relating to IEPs? Does your evidence reflect how you manage and write IEPs?

**TABLE 4-6**  *Evidence Checklist: IEPs*

To provide evidence of competence in the area of IEPs, a special education teacher might include the following in a teaching portfolio:

❑ Copies of IEPs

❑ Copies of PLOP or PLAAFP

❑ Copies of annual goals and objectives (benchmarks)

❑ Copies of documentation toward progress on IEP goals

❑ Copies of required accommodations or modifications

❑ Copies of calendars and notes regarding key dates

❑ Copies of transition plans

❑ Copies of communication with parents about IEPs and progress toward IEP goals

❑ Photos of IEP meetings

❑ Copies of documentation of incorporating self-advocacy skills into the curriculum

*Note.* Student confidentiality should be maintained. Please block out any identifying information.

## REFERENCES

Association of Service Providers Implementing IDEA Reforms in Education Partnership & IDEA Local Implementation by Local Administrators Partnerships. (2003). *Discover IDEA: Supporting achievement for children with disabilities—An IDEA practices resource guide.* Arlington, VA: Council for Exceptional Children.

Bateman, B. D., & Herr, C. M. (2003). *Writing measurable IEP goals and objectives.* Verona, WI: Attainment Company.

Bateman, B. D., & Linden, M. A. (1998). *Better IEPs: How to develop legally correct and educationally useful programs* (3rd ed.). Longmont, CO: Sopris West.

deBettencourt, L. U. (2002). Understanding the differences between IDEA and Section 504. *Teaching Exceptional Children, 34*(3), 16–23.

Fairfax County Public Schools. (2001). *Special education handbook.* Fairfax, VA: School Board of Fairfax County.

Hallahan, D., & Kauffman, J. (2006). *Exceptional learners: Introduction to special education* (10th ed.). Boston: Allyn & Bacon.

Kauffman, J., & Hallahan, D. (2005). *Special education: What it is and why we need it.* Boston: Allyn & Bacon.

Patterson, J. (2000). *Essentials for principals: School leader's guide to special education.* Arlington, VA: Educational Resource Service and National Association of Elementary School Principals.

Sabornie, E. J., & deBettencourt, L. U. (2004). *Teaching students with mild and high-incidence disabilities at the secondary level* (2nd ed.). Upper Saddle River, NJ: Pearson Education.

U.S. Department of Education. (2004a). *Family Educational Rights and Privacy Act (FERPA).* Retrieved August 29, 2005, from http://www.ed.gov/policy/gen/guide/fpco/ferpa/index.html

U.S. Department of Education. (2004b). *Individuals with Disabilities Education Act.* Retrieved August 14, 2005, from http://ideadata.org

U.S. Department of Education Office of Special Education Programs. (2000). *A guide to the individualized education program.* Washington, DC: Author.

Van Dycke, J. L., & Peterson, L. (2003, November–December). Eight steps to help students develop IEP goals. *CEC Today, 35,* 13.

Van Dycke, J. L., Martin, J., & Lovett, D. (2006). Why is this cake on fire? Inviting students into the IEP process. *Teaching Exceptional Children, 38*(3), 42–47.

Wright, D., & Wright, D. (2005). *Roadmap to IDEA 2004: What you need to know about IEPs and IEP meetings.* Retrieved January 9, 2006, from http://www.wrightslaw.com/idea/iep.roadmpap.htm

TABLE 4-7 *Complete IEP Sample*

**MADELYN T. ZALE**

Student ID: 0000002463

FTE Number: F0000002463

Date of Birth: 08/01/1986

**West Valley School District - DEMO**

Spokane, WA

---

**IEP Invitation**

---

To: _____

Student's Name: MADELYN T. ZALE _____ Date Sent to Participants: 09/12/2005 _____

This is to notify you that a/an Review team meeting has been scheduled for the above student. Your participation and attendance at this meeting are very important. This Review meeting must be scheduled at a mutually agreed upon time and place. The purpose of this meeting is to (check all that apply):

| | |
|---|---|
| ___ Develop an Initial IEP | _X_ Review Current IEP |
| _X_ Discuss Transition Services | ___ Discuss Graduation |
| ___ Discuss Annual Goal Progress | ___ Review Instructional Needs |
| ___ Consider Termination of Services | ___ Determine Placement |
| ___ Develop ESY | ___ Discuss Attendance Issues |
| ___ Manifestation Determination | ___ Behavioral Intervention Plan |
| ___ Other: | ___ |

This meeting has been scheduled for:     Date 09/19/2005     Time 10:00 AM _____

Location Conference Room _____

The following are invited to attend and participate in the Review meeting:

| | |
|---|---|
| General Education Teacher _____ | Administrator/Designee _____ |
| Kristen Zale , Parent _____ | Meredith Waters , Case Manager _____ |

* If the purpose of the meeting includes the development of transition services needs (beginning at age 14 or younger) the student will be invited. If the purpose of the meeting is the consideration of needed transition services (beginning at age 16 or younger) the student and representatives of the following agencies will be invited:

_____

The parent/adult student or school may invite individuals who have knowledge or special expertise regarding the student, including related services personnel, to participate. The determination of the knowledge or special expertise shall be made by the person/party extending the invitation. If you, the parent or adult student, are bringing other individuals to the meeting, please let us know. This will ensure that the meeting space will accommodate all team members.

If you have any questions or would like additional information or assistance to help you prepare for this IEP meeting, please contact Beth Holland at (804) 967-0700 e-mail iep.online@xperts.com.

Procedural Safeguards Notice is enclosed.

Student ID:  0000002463
FTE Number:  F0000002463
Date of Birth:  08/01/1986

**West Valley School District - DEMO**

Spokane, WA

## Excused Team Members

Student's Name: MADELYN T. ZALE                    ID#: 0000002463          Date of Birth: 08/01/1986

Attending School: Washington High                                                   Grade: 11

Home School:    Kent Middle

Parent/Guardian/Surrogate Name:    STEPHEN ZALE/ KRISTEN ZALE

Address: 3893 CAULDER RICHMOND 23224              Home#: 9998765/ 9998765        Work#: 999-1010 / 999-1010

There is a meeting in reference to your child to be held on (date) 09/19/2005      at (time) 10:00 AM
at (place) Conference Room

The following team members have requested excusal from the meeting:

| Name | Title | Reason |
|------|-------|--------|
| Meredith Waters | Case Manager | |

If the member's area of the curriculum or related service will not be discussed, the member may be excused without submitting comments in writing.  If the member's area of curriculum or related service will be discussed, they may be excused but must provide comments in writing and submit this to the team in lieu of their appearance.

☐ I agree to excuse the above team members from the meeting.

☐ I do not agree to excuse the above team members from the meeting.

_____          _____
Signature of Parent                                      Date

_____          _____
Signature of District Representative                     Date

*(continued)*

*TABLE 4-7 Continued*

**MADELYN T. ZALE**

Student ID: 0000002463
FTE Number: F0000002463
Date of Birth: 08/01/1986

**West Valley School District - DEMO**

Spokane, WA

## IEP Cover Page

Student's Name: MADELYN T. ZALE    Date: 09/19/2005

Student ID Number: 0000002463    Grade: 11

DOB: 08/01/1986    Age*: 19

Disability(ies) (if identified): Specific Learning Disablities

Parent/Guardian Name: STEPHEN ZALE/ KRISTEN ZALE

Home Address: 3893 CAULDER    Phone # (H): 9998765/ 9998765

     RICHMOND, WA 23224    Phone # (W): 999-1010 / 999-1010

| | |
|---|---|
| Most recent Eligibility date | 04/26/2005 |
| Most recent re-evaluation date | |
| Next re-evaluation must occur before this date | 04/26/2008 |
| Date of Plan meeting | 09/19/2005 |
| This IEP will be reviewed no later than this date | 08/26/2006 |
| Date parent notified of Plan meeting | 09/12/2005 |
| Date student notified of Plan meeting (if transition will be discussed) | 04/19/2005 |

Copy of Plan given to parent/student by (Name):    Date:

IEP Teacher/Manager: Beth Holland    Phone Number: (804) 967-0700

The list below indicates that the individual participated in the development of this Plan and the placement decision; it does not authorize consent. Parent or student (age 18 or older) consent is indicated on the "Prior Notice/Consent" page.

| Excused | Name of Participant | Title |
|---|---|---|
| ☐ | | General Education Teacher |
| ☐ | | Administrator/Designee |
| ☐ | Kristen Zale | Parent |
| ☒ | Meredith Waters | Case Manager |

**\* The student must be informed at least one year prior to turning 18 that the IDEA procedural safeguards (rights) transfer to him/her at age 18 and be provided with an explanation of those procedural safeguards.**

**Date informed: 09/19/2005**

If the parent did not attend, what method was used to ensure their participation:

**MADELYN T. ZALE**
Student ID: 0000002463
FTE Number: F0000002463
Date of Birth: 08/01/1986

**West Valley School District - DEMO**

Spokane, WA

## Team Considerations

Student's Name: MADELYN T. ZALE                                    Meeting Date: 09/19/2005

Student ID Number: 0000002463

During the IEP meeting the following factors must be considered by the IEP team. Best practice suggests that the IEP team document that the factors were considered and any decision made relative to each. The factors are addressed in other sections of the IEP if not documented on this page. (for example: see Present Level of Educational Performance)

☒ The strengths of the student and the concerns of the parents for enhancing the education of their child.
  Strengths of the student were considered.

☒ The results of the student's performance on any general state or district-wide assessments.
  District wide assessments were considered.

☒ The communication needs of the student. In the case of a student who is deaf or hard of hearing, consider the student's language and communication needs, opportunities for direct communications with peers and professional personnel in the student's language and communication mode, academic level, and full range of needs, including opportunities for direct instruction in the student's language and communication mode.
  Communication needs were considered.

☐ The student's assistive technology devices and services needs.

☐ In the case of a student whose behavior impedes his or her learning or that of others, consider, when appropriate, strategies, including positive behavioral interventions, strategies, and supports to address that behavior.

☐ In the case of a student with limited English proficiency, consider the language needs of the child as such needs relate to the child's IEP.

☐ In the case of a student who is blind or has a visual impairment, provide for instruction in Braille and the use of Braille unless the IEP team determines, after an evaluation of the student's reading and writing skills, needs, and appropriate reading and writing media (including an evaluation of the student's future needs for instruction in Braille or the use of Braille), that instruction in Braille or the use of Braille is not appropriate for the student.

(*continued*)

*TABLE 4-7 Continued*

## MADELYN T. ZALE

Student ID:  0000002463
FTE Number:  F0000002463
Date of Birth:  08/01/1986

### West Valley School District - DEMO

Spokane, WA

---

### Present Level of Educational Performance

---

Student's Name:  MADELYN T. ZALE                                    Date: 09/19/2005

Student's Number:  0000002463

---

The Present Level of Educational Performance describes the effects of the student's disability upon the student's involvement and progress in the general curriculum and area(s) of need. This includes the student's performance in academic achievement (reading, math, communications, etc.) and functional performance (behavior, social skills, daily life activities, mobility, extra-curricular activities, etc.) in objective terms. Test scores, if appropriate, should be self-explanatory or an explanation should be included. For preschool students this section should include how the student's disability affects the student's participation in appropriate activities. **There should be a direct relationship between the present level of educational performance and the other components of the IEP.**

**Medical-Physical**

Normal medical findings, no significant implications.

**General Education**

Madelyn is reading below grade level.  She is reading on a second grade level.  She has trouble with reading comprehension, fluency rate and vocabulary.

**Social/Emotional/Adaptive**

Madelyn is a well adjusted girl.  Teachers have not reported an emotional behaviors.  She gets along well with her peers and teachers.

**Cognitive**

Results of the cognitive evaluation reveal that Madelyn has difficulty with sound symbo relationships required for reading and decoding unfamilar words.  There is a lack of consistency on reading and spelling words that have a high predictability level.

On tasks of written expression, Madelyn avoids initiation on these tasks.  She has difficulty establishing a theme and responding to writing samples.

**Academic**

Summary indicates deficits in the areas of reading comprehension, word recognition and sound/symbol relationships.  An informal reading inventory indicated that Madelyn's independent reading level was beginning second grade, her instruction level was mid-second grade and her reading frustration level is at the mid-third grade level.

**Observation**

Teacher observations reveal that Madelyn avoids tasks involving writing.  She does not actively participate during reading time.  She is an extremely active participant during math and science time.

## Annual Goals and Objectives

Student's Name: MADELYN T. ZALE

Date: 09/19/2005

Student ID Number: 0000002463

Disability: Specific Learning Disablities

**Annual Goal: Reading Goals-Comprehension**

By 09/25/2006, when given a graded (fiction/nonfiction) passage MADELYN will silently read the passage improving reading comprehension from answering 5/10 questions correctly at 3rd grade level to answering 8/10 questions correctly at 5th grade level as measured by reading assessment

**Report of Student Progress:** [x] Monthly ☐ Quarterly ☐ Yearly ☐ Other

| Progress of Goals: | 1 | 2 | 3 | 4 | 5 | 6 | 7 | 8 |
|---|---|---|---|---|---|---|---|---|
| Date of Review: | | | | | | | | |
| Progress toward goal: | | | | | | | | |

Progress on this goal will be reported using the following codes.

ES - Emerging Skill demonstrated but may not achieve annual goal within duration of IEP.

IP - Insufficient Progress demonstrated to meet this annual goal and may not achieve annual goal within duration of IEP.

M - Mastered this annual goal.

NI - Not been provided Instruction on this goal.

SP - Sufficient Progress being made to achieve annual goal within duration of IEP.

### Short Term Objectives or Benchmarks

**Objective: Content and Processing**

By 05/03/2006, MADELYN will demonstrate comprehension and/or use of basic concepts of reading words.

**Comments:**

Last Updated: _____

**Mastery Criteria:**
80%
**Evaluation method:** _____

**Other evaluation method:** _____

(continued)

*TABLE 4-7* *Continued*

**MADELYN T. ZALE**

Student ID:  0000002463
FTE Number:  F0000002463
Date of Birth:  08/01/1986

**West Valley School District - DEMO**

Spokane, WA

## Annual Goals and Objectives

**Annual Goal: Reading Goals-Comprehension**

By 09/25/2006, when given a graded (fiction/nonfiction) passage MADELYN will identify and define targeted terms improving vocabulary acquisition from 5/10 vocabulary terms to 8/10 vocabulary terms as measured by weekly vocabulary assessments

**Report of Student Progress:**   [x] Monthly   ☐ Quarterly   ☐ Yearly   ☐ Other

| Progress of Goals: | 1 | 2 | 3 | 4 | 5 | 6 | 7 | 8 |
|---|---|---|---|---|---|---|---|---|
| Date of Review: | | | | | | | | |
| Progress toward goal: | | | | | | | | |

Progress on this goal will be reported using the following codes.

ES - Emerging Skill demonstrated but may not achieve annual goal within duration of IEP.

IP - Insufficient Progress demonstrated to meet this annual goal and may not achieve annual goal within duration of IEP.

M - Mastered this annual goal.

NI - Not been provided Instruction on this goal.

SP - Sufficient Progress being made to achieve annual goal within duration of IEP.

## Short Term Objectives or Benchmarks

**Objective:**

By _____, MADELYN will

**Comments:**                                                      Last Updated:  _____

**Mastery Criteria:**

**Evaluation method:** _____

**Other evaluation method:** _____

**MADELYN T. ZALE**

Student ID: 0000002463

FTE Number: F0000002463

Date of Birth: 08/01/1986

**West Valley School District - DEMO**

Spokane, WA

## Annual Goals and Objectives

**Annual Goal: Written Expression**

By 09/25/2006, when given a writing prompt MADELYN will write complete sentences improving writing fluency from writing sentence fragments to writing 5 complete sentences as measured by teacher data collections

**Report of Student Progress:**  [x] Monthly  [ ] Quarterly  [ ] Yearly  [ ] Other

| Progress of Goals: | 1 | 2 | 3 | 4 | 5 | 6 | 7 | 8 |
|---|---|---|---|---|---|---|---|---|
| Date of Review: | | | | | | | | |
| Progress toward goal: | | | | | | | | |

Progress on this goal will be reported using the following codes.

ES - Emerging Skill demonstrated but may not achieve annual goal within duration of IEP.

IP - Insufficient Progress demonstrated to meet this annual goal and may not achieve annual goal within duration of IEP.

M - Mastered this annual goal.

NI - Not been provided Instruction on this goal.

SP - Sufficient Progress being made to achieve annual goal within duration of IEP.

## Short Term Objectives or Benchmarks

**Objective: Written Expression**

By 05/03/2006, MADELYN will will be able to write complete sentences.

**Comments:**

Last Updated: _____

**Mastery Criteria:**

80%

**Evaluation method:** _____

**Other evaluation method:** _____

*(continued)*

*TABLE 4-7* Continued

**MADELYN T. ZALE**

Student ID: 0000002463

FTE Number: F0000002463

Date of Birth: 08/01/1986

**West Valley School District - DEMO**

Spokane, WA

---

### Supplementary Aids and Services, Program Accommodations/ Modifications, Support for School Personnel

Student's Name: MADELYN T. ZALE                                                     Date: 09/19/2005

Student ID Number: 0000002463

---

This student will be provided access to the general education, special education, other school services and activities including non-academic activities and extracurricular activities, and education related settings:

☐ with no accommodations/modifications

☒ with the following accommodations/modifications

Accommodations/modifications provided as part of the instructional and testing/assessment process will allow the student equal opportunity to access the curriculum and demonstrate achievement. Accommodations/modifications also provide access to non-academic and extracurricular activities and educationally related settings. Accommodations/modifications based solely on the potential to enhance performance beyond providing equal access are inappropriate.

Accommodations may be in, but not limited to, the areas of scheduling, setting, aids, and format. The impact of any modifications listed should be discussed. This includes the earning of credits for graduation.

**Supplementary Aids and Services, Accommodations/Modifications** (please list, as appropriate):

| Accommodation(s)/Modification(s) | Frequency | Location | Duration m/d/y to m/d/y |
|---|---|---|---|
| reduce length of assignments | Daily | Classroom | 09/26/2005 to 09/25/2006 |
| extended time on tests | Daily | Classroom | 09/26/2005 to 09/25/2006 |
| preferential seating | Daily | Classroom | 09/26/2005 to 09/25/2006 |

Supports for School Personnel ( training, professional, development etc):

West Valley School District - DEMO

Spokane, WA

## Special Education and Related Services

Student's Name: MADELYN T. ZALE                    Date: 09/19/2005

Student ID Number: 0000002463

### Least Restrictive Environment (LRE):

When discussing least restrictive environment and placement options, the following must be considered:

- To the maximum extent appropriate, the student is educated with children without disabilities.
- Special classes, separate schooling, or other removal of the student from the regular educational environment occurs only if the nature or severity of the disability is such that education in regular classes with the use of supplementary aids and services cannot be achieved satisfactorily.
- The student's placement should be as close as possible to the child's home and unless the IEP of the student with a disability requires some other arrangement, the student is educated in the school that he or she would attend if he or she did not have a disability.
- In selecting the LRE, consideration is given to any potential harmful effect on the student or on the quality of services that he/she needs.
- The student with a disability is not removed from education in age-appropriate regular classrooms solely because of needed modifications in the general curriculum.

### Special Education and Related Services:

| Service(s) | Instruction Style | Provider | Frequency | Location | Duration | Monitor |
|---|---|---|---|---|---|---|
| **Special Education** | | | | | | |
| **Setting: General Education** | | | | | | |
| Language Arts | Direct/Group | LD teacher | 30.00 Minutes / 5.00 Weekly | General Education classroom/resource room | 09/26/2005 - 09/25/2006 | Teacher |
| **Setting: Special Education** | | | | | | |
| Reading | Direct | Reading Specialist | 30.00 Minutes / 5.00 Weekly | Resource Room | 09/26/2005 - 09/25/2006 | Teacher |

**Transportation:** [X] Regular  [ ] Special
**Extended School Year:** [ ] Yes  [X] No    If Yes, must complete ESY form.
**General PE:** [X] Yes  [ ] No

*(continued)*

*TABLE 4-7 Continued*

## MADELYN T. ZALE

Student ID: 0000002463
FTE Number: F0000002463
Date of Birth: 08/01/1986

## West Valley School District - DEMO

Spokane, WA

### Special Education and Related Services

## Placement

The team may consider placement options in conjunction with discussing any needed supplementary aids and services, accommodations/modifications, assistive technology, and supports for school personnel. In considering the placement continuum options, check those the team discussed. Then, describe the placement selected in the **Placement Decision** section below.

**Placement Options:**

| Placement Options for LRE | SELECTION | | OR...REASONS REJECTED | | |
| --- | --- | --- | --- | --- | --- |
| | Considered | Selected (only 1) | Academic benefit cannot be satisfactorily achieved | Non-academic benefit cannot be satisfactorily achieved | Effect student will have on teacher and other students |
| General Education Class (80-100% of day in general education) | X | | X | | |
| Resource Room (40-79% of day in general education) | X | X | | | |
| Separate Class (0-39% of day in general education) | X | | X | X | |
| Separate Public/Private School (NPA) | | | | | |
| Public Residential | | | | | |
| Private Residential | | | | | |
| Home/Hospital | | | | | |

**Placement Decision:**

Based upon identified services and the consideration of least restrictive environment (LRE) and placement continuum options, describe in the space below the placement. Additionally, summarize the discussions and decision around LRE and placement. This must include an explanation of the extent to which the student WILL NOT be participating with students without disabilities in the general education class(es), programs, and activities.

Madelyn will recieve special education services in the resource room for reading and writing based on her identified need for specially designed instruction in those skill areas. Math skills are an area of strength for Madelyn and she will receive instruction in the general education classroom with her non-disabled peers.

[x] Parent/student rights and responsibilities have been explained in a manner that was understood by all parties involved and a copy of the IEP was provided at no cost.

## Placement Disclaimer

**REQUIRED FOR INITIAL PLACEMENT ONLY: WRITTEN PARENTAL PERMISSION** *My rights and those of my child regarding procedural safeguards have been fully explained. I understand that my child requires special education and before* <u>initial</u> *placement to receive special education, I must give consent for services. I give consent for my child to receive special education services. I understand when I give consent, it is voluntary, and that while it can be revoked, revocation is not retroactive. This means that once my child begins to receive services I cannot revoke the decision to allow my child to receive special education services. If I refuse consent I understand that the district may ask for mediation to address my childís eligibility for services. I understand the district may not ask for a due process hearing to override my consent. If I do not give consent for initial placement, the district may not provide services until I provide written consent.*

Initial Placement Only
[x] I approve of the Individualized Education Program and Placement as stated

_____         _____
Signature                                              Date

**MADELYN T. ZALE**

Student ID: 0000002463
FTE Number: F0000002463
Date of Birth: 08/01/1986

West Valley School District - DEMO

Spokane, WA

### State or Districtwide Assessments of Student Achievement

Student's Name: MADELYN T. ZALE                                    Date: 09/19/2005

Student ID Number: 0000002463

For Washington Assessment of Student Learning (WASL) or Washington Alternate Assessment (WAAS) see Guidelines for Inclusion and Accommodations for Special Populations on State-Level Assessments.

| Assessment | Participation | | Accommodations Modifications | | If YES, List Accommodation(s) and/or Modification(s) by Assessment |
|---|---|---|---|---|---|
| | Yes | No | Yes | No | |
| **Districtwide** | | | | | |
| PALS | X | | | X | |
| **ITBS/ITED** | | | | | |
| Language | | X | | | |
| Math | | X | | | |
| Reading | | X | | | |
| **Language Proficiency Test** | | | | | |
| Reading | | X | | | |
| Writing | X | | | X | |
| **WAAS** | | | | | |
| Listening | | X | | | |
| Math | | X | | | |
| Reading | | X | | | |
| Science | | X | | | |
| Writing | | X | | | |
| **WASL** | | | | | |
| Listening | | X | | | |
| Math | | X | | | |
| Reading | X | | X | | extended time on tests |
| Science | | X | | | |
| Writing | | X | | | |

*(continued)*

83

*TABLE 4-7* Continued

**MADELYN T. ZALE**

Student ID: 0000002463

FTE Number: F0000002463

Date of Birth: 08/01/1986

**West Valley School District - DEMO**

Spokane, WA

---

### Level V Graduation Standards

---

MADELYN T. ZALE will complete the district Level V requirements for the attainment of a high school diploma and will need the following accommodations and/or modifications in order to demonstrate proficiency in the Writing Standards

Graduation Plan for achieving writing standards:

☒ Proficient(1)  ☐ Proficient with accommodations(2)  ☐ Proficient with modifications(3)

☐ Proficient with Honors  ☐ Proficient with honors with accommodations(4)  ☐ Expectations

　　　　　　　　　　　　　　☐ Scheduling  ☐ Traits

　　　　　　　　　　　　　　☐ Setting  ☐ Content

　　　　　　　　　　　　　　☐ Aids

　　　　　　　　　　　　　　☐ Format

(1) Student does not need any accommodations or modifications to demonstrate proficiency

(2) Student needs accommodations to demonstrate proficiency. Accommodations do not alter graduation standards.

(3) Student needs modifications to demonstrate proficiency. Modifications are an alteration of the graduation standards, are directly related to student's disability and the qualifying areas of specially designed instruction, and are reflected in the goals and objectives of the IEP.

(4) Requires special approval.

Projected Graduation/Exit Date:_____

**Comments:**

---

**Is secondary transition being addressed?**　☐ No　☒ Yes

**If yes,** complete "Secondary Transition" pages before developing measurable annual goals.

**MADELYN T. ZALE**

Student ID: 0000002463
FTE Number: F0000002463
Date of Birth: 08/01/1986

**West Valley School District - DEMO**

Spokane, WA

## Prior Notice

**Purpose:** As a parent/guardian of a special education child suspected of needing special education services, the school district is required to provide you with prior written notice whenever it proposes or refuses to initiate or change the identification, evaluation, educational placement, or provision of a free appropriate public education to your child. This notice should be given to you after a district makes a decision and before action is taken on the decision. The notice should be given to you in a reasonable amount of time before the district takes action.

To: STEPHEN ZALE/ KRISTEN ZALE                    Date: 09/26/2005

Re: Student's Name: MADELYN T ZALE

**The purpose of this prior written notice is to inform you that we are:**

1. [X] proposing    [ ] refusing    **to**    2. [X] initiate    [ ] change    **a/an**
   (mark one of the above)                        (mark one of the above)

Mark all items below that apply:

3. [ ] Referral                                    [ ] Evaluation                [ ] Eligibility Category
   [ ] Educational Placement                        [X] IEP                      [ ] Reevaluation
   [ ] Disciplinary action that is a change of placement    [ ] Other:

Description of the proposed or refused action:
We propose to initiate this IEP.

The reason we are proposing or refusing to take action is:
Madelyn's weaknesses in reading comprehension and written expression.

Description of any other options considered and rejected:
No other options were considered.

The reasons we rejected those options were:
NA

A description of each procedure, test, record, or report we used or plan to use as the basis for taking this action is as follows:
Classroom observations, grades, work samples, WISC III

Any other factors that are relevant to the action:
NA

The action will be initiated on: _____

Your child has procedural protections under IDEA. These protections are explained in the *Notice of Procedural Safeguards for Special Education Students and Their Families.* If this prior written notice is given to you as part of your child's initial referral for evaluation, a part of a request for reevaluation or notice to you regarding disciplinary action that constitutes a change of placement the procedural safeguards accompanies this notice. If a copy of the *Notice of Procedural Safeguards for Special Education Students and Their Families* is not enclosed and you would like a copy or you would like help in understanding the content, please contact:

_____    at    _____

                                            _____
                                            Administrator/Designee

---

*Source:* © Xperts, Inc. 2006.

# CHAPTER *Five*

## Writing Unit and Lesson Plans

**OBJECTIVES**

After reading this chapter, the reader will be able to:

- identify and describe the necessary components of successful unit planning;
- identify and describe the importance of assessment planning;
- identify and describe the necessary components of successful lesson plans;
- create appropriate unit and lesson plans.

**INTRODUCTION**

This chapter provides an introduction for special educators in creating both unit and lesson plans. The first section of the chapter addresses curriculum and unit planning. The second section addresses the planning of lessons with helpful suggestions for the new special education teacher. In both sections, examples and suggestions are included to guide the teacher in developing his or her own unit and lesson planning templates.

As teachers begin developing their portfolios, important pieces of documentation or evidence to include are unit and lesson plans. The following discussion provides teachers with specific unit and lesson planning guidance as well as components that should be included in their plans. This evidence could include, but should not be limited to, samples of completed unit and lesson plans, student work samples documenting instructional sequences, and templates used for lesson and unit plans.

*My Classroom*

What a day! There was a fire drill in second period, five parents called, and his co-teacher called in sick. Finally, Mr. Kane has his planning period and time to catch his breath. His co-teacher asked him to look over the curriculum for the upcoming unit in social studies. They will need to begin planning for the unit. As Mr. Kane reads through the material, he begins making notes about unit objectives, assessment ideas, learning experiences, and where the instruction will need to be adapted for his special education students.

**FOCUS QUESTIONS**

1. How can national and state standards be incorporated into unit and lesson planning?

2. How can the "backward design" process facilitate unit and lesson planning for special education students?
3. How can a special education teacher effectively plan instruction for both units and individual lessons?

## CURRICULUM OVERVIEW

Lesson and unit planning for instruction is a foundation of teaching. Well-crafted plans ensure that instruction is focused and engaging for the learners. In many ways, a well-designed unit plan is a road map for both the teachers and the students. It tells you where you are headed, how you will get there, how long it will take, and how you know when you have arrived. A unit or lesson plan is how the curriculum is addressed in the classroom through instruction.

As previously discussed, a special education teacher may be a co-teacher in an inclusion classroom or teach in a self-contained classroom. Both situations require regular and consistent lesson planning. In a self-contained classroom, the teacher will provide a more generalized plan of how the day will be sequenced while each student's individual needs are addressed. In a co-taught classroom, the special and general education teachers will need to plan together to ensure that both the learning strategies for individual students and the curriculum needs of all the students are addressed.

While special education teachers have expertise in individual learning strategies, general education teachers have expertise in the curriculum for all students. The scope and sequence of the curriculum is comprehensive and addresses what information was previously covered, what information will be needed as a foundation for future learning, how state and national standards will be addressed, and how instruction will be sequenced (Ornstein & Hunkins, 1998). As standards-based testing has become more prevalent, individual school districts and states have focused on standardizing the curriculum as well (Protheroe, 2001). The unit and lesson plan must be aligned with the scope and sequence of the curriculum.

**Standards.** The implementation of the No Child Left Behind Act has brought an increased emphasis on standards-based testing for all students, including special education students (U.S. Department of Education, 2005). Most disciplines (or content areas) have a national organization that has established standards (e.g., the National Council of Social Studies). Some states have established their own standards (e.g., Virginia's Standards of Learning) that will need to be considered when unit or lesson planning.

Special education teachers will need to collaborate closely with general education teachers to ensure that the curriculum standards are addressed and that individual students are prepared to demonstrate their mastery of standards (Patterson, 2000). This will require special education teachers to become familiar with and knowledgeable of the standards for specific disciplines and grade levels.

**Standards-Based Assessments.** IDEA 2004 requires that individualized education programs (IEPs) contain a statement about whether a student will participate in the state- or districtwide assessment and what accommodations will be needed (Wright & Wright, 2005). The IEP team may decide that the student should not take the standardized assessment and that an alternative assessment will be conducted. In this case, the IEP must contain a statement about why the student could not participate in the state- or districtwide assessment and that the alternative assessment is appropriate to determine the student's academic achievement and functional performance (U.S. Department of Education, 2004).

For those students who will participate in the state- or districtwide assessments, special education teachers should closely align their unit and lesson planning with the curricular standards to be tested. In addition, students should be taught test-taking strategies appropriate to the tests that will be taken (e.g., answer selection for multiple choice or essay construction for writing).

## UNIT PLANNING

Planning for a thematic or curricular unit can be accomplished in different ways. Consider the elementary school teacher who plans a unit around community helpers, or the high school English teacher who plans a unit about *Lord of the Flies*. While the content of these units is very different, the process of planning for the instruction and learner experiences is similar. See Box 5-1 for information on unit planning considerations.

Many different planning tools for developing thematic units are available, and individual school districts may provide a program of studies that details how the curriculum should be addressed. Currently, it is important to align thematic units with the standards being assessed so that students have an opportunity to master the knowledge they will be tested on (Erickson, 1998). New special education teachers should actively seek out and consult with general education teachers on matters related to unit planning. However, one method of unit planning, "backward design," is especially valuable for the special education teacher (Wiggins & McTighe, 1998).

**Backward Design.** Backward design advocates that "one starts with the end-desired results (goals or standards) and then derives the curriculum from the evidence of learning (performances) called for by the standard and the teaching needed to equip students to perform" (Wiggins & McTighe, 1998, p. 8). In special education, teachers must focus on IEP goals and helping students meet assessment standards; therefore, a planning method that designs for these outcomes from the beginning is a terrific tool. Teachers begin with identifying desired outcomes. This should include a review of state and national standards for the content area being planned. This should also include what knowledge is important to understand, do, or know (Wiggins & McTighe, 1998).

**Assessment Plan.** The importance of assessing students as a measure of a school's or a teacher's performance has been recently emphasized. Effective schools (and teachers) regularly and consistently evaluate their performance. In 1997, the National Study of School Evaluation developed the following Principles

---

*BOX 5-1    Unit Planning Considerations*

Teachers should consider the following components when planning:
- Purpose of unit
- Learning objectives
- Length of time to teach unit
- Number and sequence of lessons
- Instructional activities (reading assignments, practice, experiments, homework)

- Assessments (unit tests, projects, papers, reports, presentations)
- Materials needed (texts, art supplies, computers, videos)
- Accommodations or modifications needed (see checklist in chapter 2)
- Special activities (guests, field trips)

for Assessment as part of the Principles of the Instructional Effectiveness of Schools of Quality:

- Defines clearly the expectations for student learning to be assessed. Assessments of student learning are aligned with clearly specified and appropriate achievement expectations.
- Establishes the purpose of the assessment. Assessments arise from and are specifically designed to serve instructional purposes specified by the users of the results of the assessments.
- Selects the appropriate method of assessment. Assessments are developed using a method that can accurately reflect the intended goals for student achievement and serve the intended purpose.
- Collects a comprehensive and representative sample of student achievement. The student learning assessment system provides for the collection of a comprehensive and representative sample of student performance that is sufficient in scope to permit confident conclusions about student achievement and yields generalizable results.
- Develops fair assessments and avoids bias and distortion. Assessments are designed, developed, and used in a fair and equitable manner that eliminates any source of bias or distortion which might interfere with the accuracy of the results (Fitzpatrick, 1998, p. 55).

These principles should be incorporated into all student assessments. Special education teachers should be particularly sensitive to developing assessments that measure student academic achievements and functional performance. A further discussion of assessment is provided in Chapter 6.

A unit plan should encompass an assessment plan. According to Wiggins and McTighe (1998), the following should be included in an assessment plan:

1. Identify the national or state standards to be addressed by the unit;
2. Identify the learning objectives;
3. Identify what assessment methods and criteria will measure the learning objectives; and
4. Identify what instructional methods and assignments you will use in the unit.

Box 5-2 provides specific details for assessment planning.

**Planning for Standards.** When developing an assessment plan, teachers should identify the standard that is to be addressed. While the entire standard may not be addressed in a single unit, teachers should identify the specific

---

**BOX 5-2** *Assessment Planning Considerations*

Teachers should ask:
- What is it students should know or be able to do?
  - What standards are to be assessed or measured?
  - Do you need to know where students are in relationship to benchmarks?
- How is the assessment information going to be used?
  - Is the information to gauge student learning?
  - Is it to inform instruction?
  - Is it to evaluate or provide a grade?
  - Is it to provide practice opportunities for the learners?
- Is it to evaluate or judge school or program effectiveness?
- What modifications to the curriculum are needed?
  - How will these modifications be assessed?
  - How do the modifications affect the student being assessed?
- What accommodations for assessment might be required?
  - Will students need extended time or questions read aloud for taking tests?
  - Will students need technology assistance to complete essay assignments?

objectives or benchmarks under the standard that are addressed. Consider the following math standard for grades 9 to 12:

Understand numbers, ways of representing numbers, relationships among numbers, and number systems.

- develop a deeper understanding of very large and very small numbers and of various representations of them;
- compare and contrast the properties of numbers and number systems, including the rational and real numbers, and understand complex numbers as solutions to quadratic equations that do not have real solutions;
- understand vectors and matrices as systems that have some of the properties of the real-number system; use number-theory arguments to justify relationships involving whole numbers (National Council of Teachers of Mathematics, 2004).

A teacher might develop an entire unit that addresses quadratic equations under the second objective. This unit might last from 3 to 4 weeks, while the overall standard will be addressed throughout a single school year with units developed around the specific objectives. See Tables 5-1, 5-2 and 5-3.

When determining the assessment methods and criteria, teachers should consider the development of grading or scoring rubrics. Rubrics that provide examples and specific articulation of required elements are the most helpful for facilitating student learning (McTighe & Ferrara, 1998). Rubrics can be effectively used in inclusive classrooms because they can be developed with the general curriculum in mind and incorporate benchmarks for all students. Rubrics can assist all students in learning how to evaluate their own work, thus increasing student self-efficacy. They can also incorporate IEP goals for special needs students (Whittaker, Salend, & Duhaney, 2001).

**TABLE 5-1** *Learner Objectives and Assessment Methods*

| Bloom's Taxonomy (Words to State Learning Outcomes) (Bloom, 1974) | Assessment Methods: Constructing Tests | Assessment Methods: Constructing Products (Reports) and Performances (Presentations) |
|---|---|---|
| **Knowledge**—label, name, order, state, list, define, recognize, relate | True/false, multiple choice, matching | Consider defining knowledge needed to create the product or performance. |
| **Comprehension**—classify, identify, locate, explain, select, describe, indicate | True/false, multiple choice, matching, short answer | Consider explanations needed to create the product or performance. |
| **Application**—apply, schedule, illustrate, choose, interpret, practice, write, solve | Multiple choice, short answer, essay, charts, graphs, maps | Consider applications and interpretations needed to create the product or performance. |
| **Analysis**—analyze, distinguish, compare, differentiate, categorize, contrast, criticize, examine, discriminate | Multiple choice (items may get wordy), short answer, essay, charts, graphs, maps | Consider discriminations, comparisons, and criticisms needed to create the product or performance. |
| **Synthesis**—arrange, formulate, organize, plan, construct, collect, prepare, assemble, compose | Essay | Consider formulations, organization, and planning needed to create the product or performance. |
| **Evaluation**—judge, attach, support, estimate, score, predict, choose, evaluate, assess, select, appraise | Essay | Consider judgments, assessments, and evaluations needed to create the product or performance. |

*Source.* Adapted from Bloom (1974).

TABLE 5-2 Assessment Plan Template

| National or State Standard<br><br>Step 1 | Learner Objectives<br><br>Step 2 | Unit Assessments (Essays and Tests)<br><br>Step 3 | Grading Criteria Rubrics<br><br>Step 4 | Accommodations and/or Modifications<br><br>Step 5 | Learning Experiences (Homework, Guided Practice, and Independent Work)<br><br>Step 6 |
|---|---|---|---|---|---|
| | | | | | |

TABLE 5-3 *Example of Assessment Plan*

| National or State Standard<br><br>Step 1 | Learner Objectives<br><br>Step 2 | Unit Assessments (Essays and Tests)<br><br>Step 3 | Grading Criteria Rubrics<br><br>Step 4 | Accommodations and/or Modifications<br><br>Step 5 | Learning Experiences (Homework, Guided Practice, and Independent Work)<br><br>Step 6 |
|---|---|---|---|---|---|
| 5.3 The student will describe colonial America, with emphasis on the factors that led to the founding of the colonies, and key individuals and events in the American Revolution including King George, Lord North, Lord Cornwallis, John Adams, George Washington, Thomas Jefferson, Patrick Henry, and Thomas Paine.<br><br>(Virginia Standard of Learning: History and Social Science SOL) | Students will be able to identify key figures in the American Revolution.<br><br>Students will be able to examine and distinguish the role of key figures in the American Revolution.<br><br>Students will be able to assess and evaluate the impact of key figures on the American Revolution. | Unit test with matching, multiple-choice, and short essay questions. (60 pts.)<br><br>Write a newspaper article from a colonial newspaper. (20 pts.)<br><br>Students will complete an individual KWL chart about each figure.<br><br>Report and presentation (180 pts.) Group project: Student group (20 pts. for process) | Test will be 20% of unit grade.<br><br>Comment on support of Revolution, Spell/Grammar, note key figures. (10% of unit grade)<br><br>KWL chart, Spell/Grammar, key events in lives. (10% of unit grade)<br><br>Report and presentation rubric: Spell/Grammar logical sequence, critical roles and why, oral skills. (50% of grade)<br><br>Homework completion will be 10% of unit grade. | Teacher will review test items with students. Identify mistakes and correct answers. Extended time and oral instructions as needed.<br><br>Students will peer review each other's newspaper article. Provide feedback and use rubric for grading.<br><br>KWL chart is self-assessment for learning process.<br><br>Students will review in class rubric for report and presentation. Students will submit grades for members of group project.<br><br>Other accommodations and modifications as stated on IEPs (i.e., computer use, extended time, shortened assignments, and oral instructions). | Reading assignments in text followed by classroom discussion.<br><br>Students will view Williamsburg video on the American Revolution (discusses GW, PH, and TJ).<br><br>Students will write a newspaper article for a colonial paper describing a key event of the revolution (Declaration of Independence or surrender at Yorktown).<br><br>Group project: Students will be asked to prepare a presentation (and report) on the biography of a key figure and contribution. |

**Developing a Unit.** Finally, after determining the learner outcomes and developing an assessment plan, teachers can begin planning for the instruction of the unit. Learner objectives should be written in measurable language (e.g., compare/contrast, identify, or evaluate). This is done before any lessons on the unit are taught and before lesson plans are written. See Tables 5-4 and 5-5 for an example of an elementary unit; however, if you are interested in a secondary example, see Table 5-6.

As teachers begin developing a unit plan, it is important that the plan focus the instruction on what will be assessed and how it will be taught. Wiggins and McTighe (1998) provide a helpful acronym, WHERE:

W—Where is the instruction headed?

H—Hook the students through engaging instruction.

E—Explore and enable (consider the learning experiences).

R—Reflect and rethink (guide students to "dig deeper").

E—Evaluate.

Special education teachers must consider individual learner needs and different strategies or methods to address those needs. Special education teachers should ensure that the instructional activities (homework or readings) can be modified ahead of time. To support and enhance the content being addressed, consider what learning experiences or instructional activities will be incorporated for all students.

**Integrating IEP Goals and Objectives.** When possible, the special education teacher should integrate IEP goals into a unit plan. Just as learner objectives are identified, IEP goals and objectives should also be identified. Consider that many IEPs have written and oral language goals stated and that essays or written homework often are assigned as part of a unit. By

*TABLE 5-4*  *Unit Planning Template*

| National or state standard | *(Write standard here)* |
|---|---|
| Purpose or theme of unit (consider scope and sequence of curriculum) | *(What is the purpose of the unit? Are there any processes or skills that must also be covered?)* |
| Unit assessments (list types of assessments [tests, essays, and student projects] and include criteria and rubrics) | *(List unit assessments and attach tests, rubrics, and so on)* |
| Learner objectives (state in measurable and objective terms) | *Students will be able to:* |
| IEP goals (related to curricular content) | *(Note IEP goals and accommodations or modifications needed)* |
| Learning experiences | *(How will the unit be presented? What will the students do? What homework will be assigned?)* |
| Instructional considerations | *(Consider: checks for understanding, vocabulary, guided practice, and independent work)* |
| Special events and materials | *(Consider: guest speakers, field trips, computer/technology applications, and materials that will need to be prepared)* |
| Co-teaching considerations | *(Consider: Who will teach what content? How will lesson plans be completed?)* |

*TABLE 5-5* Example of Unit Plan

| | |
|---|---|
| National or state standard | *(Write standard here)*<br>5.3 The student will describe colonial America, with emphasis on the factors that led to the founding of the colonies, and key individuals and events in the American Revolution, including King George, Lord North, Lord Cornwallis, John Adams, George Washington, Thomas Jefferson, Patrick Henry, and Thomas Paine. (Virginia Standard of Learning: History and Social Science SOL) |
| Purpose or theme of unit (consider scope and sequence of curriculum) | *(What is the purpose of the unit? Are there any processes or skills that must also be covered?)*<br>The purpose of this unit is to identify and understand the roles of key figures in the American Revolution. The differences in the American and British perspectives on the Revolution will be explored. |
| Unit assessments (list types of assessments [tests, essays, and student projects] and include criteria and rubrics) | *(List unit assessments and attach tests, rubrics, and so on)*<br>Unit test with matching, multiple-choice, and short essay questions. (60 pts.)<br>Test will be 20% of unit grade.<br>Write a newspaper article from a colonial newspaper. (20 pts.) Comment on support of Revolution, Spell/Grammar, note key figures. (10% of unit grade)<br>Homework completion will be 10% of unit grade.<br>Students will complete an individual KWL chart about each figure. Student rubric KWL chart, Spell/Grammar, key events in lives. (10% of unit grade)<br>Report and presentation (180 pts.). Process: Student group (20 pts.)<br>Report and presentation rubric: Spell/Grammar<br>Logical sequence, critical roles and why, oral skills. (50% of grade) |
| Learner objectives (state in measurable and objective terms) | *Students will be able to:*<br>Identify key figures in the American Revolution.<br>Examine and distinguish the role of key figures in the American Revolution.<br>Assess and evaluate the impact of key figures on the American Revolution. |
| IEP goals (related to curricular content) | *(Note IEP goals and accommodations or modifications if needed)*<br>Differentiation Strategies:<br>Students will develop their own KWL charts for key figures.<br>Students will develop personal learning contracts.<br>Activities will be tiered.<br>Students will have options on how to research key figures: texts, Internet, and video.<br>Accommodations:<br>Simplified text readings, peer support, extended time, shortened assignments, and other accommodations as stated on IEP.<br>List IEP Goals:<br>1. Oral language goals<br>2. Written language goals<br>3. Organizational goals |

**TABLE 5-5** *Continued*

| | |
|---|---|
| Learning experiences | *(How will the unit be presented? What will the students do? What homework will be assigned?)*<br>Reading assignments in text followed by classroom discussion.<br>Students will view Williamsburg video on the American Revolution (discuss GW, PH, and TJ).<br>Students will be asked to write the obituary of three of the key figures.<br>Group Project:<br>Students will be asked to prepare a presentation (and report) on the biography of a key figure and his or her contribution to the Revolution.<br>Students will be encouraged to consider how they might have responded to the call for freedom and revolution. |
| Instructional considerations | *(Consider: checks for understanding, vocabulary, guided practice, and independent work)*<br>ZPD Checks:<br>Introductory discussion<br>Have students write a paragraph on two of the figures<br>Ask students to list two things they do not understand about the people in the American Revolution.<br>Ongoing informal ZPD checks through discussion and homework review.<br>Thought questions relating to how did their wives think and feel about their activities (letters from Martha Washington and Abigail Adams as reading assignments).<br>Thought questions relating to pro-British or pro-American position. What may have led to each figure's beliefs about the Revolution? Discussion about what "freedom" means to you as an individual and how this relates to what the American patriots might have thought?<br>What was the British perspective? How did they see the colonists? |
| Special events and materials | *(Consider: guest speakers, field trips, computer and technology applications, and materials that will need to be prepared)*<br>Williamsburg video<br>Use of Web for research on key figures |
| Co-teaching considerations | *(Consider: Who will teach what content? How will lesson plans be completed?)*<br>Special Education Teacher: IEP goals, accommodations, and rubrics for unit assessments<br>General Education Teacher: Video preparation, project directions, and development of unit test<br>Both: Introduce unit, class discussions, supervise project work, and grade homework |

*TABLE 5-6* Example of Unit Plan (High School)

| National or state standard | (*Write standard here*)<br>PS. 10 The student will investigate and understand scientific principles and technological applications of work, force, and motion.<br>Key concepts include<br>1. speed, velocity, and acceleration;<br>2. Newton's laws of motion;<br>3. work, force, mechanical advantage, efficiency, and power; and<br>4. applications (simple machines, compound machines, powered vehicles, rockets, and restraining devices).<br>(Virginia standard of Learning) |
|---|---|
| Purpose or theme of unit (consider scope and sequence of curriculum) | (*What is the purpose of the unit? Are there any processes or skills that must also be covered?*)<br>Newton's laws of motion:<br>• First law of motion (also known as law of inertia)<br>  • An object at rest will remain at rest.<br>  • An object in motion will remain in motion at a constant velocity unless acted on by an external force.<br>• Second law of motion<br>  • If a net force acts on an object, it will cause the acceleration of the object.<br>  • Force = mass × acceleration: F = ma.<br>• Third law of motion:<br>  • For every action, there is an equal and opposite reaction.<br>  • If an object exerts a force on another object, the second object exerts an equal and opposite force on the first.<br>• Inquiry/experimental process:<br>  • Hypothesis testing<br>  • Format for writing lab report |
| Unit assessments (list types of assessments [tests, essays, and student projects] and include criteria and rubrics) | (*List unit assessments and attach tests, rubrics, and so on*)<br>• Daily homework (including F = ma calculations)<br>• Labs (including participation in experiments and lab reports in required format)<br>• Essay on Isaac Newton (biography of five to six pages with references)<br>• Unit test (format: combined multiple choice, short answer, and calculations [calculators allowed])<br>• Allocations: homework = 20%, labs = 30%, essay = 20%, and unit test = 30% |
| Learner objectives (state in measurable and objective terms) | *Students will be able to:*<br>• Demonstrate knowledge of Newton's three laws of motion both verbally and mathematically by solving problems.<br>• Demonstrate understanding of the scientific importance of Newton's contributions both verbally and in writing.<br>• Apply concepts of inertia, force, and motion to real-life scenarios, including roller coasters and sports.<br>• Evaluate data obtained through experimental processes relating to inertia, force, and motion, including an appropriate display and write-up of the data. |
| IEP goals (related to curricular content) | (*Note IEP goals and accommodations or modifications if needed*)<br>Differentiation Strategies:<br>1. Labs done in tiers<br>2. Learning contracts |

**TABLE 5-6** *Continued*

| | *Accommodations:*<br>Simplified text, extended time, shortened assignments, and other accommodations as stated on IEP.<br>List IEP Goals:<br>1. Oral language goals<br>2. Written language goals<br>3. Organizational goals—focus on sequencing lab experiments |
|---|---|
| Learning experiences | *(How will the unit be presented? What will the students do? What homework will be assigned?)*<br>• Reading assignments in text followed by classroom discussion.<br>• Review of daily homework following reading assignment discussion. Daily homework will include F = ma calculations and real-world problems to solve. (10 problems per day)<br>• Pose question relating to inertia, motion, and force on whiteboard prior to lab experiment. (Review the importance of observation, hypothesis testing, and data collection as part of the inquiry process before beginning labs.)<br>• Lab experiments—Use experiments designed and available from the National Science Teachers association (http://www.nsta.org).<br>• Lab reports—written in acceptable format.<br>• CD-ROM from text with computer simulation—used to demonstrate real-world applications for Newton's laws of motion.<br>• Essay assignment—Students will be asked to write an essay on Newton's biography and his contributions to science. |
| Instructional considerations | *(Consider: checks for understanding, vocabulary, guided practice, and independent work)*<br>ZPD Checks:<br>• Introductory discussion.<br>• Review of daily homework (will need to check calculations and process to ensure understanding by all students).<br>• Informal observations during lab experiments (pay attention to lab safety and data collection procedure).<br>Vocabulary:<br>• Definitions of inertia, force, motion, acceleration, and velocity.<br>• Will also need to mathematically define with equations.<br>Guided Practice and Independent Work:<br>• Homework will be started in class with examples on the whiteboard. It will be completed outside of class and reviewed the next day. Labs will provide another avenue of both guided practice and independent work. |
| Special events and materials | *(Consider: guest speakers, field trips, computer and technology applications, and materials that will need to be prepared)*<br>Both teachers will review the article by R. Grumbine and P. B. Alden, "Teaching Science to Students with Learning Disabilities," *The Science Teacher*, 73 (3), 26–31.<br>• Lab handouts from National Science Teachers' Association from their materials on Newton's laws of motion.<br>• Prepare lab materials (soda bottles, magnets, string, and marbles).<br>• CD-ROM from text on Newton's Laws of motion is needed.<br>• Ensure that computer lab is prepared for use by students (Internet and CD-ROM).<br>• Contact school librarian or media specialist about the need for biographical information on Isaac Newton. |
| Co-teaching considerations | *(Consider: Who will teach what content? How will lesson plans be completed?)*<br>Special Education Teacher: IEP goals, accommodations, and rubric for essay.<br>General Education Teacher: Lab preparation and development of unit test.<br>Both: Introduce unit, class discussions, supervise lab work, and grade homework. |

incorporating IEP goals into the planning of the unit, the special education teacher can ensure that IEP goals and objectives are consistently addressed. Other goals (e.g., organizational or social) may also be appropriate to integrate, depending on the unit to be taught.

Another benefit of planning a unit with IEP goals and objectives built in is that unit assessments can also function as documentation of progress on IEP goals and objectives. In the previous example of incorporating written language goals into an essay assignment, the special education teacher could keep copies of the essay and grading rubric as work samples to document progress. Initially, integrating IEP goals and objectives into the unit planning process may be time consuming; however, the gains made in student achievement and the ease of documentation for the special education teacher are worth considering.

**Instructional Considerations.** Finally, after the assessment plan has been developed, the learner objectives have been stated, and IEP goals and objectives have been considered, the unit plan should focus on what the teacher will do. How will the unit be introduced? What learning experiences will the teacher provide the students? When will the students work independently? When will the teacher provide guided practice? What informal checks for understanding will be included so that the teacher knows if the students are learning?

While each special education teacher will develop their own instructional routines and "style" for teaching over time, certain approaches can be effective. Differentiated instruction, which provides a mechanism for providing individualized instruction for all students in a classroom, could be incorporated into unit planning (Tomlinson, 2001). Another approach to unit planning, universal design for learning, incorporates elements related to universal design for access to instruction (Rose & Meyer, 2002). Finally, as diversity in schools increases, multicultural approaches may be appropriate (Garderen & Whittaker, 2006). These are only a few examples, and teachers are encouraged to make informed decisions about which approach to use.

One of the ways to ensure instructional effectiveness is to determine the student's zone of proximal development (ZPD). The ZPD is defined as "the distance between the actual developmental level as determined by independent problem solving and the level of potential development as determined through problem solving under adult guidance or in collaboration with more capable peers" (Vygotsky, 1978, p. 86). The ZPD is sometimes called the "instructional level." The ZPD is where instruction is going to be most effective. Teachers should plan to determine the ZPD through pretesting of students to determine their prior knowledge and/or through informal checks for understanding.

Once the ZPD is determined, teachers should provide opportunities for guided practice through scaffolding. Scaffolding refers to the changing quality of support over the course of a lesson. The teacher adjusts his or her assistance (guidance) to accommodate the student's current level of performance (Hedegaard, 1990). Often the teacher will assign practice to the students while walking around the classroom, providing individual assistance, as needed. As students progress in their understanding and approach mastery, the teacher will provide less assistance. Finally, students should be provided opportunities for independent practice to solidify their newly acquired knowledge and skills. See Chapter 6 for more information on instructional strategies.

As is evident in the unit planning discussion, a well-thought-out unit plan will enable the teacher to quickly create and/or change lesson plans because the overall direction of the unit has been determined. The time spent developing a comprehensive unit is well spent and will make it easier to plan instructionally effective lessons.

## LESSON PLANNING

Once a unit plan has been developed, individual lesson plans will be constructed. Lesson plans are how teachers ensure that their instruction is focused and effective; however, many teachers (both experienced and novice) simply do not spend time on planning. New teachers often feel overwhelmed by all their responsibilities. Consequently, less time is allowed for planning, and it may be done haphazardly or, sometimes, not at all. This is a critical mistake. See Figure 5-1.

Would you want your taxes prepared by an accountant who did not use spreadsheets or who created them in a haphazard fashion? Probably not, since spreadsheets are the tools that the professional accountant uses to perform the job. Similarly, a well-crafted lesson plan is a tool of the teaching profession and a professional responsibility. Simply put, lesson planning is part of the job of teaching. See Box 5-3 on lesson planning considerations.

Time should be allocated to lesson planning. If a teacher has created a unit, the time needed to create individual lesson plans will be much less because an overall plan has already been established. Planning a week at a time is another successful strategy for managing your time (Pelletier, 2004). In many classrooms, teachers use a desk planner with a monthly view to plan lessons. This can be effective when a comprehensive unit plan is in place; otherwise, it does not provide the level of detail necessary for a successful lesson plan. Time spent on lesson planning can make classroom teaching more efficient and smoother; thus helping the teacher maximize instructional time. See Box 5-4 for lesson planning for your substitute and Tables 5-7 to 5-11 for helpful lesson planning templates.

*FIGURE 5-1*

*Source:* FOR BETTER OR FOR WORSE © 2002 Lynn Johnston Productions. Distributed by Universal Press Syndicate. Reprinted with permission. All rights reserved.

---

**BOX 5-3**  *Lesson Planning Considerations*

A successful lesson plan will contain the following:
- The purpose and objective of the lesson
- The state or national standard(s) that will be addressed
- The instructional sequence that will be used

- The materials (texts and handouts) and equipment that will be used
- The evaluation tools (quizzes and homework) that will be used to monitor learning
- The accommodations or modifications that will be needed

Teachers get sick and have unexpected emergencies. Daily lesson plans are essential for helping a substitute teacher maintain classroom routines and instruction. Consider the following:

1. Leave written lesson plans in an easy-to-locate place (folder on your desk).
2. Prepare your materials the night before the lesson. The materials are then ready if you are unable to make it to class.
3. Create a substitute folder that contains worksheets, readings, or other assignments that the substitute can give the students to work on while you are absent. This folder might also contain helpful hints for the substitute (class rules, routines, and where to locate equipment).

**TABLE 5-7** *Daily Lesson Plan Sequence*

| Time | Learning Experience (Activity) | Notes | Accommodations |
|------|-------------------------------|-------|----------------|
|      |                               |       |                |
|      |                               |       |                |
|      |                               |       |                |
|      |                               |       |                |
|      |                               |       |                |
|      |                               |       |                |
|      |                               |       |                |

**TABLE 5-8**  *Example of Daily Lesson Plan Sequence (Elementary Language Arts)*

| Time | Learning Experience (Activity) | Notes | Accommodations |
|---|---|---|---|
| 9:00–9:10 | • Review previous lesson<br>• Review today's agenda<br>• Have students record homework assignment<br><br>• State the goal or objective of the lesson | This is also the time to check in and make sure everyone knows the class rules and is ready for learning. Planner checks can be done. | Ensure that learners understand the goal of the lesson. Ensure that learners understand performance criteria on the learning tasks. |
| 9:10–9:25 | • Warm-up (could be any of the following or other language arts activities)<br>• Practice test questions<br>• Practice worksheets<br>• Phonemic awareness activities | This could also be a time to do practice questions from standardized tests. This might also include learning journals to identify strategies that are helpful. | Ensure extended time or individual assistance as needed. Ensure that progress is being tracked. Note IEP goals (oral or written language goals). |
| 9:25–9:40 | • Reading time (could be any of the following)<br>• Reading with teacher (guided)<br>• Silent reading<br>• Buddy reading<br>• Computer-assisted reading program | Students circle words that they don't know. (comprehension) Students circle words they can't pronounce. (phonics) Help students be aware of their progress in reading and how they can remember specific words and sounds. | Individual or small-group assistance, as needed. |
| 9:40–9:50 | • Break time or at least some activity to move around | | May be appropriate to incorporate social goals from IEP. |
| 9:50–10:10 | • Writing/other language arts activity<br>• Vocabulary builder<br>• Poems<br>• Phonemic awareness exercises | Students could work together, or this could be a whole-group lesson. | Consider using pair and share. Have students read each other's work. Develop personal dictionaries of words that are hard for them. Have students monitor which sounds they have difficulty with. |
| 10:10–10:15 | • Closing routine<br>• Go over what we did<br>• Go over the goal or objective of lesson<br>• Remind students of homework assignment | This is the closing bracket for how you began the instructional period. Have learners note any progress they made. (Example: I got all the words with a long e today.) Documentation of progress. | Review goal or objective of lesson. Review performance criteria. Review planners for homework assignments. Collect data for documentation of IEP progress. |

**TABLE 5-9**  *Calendar Template*

| Sun | Mon | Tue | Wed | Thu | Fri | Sat |
|---|---|---|---|---|---|---|
| | | | | | | |
| | | | | | | |
| | | | | | | |
| | | | | | | |

*TABLE 5-10*  Lesson Plan Template

| Title of lesson Class, period, date | |
|---|---|
| State or national standard(s) | |
| Learner objectives (Student will be able to . . . ) | |
| Instructional sequence | |
| Materials and equipment | |
| Evaluation (include informal checks for understanding) | |
| Accommodations or Modifications | |

*TABLE 5-11*  Lesson Plan Template

| Title of lesson Class, period, date | Subject: Time frame: (minutes and period): Grade: Number of Students: |
|---|---|
| State or national standard(s) (write out relevant parts of the standard) | Topic: Rationale: |
| Rationale for instruction (state rationale given to students for how this instruction may benefit them—write in student language) | |

103

| Daily objectives (state in operational, measurable terms; objective should be directly linked to evaluation procedures; if you are working with a small group or one-on-one, individual goals may be appropriate; one to three goals per lesson) Evaluation/monitoring (description of how you will evaluate student achievement of lesson objectives; attach any quizzes, questions used for assessment, or worksheets) | Student will be able to: |
| --- | --- |
| Instructional sequence (estimate amount of time per section)<br>Start of class period<br>• Required tasks<br>• Collection of homework<br>• Warm-up activity<br>Beginning lesson (introduction or connecting to previous day)<br>• Motivation/relevance<br>• Overview<br>• Directions<br>• Purpose of lesson<br>Middle of lesson<br>• Objective<br>• Key questions<br>• Students engaged<br>• Activity<br>• Student sharing<br>• Informal check for understanding<br>Closing of lesson<br>• Wrap-Up<br>• Review of key points<br>• Collection of papers/materials<br>Ending of class period<br>• Required tasks<br>• Collection of class work | Level of instruction (acquisition, practice, or generalization): |
| Materials/equipment/preparation (list materials, attach any worksheets or assessment forms, list any Web sites needed) | |
| Reflections<br>Do I need other resources?<br>Will I be using the paraeducator?<br>How will I know I have succeeded? | |

*Source.* Used with permission from Kristen Sayeski.

---

**BOX 5-5** *Lesson Plan Resources*

---

Many different resources for lesson planning are available. National organizations, such as the National Council of Teachers of Mathematics (http://www.nctm.org) provide books or materials that can help with lesson plans. Some of these materials are available online. Another resource is Lesson Plan Search (http://www.lessonplansearch.com), which is a Web-based search engine that allows teachers to search for lesson plans by grade and content area. While these are helpful resources, not all lesson plans will be appropriate to your classroom. You may need to modify or adapt the lessons to your students' needs.

Science centers and museums are often overlooked when lesson planning. Many of these institutions have professional educators on staff who develop and provide materials for teachers. When visiting museums or other institutions, you may wish to inquire about their educational programming, as free materials may be available. The following Websites provide examples of materials and lesson plans:

**http://americanhistory.si.edu/educators/index.cfm**
National Museum of American History—Click on the Classroom Resources link.

**http://www.nmai.si.edu**
National Museum of the American Indian—Click on the Educators link, then on Education Publications.

**http://www.mfa.org/index.asp**
Museum of Fine Arts, Boston—Click on the Educator link, then on Teacher Resources.

**http://www.pbs.org**
Public Broadcasting Service—Lesson plans and activities to use PBS productions in classrooms (e.g., NOVA, Scientific American, and Reading Rainbow). Click on the Teacher Source link.

*Note*: When accessing a lesson plan from another source, verify that the content of the lesson plan is aligned with the specific national or state standard that is being addressed in the curriculum.

---

**TABLE 5-12** *Evidence Checklist: Unit and Lesson Plans*

---

To provide evidence of competency in the area of unit and lesson plans, a special education teacher might include the following in a teaching portfolio:

❑ Copies of unit plans

❑ Copies of relevant state or national standards aligned with unit or lesson plans

❑ Copies of lesson plans

❑ Copies of unit assessments showing alignment with state or national standards

❑ Copies of accommodations or modifications of curricula for special needs students

❑ Copies of materials related to unit or lesson plans (handouts or quizzes)

❑ Photos of student projects related to unit or lesson plans

---

*Note.* Student confidentiality should be maintained. Please block out any identifying information.

---

## SUMMARY

This discussion has provided a framework for developing unit and lesson plans as well as templates that can be used for such planning. When developing the documentation for a teaching portfolio, teachers should provide examples of their unit and lesson planning. Teachers should also regularly reflect on how well an individual lesson was taught. These types of reflections should be included in a reflection journal. During the course of a teaching career, teachers develop their own styles of unit and lesson planning. Resources for constructing lesson plans can be found in Box 5-5. Some school districts mandate that teachers use a particular lesson planning form. In other situations, teams of teachers may decide to use a specific form. Whatever format is chosen, planning for lessons should be done regularly and consistently. See Table 5-12 for ideas for examples of unit and lesson plans evidence for your teaching portfolio.

## ACTIVITY QUESTIONS

1. Discuss unit and lesson planning with your mentor or co-teacher. What strategies have they found to be successful? Do they have any time-saving ideas?

2. Discuss the curriculum and standards with your general education teachers. What do they think is important for you to know? How can you become more familiar with the curriculum?

3. Begin reflecting on your lessons. At least once a week, evaluate a lesson you taught. This should be written in your journal. Think about what went well. Think about what you would change.

4. Develop a portfolio of unit and lesson plan templates. As you develop lesson and unit plans, save copies so that you can modify and use similar plans in the future.

## SELECTED WEBSITES

http://www.ncss.org/message.html
*This is the site for the National Council for Social Studies, which provides curricular and instructional support for the teaching of social studies.*

http://www.teachersfirst.com/matrix.htm
*This site provides lesson plans for a variety of content areas and suggestions for teachers on how to modify lesson plans.*

http://www.ascd.org
*This is the site for Association for Supervision and Curriculum Development. You can purchase Understanding by Design materials, including books, videos, and templates.*

## REFLECTION JOURNAL ACTIVITIES

1. Reflect on the state or national standards relevant to the curriculum you are teaching. What else do you need to know? How will you incorporate the standards into your planning? How does your mentor or co-teacher ensure that the standards are addressed?

2. Reflect on a lesson you taught. What went well in the lesson? What would you change the next time you taught this lesson? (Was the instructional sequence appropriate? Did you take too long on one part, or was one part too short? Were the students engaged?) This type of reflection should be done at least once a week.

3. Reflect on your unit and lesson planning by asking experienced teachers about their planning process. Do they have any tips or strategies you could use? How do they find time to plan? Have they built a portfolio of unit or lesson plans that they use over and over?

4. Planning and lessons are fundamental to good teaching. Reflect on what evidence you will include in your teaching portfolio to demonstrate you competency in unit and lesson planning.

## REFERENCES

Bloom, B. S. (1974). *The taxonomy of educational objectives: Affective and cognitive domains.* New York: David McKay.

Erickson, L. H. (1998). *Concept-based curriculum and instruction: Teaching beyond the facts.* Thousand Oaks, CA: Corwin Press.

Fitzpatrick, K. A. (1998). *Program evaluation handbook: A comprehensive guide for standards-based program evaluation for schools committed to continuous improvement.* Schaumburg, IL: National Study of School Evaluation.

Garderen, D. van, & Whittaker, C. (2006). Planning differentiated, multicultural instruction for secondary inclusive classrooms. *Teaching Exceptional Children, 38*(3), 12–20.

Grumbine, R., & Alden, P. B. (2006). Teaching science to students with learning disabilities. *The Science Teacher, 73*(3), 26–31.

Hedegaard, M. (1990). The zone of proximal development as basis for instruction. In L. Moll (Ed.), *Vygotsky and education: Instructional implications and applications of sociohistorical psychology* (pp. 349–371). New York: Cambridge University Press.

McTighe, J., & Ferrara, S. (1998). *Assessing learning in the classroom.* Washington, DC: National Education Association.

National Council of Teachers of Mathematics. (2004). *Principles and standards for school mathematics.* Retrieved January 10, 2006, from http://www.nctm.org

Ornstein, A., & Hunkins, F. (1998). *Curriculum: Foundations, principles, and issues* (3rd ed.). Needham Heights, MA: Allyn & Bacon.

Patterson, J. (2000). *Essentials for principals: School leader's guide to special education.* Arlington, VA: Educational Resource Service and National Association of Elementary School Principals.

Pelletier, C. M. (2004). *Strategies for successful student teaching: A comprehensive guide* (2nd ed.). Boston: Allyn & Bacon.

Protheroe, N. (2001). *Essentials for principals: Meeting the challenges of high-stakes testing.* Arlington, VA: Educational Research Service and National Association of Elementary School Principals.

Rose, D. H., & Meyer, A. (2002). *Teaching every student in the digital age: Universal design for learning.* Alexandria, VA: Association for Supervision and Curriculum Development.

Tomlinson, C. A. (2001). *How to differentiate instruction in mixed ability classrooms* (2nd ed.).

Alexandria, VA: Association for Supervision and Curriculum Development.

U.S. Department of Education. (2004). *Individuals with Disabilities Education Act.* Retrieved August 14, 2005, from http://ideadata.org

U.S. Department of Education. (2005). *No Child Left Behind.* Retrieved June 21, 2005, from http://www.ed.gov

Vygotsky, L. (1978). *Mind and society: The development of higher psychological processes.* Cambridge, MA: Harvard University Press.

Whittaker, C. R., Salend, S. J., & Duhaney, D. (2001). Creating instructional rubrics for inclusive classrooms. *Teaching Exceptional Children 34*(2), 8–13.

Wiggins, G., & McTighe, J. (1998). *Understanding by design.* Alexandria, VA: Association for Supervision and Curriculum Development.

Wright, P., & Wright, P. (2005). *Roadmap to IDEA 2004: What you need to know about IEPs and IEP meetings.* Retrieved January 9, 2006, from http://www.wrightslaw.com/idea/iep.roadmpap.htm

# CHAPTER *Six*

## *Developing Instructional Competencies*

### OBJECTIVES

After reading this chapter, the reader will be able to:

- describe several basic instructional methods;
- list several assessment techniques that can be used to guide instructional decisions;
- understand the difference between accommodations and modifications provided during standardized testing procedures;
- suggest several specific instructional strategies that will increase the student's academic achievement;
- create a portfolio of evidence demonstrating the use of appropriate instructional techniques.

### INTRODUCTION

The daily decisions made by teachers concerning which instructional methods to use in their classrooms are difficult ones. The responsibility to make the choice of any single method can seem awesome, particularly for beginning teachers who see hundreds of methods introduced during their training. Special educators need to provide intensive, direct, and special education. The methods chosen are critical. This chapter provides a general discussion on developing your teaching competencies in using selected "best practices" methods. Advice on choosing and implementing effective general and specific instructional methods is provided. Included with each section is a brief discussion of the research supporting the use of the identified methods, questions, and templates that will guide your selection as well as a set of ideas for supporting evidence for your teaching portfolio.

## *My Classroom*

Mrs. Rice is getting ready for her first full day of teaching with her new students. She is nervous, as she knows she will need to spend a few days assessing her students to determine their instructional level in each of the content areas she is responsible for in her seventh grade. Yet she is at a loss as to what to do. Mrs. Rice remembers that she needs to determine each student's instructional level in each of the content areas she is responsible for, but she also needs to cover her state's standard curriculum. She has been taught so many different instructional strategies that she is not sure which one would be the best one to use or even what activities to design. She knows that she should begin with the standards of learning the district has provided, and the goals stated on the special education students' individualized education programs (IEPs), but then what? She wants to make sure that she is competent and effective, and that the students benefit from her instruction.

**FOCUS QUESTIONS**

1. Which NCATE, INTASC, and CEC standards are relevant to the development of a repertoire of instructional strategies?
2. What are several general instructional methods all effective teachers should use?
3. As an individual and a member of a team, how would you generally select and create learning experiences that are appropriate and based on principles of effective instruction?
4. Which specific teaching and learning strategies can you use to engage students in active learning opportunities that promote the development of critical thinking, problem solving, and performance capabilities?

The National Council for the Accreditation of Teacher Education (NCATE) approved the Council for Exceptional Children's (CEC's) performance-based standards for the preparation and licensure of special education teachers (CEC, 2005). The CEC Special Education Content Standards are made up of 10 narrative standards. These standards parallel those of NCATE and the 10 Interstate New Teacher and Assessment and Support Consortium (INTASC) principles (INTASC, 2001). The content standards were written to reflect a teacher's validated knowledge and skills. Two standards deal directly with developing instructional strategies: Standard 4 and Standard 7.

Standard 4, Instructional Strategies, states, "Special education teachers possess a repertoire of evidence-based instructional strategies to individualize instruction for individuals with learning needs. Special educators select, adapt, and use these instructional strategies to promote challenging learning results in general and special curricula and to appropriately modify learning environments for individuals with disabilities" (CEC, 2005).

Standard 7, Instructional Planning, states, "Special educators develop long-range individualized instructional plans anchored in both general and special curricula. In addition, special educators systematically translate these individualized plans into carefully selected shorter-range goals and objectives taking into consideration an individual's abilities and needs, the learning environment, and a myriad of cultural and linguistic factors. Individualized instructional plans emphasize explicit modeling and efficient guided practice to assure acquisition and fluency through maintenance and generalization. Understanding of these factors as well as the implications of an individual's exceptional condition, guides the special educator's selection, adaptation, and creation of materials, and the use of powerful instructional variables. Instructional plans are modified based on ongoing analysis of the individual's learning progress" (CEC, 2005).

As you will face many challenges as a beginning teacher, you may wonder which one is the most critical. Certainly two of the most critical ones are (a) knowing "what" to teach and (b) knowing how to teach the "what." Instructional strategy decision making is confounded by variability in teachers' personal teaching philosophies, training, and interventions selected (Stanford & Reeves, 2005). Teachers who use and practice certain instructional strategies and decisions are more effective and competent than teachers who do not. Effective individualized decision making and instruction is at the center of special education practice.

Certain instructional practices or competencies are strongly related to the achievement of students. The following section discusses several generally effective instructional basics. Subsequent sections discuss specific instructional methods you could use as an individual or as part of a team that are supported by research as effective techniques. Guidance is provided for you in the use of such methods in your classrooms.

## EFFECTIVE INSTRUCTIONAL BASICS

You can employ certain instructional basics to become an effective teacher and to increase achievement and improve the social behavior of your students. Rosenshine and Stevens (1986) developed a model of effective instruction highlighting the following six teaching activities: (a) reviewing or checking previous work, (b) presenting new content and skills, (c) guiding student practice, (d) providing feedback and correction, (e) organizing independent student practice, and (f) reviewing student work on a weekly and monthly basis. Mastropieri and Scruggs (2002) suggest that "important teacher effectiveness variables include time-on-task, content covered, delivery of instruction, questioning and feedback, guided and independent practice, and formative evaluation" (pp. 1–2).

Research has supported the idea that more learning occurs in classrooms where teachers consistently ensure that students are actually engaged in learning to the greatest extent possible (Haynes & Jenkins, 1986). When students are not actively engaged in instruction, they are not learning. Many new teachers have difficulty keeping students engaged because of classroom misbehavior. (Managing classroom behavior is discussed in more detail in Chapter 7.) Try to keep your students actively engaged during the entire time you have allocated for instruction. A few guidelines for keeping students on task appear in Box 6-1.

Engaged academic time can be lost during transitions. Transition activities involve students moving from one location or subject to another. As a beginning teacher, you should try to maximize transition efficiency by setting time limits and reinforcing adherence to the time limits. For example, providing a warm-up academic activity is a good way to get your students actively engaged prior to the beginning of class. When all the students arrive and the bell rings, you should have a clear outline of the class agenda posted that helps the students know where they should be and what they should be doing. You may want to provide reinforcement initially to get the students motivated to make smooth transitions (e.g., tokens, praise, stickers, and so on). For individual students who continue to have difficulty with transitions, one or more of the following suggestions may help: (a) make certain the student can do the work assigned, (b) walk near the desk of the student who is off task, (c) provide specific rewards or consequences, or, if necessary, (d) communicate with the parents for additional ideas or support.

The content of your lesson plan should be based on specific instructional objectives derived from the students' IEPs. Lesson plans force teachers to identify what they will teach and how they will do it. Many beginning teachers do not write lesson plans, yet the plans are critical because they provide the framework for each class. Daily lesson objectives should specify the content of the objective, the conditions under which students' performance will be assessed, and the criteria for acceptable performance. For example, "The student will write four causes of the Civil War with 100% accuracy." A successful teacher

---

**BOX 6-1** *Keeping Students On Task*

Make instruction relevant and at the students' level of learning

Keep eye contact with students during presentations

Have all materials for independent seat work at each student's desk

Do not digress from topic under discussion

Keep directions to tasks clear and specific

Try not to interrupt your teaching presentation to manage classroom misbehavior

Maintain a high success rate

Provide substantial amounts of positive feedback

will specify objectives and translate IEP objectives into relevant "best practices" methods using relevant materials. Most states have published curricula addressing their own standards of learning for all subjects across all grade levels. Developing creative and appropriate lesson plans to meet such standards and IEP goals is discussed in Chapter 5.

When you are delivering content information, you should include some type of questioning of the students. You should elicit answers from students to determine if the instruction needs modification. Allowing students to call out answers or write answers on whiteboards or complete problems on the chalkboard or the overhead are excellent ways to encourage all students in your class to actively respond to your questions. Developing a *Jeopardy* style of game for actively engaging everyone in the class is beneficial as well. Be careful to include all students, to keep records of students' responses, and to ask questions that require many levels of cognitive knowledge.

Providing appropriate feedback to students for many beginning teachers is often difficult. How you respond to a student's answers is as important as how the content is delivered or the questions asked. Teacher feedback should be overt so that all students know whether the response is correct. Feedback should also be prompt, direct and positive. Yet, just as too much praise can be embarrassing, nonspecific versus specific praise can be confusing to students (e.g., "That was a good answer!" versus "Number 23 is the correct answer—good job!"). Teachers can provide prompts to partially correct answers. When a student gives an incorrect response, teachers should not criticize the student; a better approach would be to call on another student or to state the correct response.

Students should be provided with guided and independent practice. Guided practice can consist of doing a few problems or related activities under the supervision of the teacher. Students should then be allowed to work independently. Make sure you choose activities that are motivating and relevant to the concepts taught. Such practice activities can serve as important supplements to your instruction. Cooperative learning groups and peer tutoring situations may be used during independent practice activities. See Box 6-2 for peer tutoring guidelines.

Evaluation of your lessons should take place on a consistent basis. One type of evaluation, called formative evaluation, will provide you with valuable information on student progress and performance. Daily quizzes or weekly tests are examples of formative evaluation procedures that can help you make instructional decisions and modifications. Summative evaluations should be completed at the end of the grading period, semester, or year. Summative evaluation results can be used to assess students' performance and progress at the completion of a unit, a grading period, or a year.

One fundamental truth in effective teaching is that assessment results should help drive your instructional decisions. A comprehensive assessment tool furnishes an academic or behavioral growth measure that aligns with IEP goals, content area objectives, and national standards, and it enables teachers to identify trends toward meeting those expectations and monitoring them.

---

**BOX 6-2**  *Peer Tutoring*

---

Involves the pairing of two peers

Consider the students' zone of proximal development when matching

Should be set up in a systematic manner

Provides one-to-one instruction

Allows for students to gain self-esteem, self-respect, and the ability to interact with each other

Helps students learn from teaching other students

Should involve monitoring student progress

**Assessment Techniques.** You may develop your own tests or use tests developed by textbook publishers that accompany adopted test materials. Any tests you use to assess your students should be reliable and valid. Reliability refers to the consistency of the test across time or items, and validity refers to the extent that the test measures what it says it measures. Many test results that beginning teachers initially encounter are results of norm-referenced tests, which are standardized tests that are given to large, representative samples of students, and appear in students' files. Intelligence tests, achievement tests, and competency tests are examples of norm-referenced tests. Often these tests are given once a year to summarize students' performances and are not used to guide the individual teacher's instruction throughout the year. In contrast, criterion-referenced tests are given to students to assess their performance in relation to a particular criterion or curriculum. If criterion-referenced tests are designed to correspond with a particular curriculum, they are called curriculum-based assessments. Many teachers give end-of-unit tests, quizzes, or other curriculum-based tests regularly. See Table 6-1 for a list of common standardized tests used to measure student progress.

Deno (1986) and others (Fuchs & Fuchs, 1986) have encouraged special educators to use curriculum-based assessment techniques to link the scope and sequence of the objectives in specific content areas to their testing. In designing curriculum-based measurement, the teacher must first determine what skills or concepts are to be developed from the instruction (Rosenfield & Kurait, 1990). These target skills are the behaviors the teacher seeks to increase, and the measure of these target skills is the curriculum-based assessment. Unlike traditional approaches to assessment, curriculum-based assessment focuses almost entirely on the performance of the individual student in response to actual instructional experiences. If a student fails to make adequate progress, the most rational explanation is that the instructional experience was inappropriate for some reason. Progress must be measured frequently throughout the instruction so that effective interventions can be implemented and so that the not-so-effective interventions can be modified. Results from such measures assist teachers in instructional decision making. Curriculum-based assessments can also be constructed to match IEP objectives.

Creating student portfolios also can be used to document students' progress toward meeting their IEP goals. Each student's portfolio could include copies of tests, samples of written work, videotapes of the student's presentations, and samples of notes taken while observing the student. Pocket folders can be used to organize the materials, and all materials should be dated. Progress can be monitored frequently and instruction modified if satisfactory progress is not being made.

---

*TABLE 6-1*  *Examples of Standardized Tests*

---

**Intelligence Tests**

Kauffman Assessment Battery for Children (Kauffman & Kauffman, 1983)

Stanford-Binet Intelligence Scale—Fourth Edition (Thorndike, Hagen, & Sattler, 1986)

Wechsler Intelligence Scale for Children—Third Edition (Wechsler, 1991)

**Achievement Tests**

Kauffman Test of Educational Achievement, Comprehensive Form (Kauffman & Kauffman, 1985)

Peabody Individual Achievement Test—Revised (Markwardt, 1989)

Wechsler Individual Achievement Test—Second Edition (Psychological Corporation, 2001)

Woodcock-Johnson III Tests of Achievement (Woodcock, McGrew, & Mather, 2001)

---

Tests are used not only to provide information on student progress but also to evaluate the performance of schools. Teachers should be aware of the different types of tests, the purposes they serve, and how their results should be interpreted. Test scores may be used to make decisions about teacher salaries and the allocation of school resources. Another consideration is whether to test individually or in a group. Many of the tests used in special education are individually administered. In this era of educational accountability, appropriate testing and reporting of assessment results has increased in importance to educators and policymakers across the nation (Bolt & Thurlow, 2004).

**Accommodations and Modifications.** Several federal laws call for accommodations to be provided for individuals with disabilities in many large-scale standardized testing procedures (Bolt & Thurlow, 2004). Accommodations are tools or procedures that provide equal access to instruction and assessment for students with disabilities. They are provided to "level the playing field." Nearly every state has developed a list of accommodations that are permissible on statewide competency tests. The types of accommodations available fall into five basic categories: presentation (e.g., read aloud); time (e.g., extended time); setting (e.g., small group); response (e.g., dictated response); and aids (e.g., calculators). Much controversy surrounds the issue of which accommodations are appropriate.

In many cases, if a student is allowed an accommodation when assessed in his or her classroom and it is noted on the IEP, they are also allowed the accommodation on the standardized test. The student's IEP/Section 504 team should select the accommodations for both instruction and assessments. They should be selected on the basis of the individual's needs, not on the basis of the disability category, grade level, or instructional setting. Ideally, you should match accommodations with a student's needs and the demands of the assessment to allow the student to perform at the best of his or her abilities without altering what the test measures (Edgemon, Jablonski, & Lloyd, 2006). In some cases, standardized statewide assessments may not be appropriate for your students with disabilities, and in those cases an alternative assessment may be used.

The term *test modification* is often used interchangeably with *test accommodation*. It is important to clarify that these terms can mean different things. Accommodations are intended to lessen the effects of the student's disability, not to reduce the learning expectations. "Modification is typically reserved for those test alterations that change the given construct" (Bolt & Thurlow, 2004, p. 142). You want to be cautious about allowing for modifications. Yet you may attempt to maximize the use of the least intrusive accommodations that do not change the construct being measured. Be certain the student has had time to experience the accommodations prior to using them in a testing situation. Lack of familiarity may limit the student's optimal use of the accommodation on the test. In addition, research has shown that providing specific instruction on test-taking strategies can improve the test performance of students with disabilities (Hughes, 1996). Thus, the need for accommodations may be lessened with such specific strategy instruction.

As you begin to design your own assessment devices or to use tests already prepared to measure your students' progress, you might want to include such completed assessment measures in your teaching portfolio. Demonstrating competency in giving tests, analyzing test results, and using the results to guide your instructional decisions is a mark of an effective teacher. See Table 6-2 for examples of assessment evidence you might provide in your teaching portfolio.

As a special educator, you will need to select, adapt, and use instructional strategies that promote learning and to appropriately modify learning

**TABLE 6-2** *Examples of Specific Assessment Evidence for Teaching Portfolio*

To provide evidence of competency in the area of assessment, you might include the following:

❑ Protocol from a completed standardized test, including analysis, that was administered by teacher
❑ Worksheets and student copies of a curriculum-based measurement project
❑ Copy of narrative description of student's present level of performance used on IEP
❑ Copies of unit assessments (tests and essays) and unit assessment plans
❑ Copies of rubrics used to guide instruction
❑ Copies of assessments (tests) that were given to students in general education classrooms with accommodations
❑ Informal checks for understanding that are used

*Note.* Student confidentiality should be maintained. Please block out any identifying information.

environments for students with disabilities. Your selections will need to enhance the students' critical thinking, problem-solving, and performance skills while increasing their self-awareness, self-management, self-control, self-reliance, and self-esteem. In addition, you will need to emphasize the development, maintenance, and generalization of your students' knowledge and skills across environments, settings, and the life span. Wow—you will be busy! The following section discusses specific instructional strategies that have been shown to be effective and that may help you get started.

## SPECIFIC INSTRUCTIONAL STRATEGIES

Many different methods have been developed to remediate problems of individual students with disabilities. The instructional methods you choose should be ones that have the greatest benefit and that will produce the greatest gains. Lloyd, Forness, and Kavale (1998, p. 198) recommend that educators do the following:

- Intervene early
- Monitor students' progress and provide positive consequences for improvement
- Teach academic and cognitive skills directly and systematically
- Teach mnemonic strategies for understanding and remembering what one learns
- Teach cognitive strategies and behavioral self-management
- Use behavioral techniques to promote acquisition of academic and social behaviors

We discuss several specific instructional methods that you can use in the classroom. Suggestions for developing competency in using each strategy are discussed. In addition, suggestions for evidence you can use in your teaching portfolio are provided at the conclusion. The instructional methods discussed are teacher-directed instruction, cognitive learning strategies, mnemonic techniques, graphic organizers, and self-management techniques.

**Teacher-Directed Instruction.** Most instruction begins with teacher-delivered presentations. Mastropieri and Scruggs (2002) suggest that when teachers are presenting information and communicating content, they should employ the techniques easily remembered with the following acronym:

S (structure)—Provide a structured presentation

C (clarity)—Speak clearly and directly to the point of the objective

R (redundancy)—Emphasize and reinforce the most important aspects of the lessons

E (enthusiasm)—Display enthusiasm for the content and the lesson

A (appropriate rate)—Provide a brisk pace of instruction

M (maximized engagement)—Select material that is at the correct level of difficulty for the students

Teacher-directed instruction involves a systematic approach that includes well-sequenced, highly focused lessons that are presented briskly (Gersten, Woodward, & Darsch, 1997). One of the most widely used teacher-directed approaches is the use of direct instruction. Many different versions of direct instruction are suggested in teaching methods textbooks. Typically, if you were to use direct instruction to teach a student a certain skill, you would explain, teach, model, and practice the skill with the student and then give feedback on the student's skill performance. Polloway, Patton, and Serna (2005) suggest the following acronym for beginning teachers to use to remember the direct instruction format: PURPOSE (see Box 6-3).

Teacher-directed, explicit instruction is essential for students with disabilities to make the associations they need for both skill acquisition and generalization (Carnine, Silbert, Kameenui, & Tarver, 2004). Beginning readers especially need to be provided with instruction that is both explicit and systematic (National Reading Panel, 2000; Snow, Burns, & Griffin, 1998). Most students need explicit decoding instruction in order to gain an understanding of the alphabetic principle and to become good readers (Beck & Juel, 1995; Foorman, Francis, Fletcher, Schatschneider, & Mehta, 1998). Curriculum materials are available that contain a code-emphasis approach to reading instruction, such as *Reading Mastery* (Engelmann & Bruner, 1995), and *Corrective Reading: Decoding Series* (Engelmann, Becker, Hanner, & Johnson, 1988). Both of these series use scripted teacher modeling and demonstration, frequent student responding and feedback, and practice with controlled materials.

Teacher-directed instructional strategies, when used appropriately, can offer well-designed scripted lessons for the beginning teacher. Keep the pace brisk and the instruction explicit.

**Cognitive Learning Strategies.** Learning strategies are task-specific techniques that students use in responding to classroom tasks. Using a learning strategies approach teaches students how to learn rather than what to learn. Students are taught specific cognitive strategies that can be generalized to

---

*BOX 6-3  PURPOSE*

Polloway, Patton, and Serna (2005) suggest the following acronym for remembering the direct instruction steps:

P—Prepare the student to learn (define the skill, tell why it is important, and explain where it can be used)

U—Understand the skill steps (review components of the skill, give example of each, and state why each step is essential)

R—Rehearse the skill (model the skill and have students rehearse the skill)

P—Perform a self-check (have students perform a self-check on each skill component)

O—Overcome any performance barrier (may need to develop supplemental materials)

S—Select another situation where the skill can be performed (work on generalization of skill)

E—Evaluate skill performance (have students evaluate their performance)

*Source:* From Polloway, Edward; Patton, JR; Serna, L, *Strategies for teaching learners with special needs*, 8th Edition, © 2005, pp. 95–97. Adapted by permission of Pearson Education, Inc., Upper Saddle River, NJ.

general education classrooms and later to a postsecondary environment. Ellis and Lenz (1996, p. 38) suggest using the following steps to teach learning strategies:

1. Pretest the strategy to be taught and obtain a commitment from the student to learn
2. Describe the particular strategy to be taught
3. Model the use of the strategy
4. Engage the student in the verbal elaboration and rehearsal of the strategy
5. Provide practice in the application of the strategy in controlled materials (e.g., reading materials at the instructional level of the student)
6. Provide advanced practice in the application of the strategy in content materials (e.g., regular social studies textbook) and provide feedback
7. Confirm acquisition and obtain the student's commitment to generalize the strategy
8. Achieve generalization through four phases: (a) orientation as to where it can be applied, (b) activation of the strategy by moving from explicit to less explicit instructions and assignments, (c) adaptation through understanding the strategy and being able to make changes to meet different setting demands, (d) strategy maintenance over time

A learning strategies approach teaches students to learn how to learn and focuses on the development of independence. The approach stresses using the strategies across classrooms and environments. Specific strategies can be effective in enhancing reading comprehension, test taking, proofreading, and note taking. Many examples of learning strategies exist in the special education professional literature (e.g., Sabornie & deBettencourt, 2004).

Two examples are (a) RAP, a paraphrasing strategy appropriate for elementary school students with reading content area paragraphs or papers (Ellis, 1996), and (b) PIRATES, a test-taking strategy appropriate for students taking a multiple-choice test (Hughes, 1996). See Box 6-4 for more detail on these two examples of learning strategies. See also the following Web site for more strategies and information on learning strategy instruction: http://www. ku-crl.org/sim/index.html.

These two examples represent only a few of the many cognitive strategies currently discussed in the literature. It is critical to give students training in cognitive

---

**BOX 6-4**  *Examples of Learning Strategies*

The paraphrasing strategy (Ellis, 1996) suggests the following cognitive steps:

RAP:

- Read a paragraph
- Ask yourself what the paragraph was about
- Put the main idea and two details in your words

PIRATES (Hughes, 1996) has the following steps:

- P—Prepare for the test and prepare to succeed
  - Put your name and PIRATES on the test
  - Allot time and order to sections
  - Say affirmations

- Start within 2 minutes
- I—Inspect the instructions
  - Read instructions carefully
  - Underline what to do and where to respond
  - Notice special requirements
- R—Read each question
- A—Answer or abandon each question
- T—Turn back
- E—Estimate answers for the remaining questions
  - Avoid absolutes
  - Choose the longest and most detailed choice
- Estimate similar choices
- S—Survey your test

---

*Source:* From *Teaching adolescents with learning disabilities* (2nd ed.), by Deshler, DD, Ellis ED, & Lenz, BK, 1996, pp. 73, 251. Reproduced by permission of Love Publishing Company.

strategies under controlled conditions so that they are encouraged to generalize across settings. Ellis, Lenz, and Sabornie (1987, p. 8) suggest the following:

1. The learning strategy should contain a set of steps that lead to a specific outcome.
2. The learning strategy should be designed to cue the use of cognitive strategies and metacognitive processes.
3. The strategy should contain no more than seven steps.
4. Each step should begin with a verb or other word that directly relates to the action being cued.
5. A remembering system should be attached to the strategy to facilitate recall.
6. The learning strategy should be task specific.

**Mnemonic Techniques.** Several research studies have investigated using mnemonic instruction with students with disabilities (e.g., Scruggs & Mastropieri, 1992; Scruggs, Mastropieri, Levin, & Gaffney, 1985). Research on teaching mnemonic strategies to students with disabilities has occurred across the elementary through secondary levels (Wong, Harris, Graham, & Butler, 2003).

In their meta-analysis of 24 studies involving instruction in key-word and key-word–peg-word mnemonics, Mastropieri and Scruggs (1989) reported an overall effect size of 1.62. "An effect size for any one comparison can be calculated by subtracting the average score of the students in the control group (say, 19) from the average score for the students in the treated group (say, 20); this difference is divided by a measure of the variance in the sample, the standard deviation (say, 3) to obtain the effect size (0.33 in our example). Effect size may be thought of as a z-score or standard deviation unit—that is, 0 is average and an effect size of +1.0 is above average" (Lloyd et al., 1998, p. 197). The use of mnemonics in many research studies has shown an above average effect size.

According to Scruggs and Mastropieri (1990), a mnemonic is a specific reconstruction of target content that is intended to tie new information to the learner's existing knowledge base and therefore facilitate retrieval. The use of mnemonic instruction can help students remember and retain information that is difficult to recall. See Box 6-5 for an example of the use of mnemonics.

Mastropieri and Scruggs (2004, p. 292) suggest that mnemonic strategies are most effective when they are

- used to reinforce objectives to remember specific content,
- taught and practiced directly,
- combined with comprehension instruction, and
- included with application activities.

Three specific types of mnemonic strategies are the key-word method, the peg-word method, and letter strategies (Mastropieri, Scruggs, Whittaker, &

---

**BOX 6-5**  *Example of Mnemonics*

HOMES—a mnemonic used to remember the Great Lakes:

H—Huron
O—Ontario

M—Michigan
E—Erie
S—Superior

Bakken, 1994). The key-word method is used to strengthen the connection between a new word and associated information. The key word is known to the student and sounds like the new word. A picture is used to help the student remember. Mastropieri, Scruggs, Bakken, and Brigham (1992) used a key-word method for memorizing the states and capitals. For example, for Arkansas (Ark) and Little Rock (little rock), students were given a picture of Noah's Ark landing on a little rock. Peg words are rhyming words for numbers and are helpful in learning information in order. Mastropieri and Scruggs (2004) suggest, "To remember that insects have six legs, picture an insect crawling on sticks (peg-word for six)," and "to remember that spiders have eight legs, picture a spider spinning a web on a gate (pegword for eight)" (p. 296). Letter strategies help remember lists of things. The use of the acronym HOMES is an easy way to remember the Great Lakes. An acronym or a phrase can be used to help remember a list of items. To remember the planets in order, one only needs to remember, "My very educated mother just served us nine pizzas," which would help remember the following names: Mecury, Venus, Earth, Mars, Jupiter, Saturn, Uranus, Neptune, and Pluto. Letter strategies can be combined with key words or peg words. Using mnemonic strategies such as the key-word method, the peg-word method, and letter strategies promotes students' learning of unfamiliar content. See the following Web site for more details on using the mnemonic strategies discussed here: http://www.ldonline.org/ldindepth/teachingtechniques/mnemonicstrategies.html.

**Graphic Organizers.** Graphic organizers (i.e., visual formats or structures) are any types of visual representation of concepts that help students organize information in a manner that makes the information easier to learn. When graphic organizers are coupled with mnemonics (e.g., key-word mnemonics), students often remember the information with greater ease. The visual representations organize concepts in a manner that facilitates students' understanding and learning (Fisher, Schumaker, & Deshler, 1995). The organizer can be used before instruction to elicit students' prior knowledge, during the instruction to help students conceptualize the information, or at the end of instruction to summarize or review concepts as well as to assess students' understanding. Graphic organizers include such items as Venn diagrams, flowcharts, concept maps, time lines, and two-column notes.

Several studies have investigated using graphic organizers with students with disabilities (e.g., Bulgren, Schumaker, & Deshler, 1988; DiCecco & Gleason, 2002; Horton, Lovitt, & Bergerud, 1990). Graphic organizers can be used across different content areas and grade levels. See Figure 6-1 for an example of a

**FIGURE 6-1** *Example of a Graphic Organizer.*

| Compare/Contrast Matrix | | |
|---|---|---|
| **Date:**<br>**Class:** | **Topic A:** | **Topic B:** |
| Main idea | | |
| Similarities | | |
| Differences | | |
| Points to remember | | |

**TABLE 6-3**  *Template for Self-Monitoring at the Secondary Level*

---

**(Can be put on a small index card)**

Name: *Justin*                                                              Date: *9/12/06*

Identified task to monitor: *Working on my math worksheets during study ball*

Time of monitoring: *3rd Period week of 9/18-9/22*

Directions: *Mark an X in the box under the correct heading every 5-6 min of the period. Stop and ask yourself if you are on-task.*

**Am I on Task?**

| On Task | Off Task |
|---------|----------|
|         |          |
|         |          |
|         |          |
|         |          |
|         |          |
|         |          |

---

graphic organizer. See the following Website for more details on graphic organizers and easy-to-use templates: http://www.graphicorganizers.com.

**Self-Management Techniques.** Another consideration when attempting to change student behavior is the ability of the student to manage his or her own behavior. The goal of self-management programs is to try to make students more aware of their own thinking processes and their strategies for approaching tasks and to give them responsibility for their own reinforcement (Reeve, 1990). Self-management of behavior is often broken into three types: self-monitoring, self-reinforcement, and self-evaluation (Vallecorsa, deBettencourt, & Zigmond, 2000). In self-monitoring, the student is taught to recognize the behavior and record how often it may occur (Reid, Trout, & Schartz, 2005). A middle or high school student may be asked to note how many times he or she is off task during a specific instructional period. An elementary school student may be asked to circle a happy or sad face at a specific time period throughout the day to begin understanding his or her feelings. See Table 6-3 for an example of a template for self-monitoring at the secondary level.

In self-reinforcement and self-evaluation, students are asked to self-evaluate their progress or achievement on the behavior and to reward themselves. Self-evaluation or self-reinforcement involves the learner in determining the need for change in the behavior and then measuring (in some form) the change. Self-evaluation is an important skill for students to learn, as it helps them develop a sense of personal responsibility.

This section provided a review of a few specific instructional strategies. It is critical that you know what to teach and how to teach so that the most learning can occur. See Table 6-4 for suggestions on instructional strategies evidence for your teaching portfolio.

**TABLE 6-4** *Examples of Specific Instructional Strategies Evidence for Teaching Portfolio*

To provide evidence of competency in the area of instructional strategies, a special education teacher might include the following in a teaching portfolio:

- ❑ Copies of lesson or unit plans describing instructional activities and accommodations or modifications for special needs students
- ❑ Copies of handouts with specific strategies noted (mnemonics)
- ❑ Copies of student homework
- ❑ Copies of graphic organizers used by students (hamburger paragraph for writing)
- ❑ Copies of documentation of progress toward academic IEP goals
- ❑ Photos of student engaged in learning activities (circle time or silent reading)
- ❑ Photos of classroom posters and posted student work

*Note.* Student confidentiality should be maintained. Please block out any identifying information.

## SUMMARY

As more and more students with disabilities enter general education classrooms, it becomes increasingly important to examine the instructional strategies associated with learning in these environments. Research has shown that adequately meeting the needs of diverse learners, particularly students with high-incidence disabilities in general education content area classrooms, has been a problem under traditional instructional circumstances (Zigmond & Baker, 1994). These challenges are more acute in this era of high standards and student outcomes. You and your coteachers need to select direct, intense, and specific instructional strategies that have been shown to be effective.

## ACTIVITY QUESTIONS

1.  Discuss instructional techniques and ideas with your mentor or another teacher. Do they have suggestions that you can incorporate?

2.  Observe other classroom teachers. What instructional techniques do they employ? Which ideas can you use in your classroom?

3.  Review your instructional plans based on the IEP goals for the students on your caseload. Consult with your supervisor about the match.

## SELECTED WEBSITES

http://www.teachingld.org
*TeachingLD is a service of the Division for Learning Disabilities (DLD) of the Council for Exceptional Children. DLD is the largest international professional organization focused on learning disabilities. The purpose of TeachingLD is to provide trustworthy and up-to-date resources about teaching students with learning disabilities.*

http://curry.edschool.virginia.edu/sped/projects/ose/information/mega
*This site illustrates John Lloyd's presentation about the relative effectiveness of various familiar special education interventions. The slides included are from a presentation but are not accompanied by the*

*spoken narrative that one would hear at the presentation. Other research links are included, as is a link to the article published discussing the meta-analysis conducted.*

http://www.sraonline.com/index.php/home/curriculumsolutions/di/correctivereading/102
*This site offers information on the Corrective Reading program, which provides intensive intervention for students in grades 4 to 12 who are reading 1 or more years below grade level. This program delivers tightly sequenced, carefully planned lessons that give struggling students the structure and practice necessary to become skilled, fluent readers and better learners.*

http://www.mindtools.com/pages/main/new
    MNTIM.htm
*This site contains an overview of mnemonic techniques and gives several specific strategies.*

http://www.ku-crl.org/sim/index.html
*This site gives more details on the strategy intervention model (SIM) developed at the*

*University of Kansas Center for Research. SIM strives to help teachers make decisions about what is of greatest importance, what we can teach students to help them learn, and how to teach them well.*

## REFLECTION JOURNAL ACTIVITIES

1. In what ways can you encourage efficient transitions from one activity to another with the students in your classroom?

2. In what ways are student portfolios similar to your teaching portfolio, and in what ways are they different?

## REFERENCES

Beck, I. L., & Juel, C. (1995). The role of decoding in learning to read. *American Educator, 22*, 8–42.

Bolt, S. E., & Thurlow, M. L. (2004). Five of the most frequently allowed testing accommodations in state policy: Synthesis of research. *Remedial and Special Education, 25*, 141–152.

Bulgren, J., Schumaker, J. B., & Deshler, D. D. (1988). Effectiveness of a concept teaching routine in enhancing the performance of LD students in secondary-level mainstream classes. *Learning Disability Quarterly, 11*(1), 3–17.

Carnine, D., Silbert, J., Kameenui, E., & Tarver, S. (2004). *Direct instruction reading* (4th ed.). Upper Saddle River, NJ: Merrill/Prentice Hall.

Council for Exceptional Children. (2005). *CEC performance- based standards*. Retrieved January 11, 2006, from http://www.cec.sped.org/ps/perfbasedstds/standards.html#standards

Deno, S. L. (1986). Curriculum-based assessment: The emerging alternative. *Exceptional Children, 52*, 219–323.

DiCecco, V. M., & Gleason, M. M. (2002). Using graphic organizers to attain relational knowledge from expository text. *Journal of Learning Disabilities, 35*, 306–320.

Edgemon, E. A., Jablonski, B. R., & Lloyd, J. W. (2006). Large-scale assessments: A teacher's guide to making decisions about accommodations. *Teaching Exceptional Children, 38*(3), 6–11.

Ellis, E. S. (1996). Reading strategy instruction. In D. D. Deshler, E. E. Ellis, & B. K. Lenz (Eds.), *Teaching adolescents with learning disabilities: Strategies and methods* (pp. 61–125). Denver: Love.

Ellis, E. S., & Lenz, B. K. (1996). Perspectives on instruction in learning strategies. In D. D. Deshler, E. E. Ellis, & B. K. Lenz (Eds.), *Teaching adolescents with learning disabilities: Strategies and methods* (pp. 9–60). Denver: Love.

Ellis, E. S., Lenz, B. K., & Sabornie, E. S. (1987). Generalization and adaptation of learning strategies to natural environments: Part 2: Research into practice. *Remedial and Special Education, 8*(2), 6–23.

Engelmann, S., Becker, W., Hanner, S., & Johnson, G. (1988). *Corrective reading: Decoding strategies*. Chicago: Science Research Associates.

Engelmann, S., & Bruner, E. (1995). *Reading mastery*. Blacklick, OH: Science Research Associates.

Fisher, J. B., Schumaker, J. B., & Deshler, P. D. (1995). Searching for validated inclusive practices: A review of the literature. *Focus on Exceptional Children, 28*(4), 1–20.

Foorman, B. R., Francis, D. J., Fletcher, J. M., Schatschneider, C., & Mehta, P. (1998). The role of instruction in learning to read: Preventing reading failure in at-risk children. *Journal of Educational Psychology, 90*, 37–55.

Fuchs, L. S., & Fuchs, D. (1986). Curriculum-based assessment of progress toward long- and short-term goals. *Journal of Special Education, 20*, 69–82.

Gersten, R., Woodward, J., & Darsch, C. (1987). Direct instruction: A research-based approach to curriculum design and teaching. *Exceptional Children, 33*, 17–31.

Haynes, M. C., & Jenkins, J. R. (1986). Reading instruction in special education resource rooms. *American Educational Research Journal, 23*, 161–190.

Horton, S. V., Lovitt, T. C., & Bergerud, D. (1990). The effectiveness of graphic organizers for three classifications of secondary students in content area classes. *Journal of Leaning Disabilities, 23*, 12–22.

Hughes, C. (1996). Memory and test-taking strategies. In D. D. Deshler, E. S. Ellis, & B. K. Lenz (Eds.), *Teaching adolescents with learning disabilities* (2nd ed., pp. 209–266). Denver: Love.

Interstate New Teacher Assessment and Support Consortium. (2001). *Model standards for licensing general and special education teachers of students with disabilities: A resource for state dialogue*. Washington, DC: Council of Chief State School Officers.

Kauffman, A. S., & Kauffman, N. L. (1983). *Kauffman Assessment Battery for Children: Administration and scoring manual.* Circle Pines, MN: American Guidance Service.

Kauffman, A. S., & Kauffman, N. L. (1985). *Kauffman Test of Educational Achievement, Comprehensive Form.* Circle Pines, MN: American Guidance Service.

Lloyd, J. W., Forness, S. T., & Kavale, K. A. (1998). Some methods are more important than others. *Intervention in School and Clinic, 33,* 195–200.

Markwardt, F. C. (1989). *Peabody Individual Achievement Test—Revised.* Circle Pines, MN: American Guidance Service.

Mastropieri, M. A., & Scruggs, T. E. (1989). Constructing more meaning relationships: Mnemonic instruction for special populations. *Educational Psychology Review, 1,* 83–111.

Mastropieri, M. A., & Scruggs, T. E. (2002). *Effective instruction for special education* (3rd ed.). Austin, TX: PRO-ED.

Mastropieri, M. A., & Scruggs, T. E. (2004). *The inclusive classroom: Strategies for effective instruction* (2nd ed.). Upper Saddle River, NJ: Merrill/Prentice Hall.

Mastropieri, M. A., Scruggs, T. E., Bakken, J. P., & Brigham, F. J. (1992). A complex mnemonic strategy for teaching states and capitals: Comparing forward and backward associations. *Learning Disabilities Research & Practice, 7,* 96–103.

Mastropieri, M. A., Scruggs, T. E., Whittaker, M. E. S., & Bakken, J. P. (1994). Applications of mnemonic strategies with students with mental disabilities. *Remedial and Special Education, 15,* 34–43.

National Reading Panel. (2000). *A report of the national reading panel: Teaching children to read.* Washington, DC: National Institute of Child Heath and Human Development.

Polloway, E. A., Patton, J. R., & Serna, L. (2005). *Strategies for teaching learners with special needs* (8th ed.). Upper Saddle River, NJ: Merrill/Prentice Hall.

Psychological Corporation. (2001). *Wechsler Individual Achievement Test, Second Edition.* San Antonio, TX: Author.

Reeve, R. E. (1990). ADHD: Facts and fallacies. *Intervention in School and Clinic, 26,* 71–78.

Reid, R., Trout, A. L., & Schartz, M. (2005). Self-regulation interventions for children with attention deficit/hyperactivity disorder. *Exceptional Children, 71,* 361–377.

Rosenfield, S., & Kurait, S. K. (1990). Best practices in curriculum based assessment. In A. Thomas & J. Grimes (Eds.), *Best practices in school*

*psychology—II.* (pp. 275–286). Washington, DC: National Association of School Psychology.

Rosenshine, B., & Stevens, R. (1986). Teaching functions. In M. C. Wittrock (Ed.), *Handbook of research on teaching* (3rd ed., pp. 376–391). Upper Saddle River, NJ: Merrill/Prentice Hall.

Sabornie, E. J., & deBettencourt, L. U. (2004). *Teaching students with mild and high-incidence disabilities at the secondary level* (2nd ed.). Upper Saddle River, NJ: Merrill/Prentice Hall.

Scruggs, T. E., & Mastropieri, M. A. (1990). Mnemonic instruction for students with learning disabilities: What it is and what it does. *Learning Disability Quarterly, 13,* 271–280.

Scruggs, T. E., & Mastropieri, M. A. (1992). Classroom applications of mnemonic instruction: Acquisition, maintenance, and generalization. *Exceptional Children, 58,* 219–229.

Scruggs, T. E., Mastropieri, M. A., Levin, R. L., & Gaffney, J. S. (1985). Facilitating the acquisition of science facts in learning disabled students. *American Educational Research Journal, 22,* 575–586.

Snow, C. E., Burns, M. S., & Griffin, P. (Eds.). (1998). *Preventing reading difficulties in young children.* Washington, DC: National Academy Press.

Stanford, P., & Reeves, S. (2005). Assessment that drives instruction. *Teaching Exceptional Children, 37*(4), 18–22.

Thorndike, R. L., Hagen, E. P., & Sattler, J. M. (1986). *Stanford-Binet Intelligence Scale* (4th ed.). Chicago: Riverside.

Vallecorsa, A. L., deBettencourt, L. U., & Zigmond, N. (2000). *Students with mild disabilities in general education settings: A guide for special educators.* Upper Saddle River, NJ: Merrill/Prentice Hall.

Wechsler, D. (1991). *Wechsler Intelligence Scale for Children—Third Edition: Manual.* San Antonio, TX: Psychological Corporation.

Wong, B. Y. L., Harris, K. R., Graham, S., & Butler, D. L. (2003). Cognitive strategies instruction research in learning disabilities. In H. L. Swanson, K. R. Harris, & S. Graham (Eds.), *Handbook of learning disabilities* (pp. 383–402). New York: Guilford Press.

Woodcock, R. W., McGrew, K. S., & Mather, N. (2001). *Woodcock-Johnson III Tests of Achievement.* Itasca, IL: Riverside.

Zigmond, N., & Baker, J. (1994). Is the mainstream a more appropriate educational setting for Randy? A case study of one student with learning disabilities. *Learning Disabilities Research & Practice, 9,* 108–117.

# CHAPTER *Seven*

## *Developing Management Skills*

**OBJECTIVES**

After reading this chapter, the reader will be able to:

- identify important characteristics of successful classroom and individual behavior management techniques;
- describe several appropriate classroom and behavior management techniques that can be used in classrooms;
- understand the parameters of a functional behavioral assessment and behavior intervention plans;
- create a portfolio of evidence demonstrating use of appropriate classroom and behavior management techniques.

**INTRODUCTION**

The daily decisions made by teachers concerning classroom behavior management are critical components of effective teaching. Teachers who are most effective in managing behavior are also usually the most effective in improving students' achievement. Managing students' behavior is a demanding task and one that is not easy for beginning teachers. This chapter provides a general discussion on developing your basic classroom management procedures and a more specific discussion of behavior management techniques. Advice on choosing and implementing effective general and specific behavior management techniques is provided. Included with each section is a brief discussion of the use of the identified methods, questions, and templates that will guide your selection as well as a set of ideas for supporting evidence for your teaching portfolio.

### *My Classroom*

Ms. Antenucci is not sure she has tried the simplest and most obvious behavior management strategies with her third-period civics class. She knows from her training that she should ask the following questions: What is the simplest, most direct approach I can take to solve this problem? Have I overlooked an obvious solution? Maybe I have not been consistent in my implementation? Yet nothing seems to be working. The ninth graders in her class do not seem interested in the subject, and do not care about their work. She decides she will look at her instruction and make it clearer. She might also give the students choices in the final projects. She also decides to use tokens for free time as a reward for those students who complete their projects. All ninth graders love to have free time to chat with their friends. Of course, it's too soon to know if these strategies are going to work.

**FOCUS QUESTIONS**

1. What are the foundations of classroom and behavior management?
2. How can special education teachers establish good classroom and individual behavior management for all their students?
3. What are specific behavioral techniques that are supported by research as effective?
4. What are the needs and the procedures for a functional behavioral assessment?

## CLASSROOM MANAGEMENT TECHNIQUES

A critical component of effective teaching is effective classroom management. Research has shown that teachers who are the most effective in managing classroom behavior are also usually the most effective in improving classroom achievement (Mastropieri & Scruggs, 2002). When observing a well-managed classroom, an observer focuses on the instructional activities; however, when observing a poorly-managed classroom, the observer often notices how little instruction is accomplished. In the first classroom, the observer may not notice how the teacher has arranged the classroom, described her expectations for student behavior, or engaged the students in the learning activity. The importance of these structures is noted more often when they are absent (e.g., as in the second classroom). It is a cliché in education that "classroom chaos does not promote learning," but it is true.

Classroom management is one of the most significant factors in student achievement (Wang, Haertel, & Walberg, 1993). Students in classes taught by teachers with good classroom management skills show higher achievement of learning goals. As a new teacher, you may be inclined to overlook the fact that what and how you teach may have contributed directly to your students' behaviors. Yet the behavior problems in your classroom may be a result of poor choices of curriculum or teaching strategies. Thus, the first factors you should examine are your instructional practices. Kauffman, Mostert, Trent, and Pullen (2006, p. 17) use the acronym CLOCS-RAM to help teachers remember the characteristics of best instructional practices:

- Clarity—The student must know exactly what to do.
- Level—The student must be able to do the task with a high degree of accuracy.
- Opportunities—The student must have frequent opportunities to respond.
- Consequences—The student must receive a meaningful reward for correct performance.
- Sequence—The tasks must be presented in logical sequence so that the student gets the big idea.
- Relevance—The task is relevant to the student's life, and, if possible, the student understands how and why it is useful.
- Application—The teacher helps the student learn how to learn and remember by teaching memory and learning strategies and applying the knowledge and skills to everyday problems.
- Monitoring—The teacher continuously monitors student progress.

After reflecting on your academic instruction, you should consider your expectations for students' behavior. What you demand of your students and what you will not tolerate in terms of both their academic performance and their social behavior are critical. In some situations, management problems are not so much a result of students' behavior as a result of your inappropriate expectations.

Make a list of the types of behaviors you feel are critical to success in your classroom. Examples include following the established classroom rules, complying with teacher instructions, following written instructions, doing in-class and homework assignments, and producing work of acceptable quality. In addition, consider what you will not accept. Such examples might include disturbing others, cheating, creating disturbances during class activities, and using inappropriate language. Teachers have very different tolerances for classroom noise, movement, and other behaviors, and they have pet peeves. Know what your tolerances and pet peeves are, then communicate your expectations clearly and consistently to your students, whatever expectations you choose. In addition, you should try to limit your rules to a small number. Too many rules become hard to follow.

**Components of Good Classroom Management.** The following four components are the foundations of good classroom management: (a) teacher attitude; (b) established rules, routines, and procedures; (c) motivation and management; and (d) data collection. Teaching is a leadership function, and teachers need to be "in charge" of the classroom. Teachers should be assertive in both body language and tone of voice. Specifically, teachers should show good posture, maintain eye contact, match facial expressions with content of verbal messages, speak clearly and deliberately, and use a "firm" tone of voice—neither too soft nor too threatening (Emmer, Evertson, & Worsham, 2003). It may take some practice to master all these behaviors; however, it is important that a new teacher assert his or her classroom management skills from the very first day of teaching. This helps establish appropriate behavior and expectations for the students.

Every classroom has procedures or routines that help it to function as a learning environment (Marazano, 2003). Before entering the classroom, new teachers should carefully consider their general classroom behavior expectations. For example, will you have posted class rules? In an elementary classroom, class rules should be limited to no more than five, and the rules should always be stated in an affirmative or a positive tone (e.g., "listen to others when they are talking" or "think before you speak"). A middle or high school class may have a few more rules, but they should also be stated in positive terms.

You should prepare beginning-of-day and end-of-day routines. For example, will you take attendance at the beginning of each day? Do you plan to arrange the desks and chairs before leaving for the day? How do you plan to send students home with their homework? Planning these routines helps you establish clear expectations for your students.

Reflect on your communication with students. Have you made the instructions as simple and clear as possible? Have you given the instructions in a clear, firm, nontentative way? Have you given one instruction at a time? Have you provided appropriate consequences for non-compliance?

Transitions, as mentioned earlier, need to be planned. Think about what prompts or cues you will use with students so that they know when an activity is changing. How will you manage the class before leaving for lunch? In elementary classrooms, cues such as "1-2-3—Eyes on Me" or flashing the lights on and off may help students focus their attention. In middle or high school classrooms, cues may be more subtle, such as turning off the overhead projector and waiting for silence. In either case, it is important to carefully consider what cues you will use, when transitions will occur, and how you can help students self-manage transitions (Pelletier, 2004). Specific expectations for instructional activities, such as a cooperative learning activity or a silent reading activity, need to be determined. When working with a partner, will students be allowed to move around the classroom? What about the noise level? In all classrooms, teachers

---

**BOX 7-1** *Setting Up Your Classroom*

Prior to the start of school, teachers spend time setting up their classrooms. Consider the following:

- Can you see all the students from different points in the room?
- How will you arrange desks and tables? Will the desks be in rows or in groups? Will you use assigned seating? Consider how different personalities of students may interact. Consider using a seating chart.
- Where will you place your desk?
- What types of items do you want on the walls? Consider the classroom environment you want to promote. Do you want to post class rules? Do you want a space to display student work?

- Can all the students see the blackboard, video monitor, and your desk?
- How can you ensure ease of movement around the classroom? Consider traffic flow (Where are the cubbies? Where will backpacks be kept?).
- Where will often-used materials and books be kept?
- Consider placing materials where they can be easily accessed.
- Will certain items or places be "off limits" or by invitation only? Consider where any centers, small-group areas, or computers are located and when they will be used.

---

should consider what the purpose of the instructional activity is and develop expectations and rules that are appropriate to the activity. Box 7-1 gives some ideas on how to set up your classroom.

Students who are engaged and motivated to participate in learning activities are less likely to cause classroom disruptions. Teachers who use effective instructional strategies that are interesting have fewer classroom management problems; however, all new teachers may have some difficulty because students are human. They have lives outside the classroom that can affect their mood, behavior, and interactions with others. Effective classroom managers plan to engage and motivate students; however, they also respond to individual circumstances and recognize that even the best plans can go awry.

Despite the changeable nature of classroom plans, careful planning of instruction can prevent or minimize some disruptive student behaviors. All students may cause disturbances when bored or frustrated with a lesson; so, when planning a lesson, address the following to keep students motivated and engaged:

- Hook the students—How can you introduce the lesson in an interesting way? Is there something that the students can do? Is there a demonstration that would encourage students to be curious about the lesson? Can you pose a problem for the students to consider? (Wiggins & McTighe, 1998).
- Pace of lesson—How long will each activity take? Have you built in some time for the students to work together? Is there a break time? Is there a time for students to move around the room (stretch)?
- Level of instruction—How will you know if the students are understanding the lesson? What informal checks for understanding will you use? How will you change the level of instruction if students do not have adequate prior knowledge?

As a teacher, you must simultaneously teach the lesson and manage the entire classroom. You should consider the following questions:

1. Will you move around the classroom? Just being in proximity of a misbehaving student often will eliminate the behavior.
2. In what ways will you redirect students' inappropriate verbal questions or responses? Recognize that different students may need different

strategies. In some cases, it might be best to ignore students who are "talking out" without raising their hands. In other cases, it might be best to restate the expectation of a raised hand to ask a question.

3. How will you address off-task behavior (talking with a neighbor or playing with a cell phone)? Consider which students are seated in close proximity. In some cases, moving students to other places in the classroom may be helpful. In other cases, a gentle reminder of the task may be more appropriate (Pelletier, 2004).

4. How will you ensure that homework is completed? What about students who never complete homework? It is disruptive to stop a lesson while one student tries to locate his or her homework or has not finished it.

You might want to consider establishing a system for collecting or noting completed homework at the start of each class (Welton, 1999). You should also have established worksheets or other seat-work activity readily available should students finish early or while the rest of the class reviews their homework. (Note: Homework given in the last few minutes of a class period often does not get recorded because students are already mentally planning their after-class time. Have students write down their homework at the beginning of class or provide a place on their class Web page for it to be recorded daily.)

Effective classroom teachers analyze what is working about their classroom management and what needs to be adjusted (Marazano, 2003). Any adjustments or modifications to classroom management should be based on the collection of data. This data collection can be used for one student, a small group of students, or the entire class, depending on teacher concerns (Jandris, 2001). Data collection can occur by asking students for completion of one activity as a ticket out of class or completion of a frequency chart by a para-educator or co-teacher. Consider using behavior frequency charts or tracking homework completion with a chart. The process of collecting data can help the teacher by providing objective facts to dispel inaccuracies in their classroom perception (e.g., all the students talking out of turn may become only two students talking out of turn). See Table 7-1 for an example of a behavior frequency chart a teacher may use to collect data.

After clear general classroom management techniques are set in place and objectives are established that take into consideration the appropriate level and type of learning, effective behavior management strategies best suited for each objective and each student can be selected if needed.

**Analysis of Behavior Problems.** You may notice a student who is demonstrating behaviors that potentially cause problems for him- or herself or others. Before you can solve any behavioral problems by this student or others that occur in your classroom, you will need to analyze why the problems exist. The time you spend in such analysis can save instructional and planning time in the long run. Kauffman and his colleagues (2006) suggest the following questions to reflect on as part of your analysis:

(a) What are my assumptions about why students behave the way they do?
(b) Can I identify causal factors that I can change?
(c) What is sufficient evidence that I am making progress in changing behavior?
(d) Exactly what am I trying to accomplish?
(e) What is the student trying to get?
(f) Could I help this student get what he or she is after in a better way? (p. 33).

Careful analysis of a problem prior to developing a plan will assist you in screening for behavior problems. The Individuals with Disabilities Education Act (IDEA) requires that teachers screen for problems (Turnbull, Turnbull, Shank, &

*TABLE 7-1*  *Behavior Frequency Chart*

Student Name: _____
Target Behavior: _____
Directions: Use tally marks to note each occurrence of the target behavior during the designated time period.

| Date | Period 1 Time: | Period 2 Time: | Period 3 Time: | Period 4 Time: | Period 5 Time: | Period 6 Time: |
|------|----------------|----------------|----------------|----------------|----------------|----------------|
|      |                |                |                |                |                |                |
|      |                |                |                |                |                |                |
|      |                |                |                |                |                |                |
|      |                |                |                |                |                |                |
|      |                |                |                |                |                |                |
|      |                |                |                |                |                |                |
|      |                |                |                |                |                |                |
|      |                |                |                |                |                |                |
|      |                |                |                |                |                |                |
|      |                |                |                |                |                |                |
|      |                |                |                |                |                |                |
|      |                |                |                |                |                |                |
|      |                |                |                |                |                |                |
|      |                |                |                |                |                |                |

Smith, 2004). You can begin by identifying the problem in observable terms and collecting data on the frequency or nature of the problem using checklists, rating scales, or teacher interviews and rankings. Such screening procedures should be brief and brought to a school-based committee for review.

After teachers and others have reviewed the collection of data, often a discussion is warranted to determine if the student has any medical problems that may be causing the behavior problems. To rule out such a decision, a school nurse, physician, or mental health professional may be asked to assist you. If the decision is made to develop an intervention plan for a target behavior, the following sections may help in your planning.

## BEHAVIOR MANAGEMENT PLANS AND TECHNIQUES

You may be asked to develop, implement, and manage the behavior of individual students. In some cases, you and other teachers may be involved in conducting a careful analysis of a student's problem to determine if an individual behavior management plan is needed. In addition, many students with disabilities may have individual behavioral goals mandated on their individualized education programs (IEPs), and you may be asked to monitor their programs. As a special education teacher, you need to be adept at providing individualized behavior planning and management.

Often amid the demands of your first years of teaching, you may forget the simple, direct approaches to changing behavior. When the simple strategies work, they have the advantage of saving time and energy. As you begin to develop a plan to change behavior, ask yourself if you have tried the simplest and most obvious strategies first. It may be that modifying teacher instructions, giving students choices, or providing appropriate consequences for compliance will change the behavior in question.

If the direct approaches are attempted and the problem behavior continues, you should consider another more involved approach. Make sure the approach you choose is consistent with professional practice and is supported by empirical research. Several approaches supported by research are described in the following sections.

**Basic Behavioral Operations.** Most teachers are familiar with the concept of positive reinforcement. If a student behaves a certain way, the consequences will be positive. It is critical that you provide a consequence that is rewarding to the student. Some familiar rewards are not always appropriate for all students. You should also be able to control access to the consequence. See Box 7-2 for examples of possible reinforcers.

If you want to be successful in using positive reinforcement, you need to make sure it is given immediately after the desirable behavior occurs. You should give the reward frequently and describe to the student what he or she has done to earn the reward while making eye contact. Be certain the reinforcer chosen is not freely available but is available only contingent on when the behavior is exhibited. Another factor to consider is the immediacy of the reward. Make certain the reward is given immediately after the appropriate behavior is displayed. You will strengthen whatever behavior is immediately prior to the receiving of the reward. Be careful of your timing. Finally, make certain the reward is fair. It might help to talk with the student about the reward in terms of its appropriateness. Not all educators believe that positive reinforcement is appropriate in classrooms because it may inhibit students' intrinsic motivation to learn or may teach students to work only for a reward (Kohn, 1993). Yet most of us would agree that we all work for some reward—it may be a paycheck or a professional advancement or a simple "good job."

*Negative reinforcement* is a term that is frequently misunderstood. The term refers to strengthening a behavior by removing something unpleasant (e.g., getting good grades for fear of failure). You should rely more on positive reinforcement and less on negative reinforcement in your classroom.

---

**BOX 7-2** *Examples of Reinforcers*

**Social Reinforcers**

Teacher attention

Praise

Handshake

**Activity Reinforcers**

Talking with friends

Reading

Playing a game

Working at the computer

Watching a video or playing a video game

**Tangible Reinforcers**

Toys

Food

Money

Tokens

---

**BOX 7-3**  *Behavioral Operations*

---

Behavioral operations are based on the principles of operant conditioning first described by B. F. Skinner and include positive reinforcement, negative reinforcement, and punishment (Weiten, 2000):

- Positive reinforcement—A desired student behavior (completed homework) is increased by giving the student a reinforcer (sticker) after the student exhibits the behavior. This will increase the likelihood of the behavior reoccurring.
- Negative reinforcement—A desired student behavior (studying for algebra test) is increased

by removing an aversive or unwanted stimulus (failure). This will increase the likelihood of the behavior reoccurring.

- Punishment—An undesired student behavior (talking with friend) is decreased by applying something the student dislikes or wants to avoid (extra homework problems) after the student exhibits the undesired behavior. This will decrease the likelihood of the behavior reoccurring.

---

Punishment is used in many classrooms. The term *punishment* means providing a consequence that decreases the likelihood that a behavior will be repeated. It is best to try to manage behavior using more positive procedures first. Determine if you are generally positive toward your students by giving praise and other forms of positive attention. If you choose to set a punishment, make certain it is immediate, fair, and consistent. The student must know what behavior will result in a punishment and that the punishment will be consistent across all students. See Box 7-3 for examples of basic behavioral operations.

**Group Contingencies.** You will need to manage groups of students and to foster positive peer relations during your first years of teaching. It is always important to remember the strength and influence of peer groups in your students' lives. Social pressure from peers is more obvious in some classrooms than in others. Teachers who are good managers make use of vicarious effects to encourage good behavior. For example, you ignore a minor misbehavior and then show obvious approval of an appropriate behavior of another student, maybe one in close proximity to the one who is misbehaving. You focus on the desirable behavior rather than giving attention to the inappropriate behavior. If you choose to use a group contingency of reinforcement, keep in mind that it will create some level of peer pressure.

Kauffman et al. (2006) suggest several types of group contingencies you could use in your classroom. Independent group contingencies are those that apply to each student regardless of the performance of the group: "Those who turn in their project can spend 5 minutes at the end of the period talking with their friends." Dependent group contingencies are those that have rewards available for all group members only when requirements are met by one member or a small subset of the group: "If Billy behaves during the field trip, the entire class will get a reward when we return to school." Interdependent group contingencies are those that have a specific requirement for a reward, and the reward applies to all members of the group. The reward depends on the combined or total performance as well as the behavior of the individuals: "We will be dividing into teams to play *Jeopardy* for review of the history test. The team that wins will receive candy."

When choosing to use group contingencies, you need to make certain that the behavior you set as a goal is not too high a standard. In addition, make certain you emphasize rewarding the appropriate behavior rather than using punishment. Always keep the competition among peers fair.

**Individual Contingencies.** Designing individual contingency contracts represents a potentially effective, versatile management system. Contracts should be perceived as binding written agreements between student and

***TABLE 7-2***   *Template for Behavioral Contract*

Student: _____          Teacher: _____

Desired behavior (state in terms that the student can understand and agree to):

_____

_____

Date Contract Begins: _____

Student and teacher agree to the following: (student and teacher should negotiate):

1. State behavior student is to exhibit (include how often and how it will be measured):




2. State reward for student achieving the behavior (this needs to be mutually agreed on in the negotiation):




3. State penalty if student does not achieve the behavior (may or may not use or want to focus on a deadline for achieving the behavior):




Student Signature: _____

Teacher Signature: _____

Parent Signature:  _____

---

teacher; signatures on written contracts emphasize this perception. See Table 7-2 for an example of a template for behavioral contracts.

Contingency contracts can be used to facilitate self-monitoring and to help students gain more control over their own learning. Contracts also have the advantages of encouraging you to communicate your expectations clearly and providing students with a good understanding of the rewards and consequences available for their behavior. The behavioral expectations of both you and the student should be outlined. You should also feel free to modify or rewrite as necessary.

## FUNCTIONAL BEHAVIORAL ASSESSMENT AND BEHAVIORAL INTERVENTION PLANS

When a student is having extraordinary difficulty in school because of behavior problems, IDEA requires that functional behavioral assessment (FBA) and behavioral intervention plans (BIPs) be conducted. Actually, neither the federal special education law (IDEA 2004) nor professionals in special education agree on just what an FBA is or how to do it (Kauffman et al., 2006). Functional behavioral assessment is generally considered to be a problem-solving process for addressing student problem behavior. The basic idea is to look at the pattern of the student's behavior within the school's context. It relies on a variety of techniques and strategies to identify the purposes of a specific behavior and to help IEP teams select interventions to directly address the problem behavior. Functional behavioral assessment should be integrated, as appropriate, throughout the process of developing, reviewing, and, if necessary, revising a student's IEP.

An FBA looks beyond the behavior itself. The focus when conducting an FBA is on identifying significant pupil-specific social, affective, cognitive, and/or environmental factors associated with the occurrence (and nonoccurrence) of

---

**BOX 7-4**   *Steps in Functional Behavioral Assessment*

**Step 1:** Define the problem. Create a definition of the problem behavior and the conditions under which it typically occurs.

**Step 2:** Gather information regarding environment and behavior. Use data collection procedures, including interviews, questionnaires, record review, and direct observations.

**Step 3:** Hypothesize the function of the behavior. Use collected information and data to hypothesize the function or purpose the behavior serves for the student.

**Step 4:** Develop a behavioral plan. Determine and teach an appropriate behavior that serves the same function for the student. Arrange the environment to prompt desired behavior and develop plans for providing consequences for both desired and undesired behavior.

**Step 5:** Monitor behavior to verify hypotheses and validate intervention.

---

*Source*: From Zirpoli, TJ, *Behavior management: Applications for teachers*, 4th Edition, © 2005, p. 174. Adapted by permission of Pearson Education, Inc., Upper Saddle River, NJ.

specific behaviors. This broader perspective offers a better understanding of the function or purpose behind student behavior. See Box 7-4 for steps involved in an FBA as suggested in Zirpoli (2005).

Positive behavioral interventions (PBIs) are used to change student behavior. The purposes of the PBI are to help schools educate all students, including those with behavioral problems, using a range of appropriate services. These types of interventions and supports are often used following an FBA. The purposes of the PBI are (a) to reduce or eliminate specific behaviors, (b) to replace a difficult or problem behavior with a more acceptable behavior, and (c) to increase the student's ability to achieve in a classroom and develop personal skills for increased quality of life.

A behavioral intervention plan (BIP) based on an understanding of why a student misbehaves is extremely useful in addressing a wide range of problem behaviors. Once an analysis or evaluation of the student's behavior or an FBA has been conducted, the special education teacher should develop a plan for modifying or changing the behavior or for reinforcing an emerging behavior. The development of BIPs may involve other IEP team members or any other personnel who might provide assistance. When developing a plan for students in inclusion classes, it is critical that both the general education and the special education teachers collaborate to effectively design a plan that can be used by both teachers.

Scott and Nelson (1999) have proposed a 10-step process to help school personnel infuse the FBA data into the BIP:

1. Determine the function of the undesired behavior
2. Determine an appropriate replacement behavior
3. Determine when the replacement behavior should occur
4. Design a teaching sequence
5. Manipulate the environment to increase the probability of success
6. Manipulate the environment to decrease the probability of failure
7. Determine how positive behavior will be reinforced
8. Determine consequences for instances of problem behavior
9. Develop a data collection system
10. Collect data

As a new teacher, you should consult with your administrators for the details of the legal requirements for the FBA and the BIP prior to beginning to work on one for your students. Careful analysis of problem behavior is acceptable prior to designing a plan for change, but you should make sure you are following any specific rules of your school district. Students who receive special education as a result of behavior problems must have IEPs that include behavior goals, objectives, and intervention plans. While the current laws driving special education do not require specific procedures and plans for these students, it is recommended that their IEPs be based on FBAs and include proactive positive behavioral interventions and supports.

## DISCIPLINE ISSUES

Teachers have been challenged for years by student discipline issues. Keeping schools safe and orderly is encouraged by many parents, police officers, members of Congress, and other public entities, and their voices are often heard in the public discussions of schoolwide discipline issues. Teachers and school administrators have been recognized by the public as having the authority to discipline students. Yet the students do have rights. "The Supreme Court in Gross v. Lopez (1975; hereafter Gross) held that students have the constitutional protection in the form of due process rights when school officials use disciplinary procedures such as suspension" (Zirpoli, 2005, p. 380).

Guidelines have been established by special education law that ensures appropriate discipline of students who are eligible for special education programs; the procedures for discipline are often not known by new teachers. You should be aware of your schoolwide discipline procedures as well as the procedures in place for students with disabilities. See Boxes 7-5 and 7-6.

In most cases, school officials may discipline a student with disabilities in the same manner that they discipline students without disabilities, with a few exceptions. However, if suspended for more than 10 days, a student with disabilities must receive educational services. If a student with disabilities is suspended for less than 10 school days, a school district is not required to continue educational services (OSEP Discipline Guidance, 1997). If a student with disabilities is suspended for a series of short-term suspensions and if they constitute a pattern of exclusion, the school is "changing the placement" of the student, and that process is illegal under the latest IDEA.

If a student brings a weapon to school or knowingly possesses drugs or other controlled substances on school property, school officials may unilaterally place the student in an appropriate interim alternative educational setting for 45 days. A hearing officer should be involved. During this time, the IEP team should meet

---

**BOX 7-5**  *School Disciplinary Procedures: Find Out What They Are!*

Despite our best efforts at using positive classroom management strategies, sometimes student behavior requires disciplinary action. Every school has stated policies and procedures that govern discipline. You should carefully review this material and know whom to contact for clarification. You should know the school's policies and procedures for the following:

- Removal of a disruptive student from classroom—Is there a time-out room? Can students be assigned to work silently in the hallway? Is there a process for sending a student to the principal or

assistant principal? Who monitors the student when he or she is out of the classroom?
- Physical aggression toward other students or teachers—How do you get help? Who should be contacted? What paperwork needs to be completed?
- Suspected or observed drug use—Who is this reported to? What are you required to do or say to the student?
- Suspension or expulsion from school—What is the process? What are the rights of the student? Are homework assignments to be prepared?

---

***BOX 7-6***    *Expulsion or Suspension of Special Needs Students*

---

In some cases, a special needs student may be removed from a classroom or suspended from school for disciplinary infractions. Two questions to consider before this action is taken are the following:

1. Does a relationship exist between the student's disability and the behavior, and is the behavior a manifestation of the disability? If no relationship exists between the student's behavior and his or her disability, then regular disciplinary procedures should be implemented. If the behavior is related to the student's disability, then another question must be addressed.
2. How does a student with disabilities continue to receive a free and appropriate public education, and what must the school do to ensure the IEP services are maintained? The IEP team must

conduct an assessment of the behavior and develop a plan that reduces the behavior. This can be done by convening the IEP team, conducting a manifestation determination, and seeking permission to do so from the student's parents.

Students with disabilities may be removed from school for up to 10 cumulative or consecutive school days as long as the suspensions are used with nondisabled students as well. if a suspension exceeds this limit it becomes a change in placement. In this situation, if school officials do not follow the IDEA change of placement procedures (i.e., written notice to the student's parents, convening the IEP team) the suspension is a violation of the law.

---

to determine what actions should take place. If a change of placement, including suspension or expulsion, is discussed, IDEA requires a manifestation determination. A manifestation determination is a review of the relationship between a student's disability and the misconduct. The manifestation determination must be conducted by the IEP team, and they will need to consider all relevant information. They need to determine if the student understood the consequences of his or her behavior and was capable of controlling it.

Maintaining a safe and orderly classroom environment is one of the most important duties you will face as a teacher. Certainly, it can be a very difficult aspect of your job. As a teacher of students with disabilities, you face a complex situation when applying disciplinary rules, and you must follow the legal guidelines. If you need assistance, make sure you ask your supervisors, and you may find that your district provides multiple workshops and support on this topic.

As you master classroom and behavior management and begin to implement the techniques that work for you and your students, you may want to include evidence of such in your teaching portfolio. Review the ideas in Table 7-3 for classroom and behavior management evidence suggestions.

---

***TABLE 7-3***    *Examples of Classroom/Behavior Management Evidence for Teaching Portfolio*

---

To provide evidence of competency in the area of classroom and behavior management, a special education teacher might include the following in a teaching portfolio:

- ❑ Photos of class rules, wall art, posted behavior charts, or other classroom items
- ❑ Classroom floor plans with traffic flow patterns noted
- ❑ Copies of behavior plans
- ❑ Copies of frequency charts
- ❑ Copies of behavioral contracts
- ❑ Copies of IEP with behavioral goals and documentation of progress
- ❑ Copies of FBAs

---

*Note.* Student confidentiality should be maintained. Please block out any identifying information.

## SUMMARY

Good behavior can be taught to students using many of the same procedures you use in instructional delivery. This chapter discussed several specific techniques that will help you design positive classroom environments using many basic behavioral operations. Always review your instructional procedures as the first step in good behavior management. Establishing a dialogue with your students, parents, and administrators can help you establish clear, appropriate behavioral plans for your classroom.

## ACTIVITY QUESTIONS

1.  What are different types of reinforcement used by teachers in your school? Ask a co-teacher what he or she has found to work in his or her classroom.

2.  What are the important elements of contingency contracts? Collect several samples of contracts that other teachers have used.

3.  What are the advantages of data collection when determining the need for a behavior intervention plan? What are the variables that may influence the accuracy of data collection procedures?

4.  Discuss with your administrators what the due process protections are for your students. How does your school assure students and their families that due process protections are followed?

## SELECTED WEBSITES

http://www.ccbd.net
*This is the site for the Council for Children with Behavioral Disorders. This site provides resources and suggestions for working with challenging behaviors and students with emotional disorders.*

http://www.nasponline.org
*This is the site for the National Association of School Psychologists. This site provides general guidelines and resources for addressing behavior concerns.*

http://www.pbis.org
*This is the site for the Office of Special Education Programs Center on Positive Behavioral*
*Interventions and Supports. This site provides information on IDEA guidelines and suggestions for school personnel.*

http://www.edjj.org
*This is the site for the National Center on Education, Disability and Juvenile Justice. This site examines the overrepresentation of youth with disabilities at risk for contact with the courts or already involved in the juvenile delinquency system. They provide professional development and technical assistance, conduct research, and disseminate resources.*

## REFLECTION JOURNAL ACTIVITIES

1.  Reflect on how you will establish rules, routines, or procedures. What are three rules that students must adhere to? Consider your body language and tone of voice. Do they work for you? Do you need more practice? Do you feel "in charge" of your classroom? Why or why not?

2.  Review or create a data collection procedure for homework assignments for your third-period class. Keep it for a week and then review. Is collecting the data working to increase homework completion rates? Do you need to modify it to include the homework assigned?

3.  Create a behavior contract for a student on your caseload. What about the contract is working? Does it need to be changed or modified? How is progress being communicated with parents? Do the parents have any suggestions or concerns?

4.  Reflect on the different types of situations in which you must manage behavior. Consider both individual and whole-class behavior management. How can you demonstrate your competency with behavior management? What evidence of your competency can you provide? What areas do you need more experience or guidance in?

## *REFERENCES*

Emmer, E. T., Evertson, C. M., & Worsham, M. E. (2003). *Classroom management for secondary teachers* (6th ed.). Boston: Allyn & Bacon.

Jandris, T. P. (2001). *Essential for principals: Data-based decision-making.* Arlington, VA: National Association of Elementary School Principals and Educational Research Service.

Kauffman, J. M., Mostert, M. P., Trent, S. C., & Pullen, P. L. (2006). *Managing classroom behavior: A reflective case-based approach* (4th ed.). Boston: Allyn & Bacon.

Kohn, A. (1993). *Punished by rewards: The trouble with gold stars, incentive plans, A's, praise and other bribes.* New York: Houghton Mifflin.

Marazano, R. (2003). *Classroom management that works: Research-based strategies for every teacher.* Alexandria, VA: Association for Supervision and Curriculum Development.

Mastropieri, M. A., & Scruggs, T. E. (2002). *Effective instruction for special education* (3rd ed.). Austin, TX: PRO-ED.

OSEP Discipline Guidance, 26 IDELR 923 (OSEP 1997).

Pelletier, C. M. (2004). *Strategies for successful student teaching: A comprehensive guide* (2nd ed.). Boston: Allyn & Bacon.

Scott, T. M., & Nelson, C. M. (1999). Functional behavioral assessment: Implications for training and staff development. *Behavior Disorders, 24,* 249–252.

Turnbull, A. P., Turnbull, R., Shank, M., & Smith, S. J. (2004). *Exceptional lives: Special education in today's schools* (4th ed.). Upper Saddle River, NJ: Merrill/Prentice Hall/Pearson.

Wang, M. C., Haertel, G. D., & Walberg, H. J. (1993). Toward a knowledge base for school learning. *Review of Educational Research, 63,* 249–376.

Weiten, W. (2000). *Psychology: Themes and variations* (4th ed.). Belmont, CA: Wadsworth.

Welton, E. N. (1999). How to help inattentive students find success in school: Getting the homework back from the dog. *Teaching Exceptional Children, 31*(4), 12–18.

Wiggins, G., & McTighe, J. (1998). *Understanding by design.* Alexandria, VA: Association for Supervision and Curriculum Development.

Zirpoli, T. J. (2005). *Behavior management: Applications for teachers.* Upper Saddle River, NJ: Merrill/Prentice Hall/Pearson.

# PART 3

*Evaluating Initial Teaching Experiences*

# CHAPTER *Eight*

## Developing Your Teaching Portfolio

### OBJECTIVES

After reading this chapter, the reader will be able to:

- describe how teaching portfolios can be helpful for a beginning teacher;
- list suggested components of a teaching portfolio;
- link evidence given in one's portfolio to CEC standards for special education teachers;
- suggest ways in which portfolios are evaluated;
- list several ideas to use to create a digital portfolio.

### INTRODUCTION

This chapter provides guidance on how to design, organize, and package a professional portfolio illustrating a teacher's growth in self-selected competency areas that are believed pertinent to effective teaching. A portfolio may serve as an instrument guiding self-reflection about realistic teaching situations and corresponding decisions made by the teacher before, during, and after their first few years of teaching. A portfolio also may serve as a real assessment device at the end of a student teaching assignment demonstrating successful completion of the experience or as a means to demonstrate a teacher's competencies during the first years of teaching. The first section of this chapter guides teachers in designing and packaging their own portfolio. In addition, because we continue to move into a more technologically supported society, the second section provides guidance on how to electronically prepare and submit a finished portfolio.

*My Classroom*

Ms. Kim, a first-year special educator, wants to develop a portfolio to show her principal her knowledge, skills, and abilities, especially in the use of behavior management techniques, but is not sure where to begin. She purchases a three-ring binder and begins collecting evidence the week prior to school. She begins to draft her teaching philosophy and a statement about her use of behavioral management procedures. She takes digital pictures of the behavioral charts she plans to put on the walls in her classroom. She copies several lesson plans she prepares to use to explain several group contingencies to the students. She realizes that she will collect more evidence including students' work as the year progresses, but she feels good that she has begun collecting evidence and plans to add her reflections on the use of the evidence once the children arrive. Ms. Kim is convinced that some ideas will work better than others as she begins the process.

**FOCUS QUESTIONS**

1. What is a teaching portfolio, and how does one get started creating one?
2. What standards and competencies am I addressing in my portfolio?
3. What are the purposes of a teaching portfolio?
4. How should a portfolio be organized?
5. How do I create a digital portfolio?

## *CREATING THE PORTFOLIO*

Portfolios have been defined as purposeful compilations of student work collected over time to demonstrate progress and achievement (Campbell, Cignetti, Melenyzer, Nettles, & Wyman, 1997). Portfolios have also been used as an opportunity for multidimensional assessment (Adams-Bullock & Hawk, 2005). In the field of education, teaching portfolios are useful tools for preservice and practicing teachers. Portfolios can support a teacher's first years of teaching in the following ways: (a) providing a richer and more realistic portrait of a person's teaching abilities; (b) offering an opportunity for self-reflection, which is arguably a good way to improve skills; (c) communicating in a powerful way a person's teaching abilities to others; and (d) providing much more detailed and useful feedback about what standards and competencies teachers have met and where teachers might need more help (Barrett, 2000b).

Portfolios also serve as effective techniques for teacher evaluation. Teacher portfolios provide a much more effective presentation of a teacher's capabilities than traditional paper-based evaluation forms. "Portfolios build a professional model of assessment, not a bureaucratic model" (Adam-Bullock & Hawk, 2005, p. 10). In a teacher's portfolio, selected work exhibits can highlight important information about a teacher's competencies and abilities to meet certain professional standards. Creation of a portfolio also serves to enhance the marketability of teachers, giving them an "edge" over other teachers possessing equivalent qualifications (Verkler, 2000). Portfolios provide a way for teachers to document their professional development, for preservice teachers to measure knowledge, or for provisionally licensed teachers to use in the certification process: (Adams, 1995). As teachers assemble their professional portfolio, they receive invaluable experience in the portfolio process: experience they can eventually utilize as they incorporate this means of assessment in their own classrooms (Verkler, 2000). Some teachers find the portfolios time consuming to compile, but they report experiencing much professional growth from the process.

Putting a portfolio together should not be so overwhelming that you feel the process to be too difficult and therefore are hesitant to complete the task. Often a teaching portfolio reflects your competency in several areas. Table 8-1 lists potential competency areas (linked to the standards of the Council for Exceptional Children [CEC]) that may be included in your portfolio (CEC, 2005). In addition, you should include a general introduction, including a teaching philosophy, and a reflection section, including daily journal entries. In some cases, developing a portfolio may be required as part of a course requirement (e.g., student teaching) or practicum placement, or it may be developed by you for your own professional development. The following sections outline the procedures that will allow you to develop a portfolio without too much stress.

*TABLE 8-1*  *Examples of Teacher Competencies in Teaching Portfolios*

| Competency/CEC Standards | Description |
| --- | --- |
| Instructional methods<br>Standard 4: Instructional Strategies;<br>Standard 7: Instructional Planning | The teacher is expected to provide a discussion for and evidence of the use of effective instructional practices in the classroom for improving academic skills of students. |
| Behavioral interventions<br>Standard 5: Learning Environments and Social Interactions | The teacher is expected to provide a discussion for and evidence of the use of best practices for managing and improving student behavior either in general education classrooms or in pullout settings. Such behaviors may include social or academic skills. |
| Classroom structure<br>Standard 3: Individual Learning Differences | The teacher is expected to provide a discussion for and evidence of the use of a classroom structure that is flexible enough to accommodate the diverse needs of all students. |
| Assessment techniques<br>Standard 8: Assessment | The teacher is expected to provide a discussion for and evidence of the use of appropriate assessment strategies such as curriculum-based assessment, anecdotal records, and portfolio assessment. |
| Collaboration<br>Standard 10: Collaboration | The teacher is expected to provide a discussion for and evidence of one's ability to work collaboratively with parents, teachers, and other professionals. |
| Professional development<br>Standard 9: Professional & Ethical Practice | The teacher is expected to demonstrate and provide evidence of participation in professional activities and to demonstrate individual transition from the role of a teacher in training to that of a professional educator. |

*Source.* CEC, 2005.

## DESIGNING A PORTFOLIO

Designing portfolios for the specific purpose of illustrating your knowledge, skills, and abilities involves only a few steps. Initially, you begin by writing a short philosophical statement outlining your teaching goals and skills. Second, in support of your teaching philosophy, you need to describe your abilities as a teacher by selecting a set of competencies that you feel you can provide evidence for from your teaching. The number of competencies you should select from the list is not set in stone. Often the purpose of the portfolio dictates the number of competencies chosen. Next, you should begin collecting work samples (e.g., worksheets completed by your students and parent contact logs or other data collection items from your classroom). These samples, called evidence or exhibits, may include but are not limited to lesson plans, behavioral charts, materials used for a unit of study, evaluation forms, and communication logs.

The pieces of evidence must be a purposeful collection of work guided by the nature of each selected competency and assembled for the particular purpose (e.g., to share with a principal or professor). Remember to keep names and identities confidential by blacking them out on the copy used in your portfolio. It often is the case that some teachers collect much more evidence than they need, but until the purpose is clearly defined and the evidence reviewed, it is difficult for beginning teachers at the collection stage to limit the number of work samples. After completion of the evidence gathering, you will review and select the best evidence. In addition, because the portfolio includes sections in which you can provide comments or reflections on each competency, you will have time to collect more or to limit the inclusion of evidence pieces. Many portfolios also include a reflection journal that may be written daily or weekly. See Table 8-2 for examples of components of one teacher's portfolio.

*TABLE 8-2*  *Examples of Components of Teaching Portfolios*

| Components | Description |
|---|---|
| Philosophy | Teaching philosophy including why you teach, who you teach, and where you teach |
| Competency #1: (list name) | Selection of one competency area—evidence supporting this competency included |
| Reflection #1 | Written reflection on evidence provided in first competency |
| Competency #2 (list name) | Selection of second competency area—evidence supporting this competency included |
| Reflection #2 | Written reflection on evidence provided in second competency |
| Competency #3 (list name) | Selection of third competency area—evidence supporting this competency included |
| Reflection #3 | Written reflection on evidence provided in third competency |
| Reflection daily journal Final comments | Daily entries reflecting on teaching activities Written reflection on portfolio process |

*Note.* You may be required to consider more than three competencies.

## ORGANIZING AND DEVELOPING A PORTFOLIO

"The portfolio development process consists of four basic steps: collection, selection, reflection and projection" (Danielson & Abrutyn, 1997, p. 10). First, you need to collect materials in your classroom that support your selected competencies. Second, you need to select which evidence supports each chosen competency and whether you need to design new evidence. Third, you need to include reflections on every item selected. Finally, you need to provide an overall written reflection, including your goals for the future. See Box 8-1 for tips on developing your own portfolio.

Danielson and Abrutyn (1997) suggest the following eight steps in organizing and developing a portfolio:

1. Determine the curricular objectives (i.e., competencies) to be addressed through the portfolio
2. Determine the decisions that will be made on the basis of the portfolio (e.g., passing a course or getting hired by a new employer)
3. Determine which teaching tasks (e.g., teaching methods) are needed to provide evidence to support the curricular objectives (i.e., competencies)
4. Define the criteria for each objective and establish performance criteria (e.g., how many pieces of evidence are needed or if new evidence needs to be designed)
5. Determine who will evaluate your portfolio entries and when (e.g., will faculty or teaching assistants provide feedback, and will feedback be provided as "parts" are completed or only at the conclusion of the process?)
6. Train faculty or teaching assistants to score the components of the portfolio (this task is not completed by the teacher)

---

*BOX 8-1*  *Tips for Portfolio Development*

- Review previous teachers' portfolios
- Select standards you will be addressing
- Start collecting materials early
- Review the requirements if completing the portfolio as part of a class assignment
- Collect multiple copies of your students' work

- Document classroom organization and activities with digital pictures
- Mark out names and faces to retain confidentiality
- Keep a large box (or file) for materials
- Keep a reflection journal

7. Complete the tasks needed to supply the evidence and collect copies for support (e.g., conduct a functional behavioral assessment and copy all materials for the portfolio)
8. Make decisions on the basis of the evidence collected (i.e., review your evidence and add your reflections and package the portfolio)

The portfolio's purpose, audience, and future use will determine what evidence you need and how much you need to collect. Once you have determined which competencies you would like to select, you will need to generate a list of evidence or exhibits that you will collect to support your knowledge in each competency. For example, if one of the competencies selected is behavior management, then you might list such items as a behavioral contract you are using with one child, a functional behavioral assessment you just completed with another student, a home-to-school contract you developed to use with another child, and so on. You may need to design new pieces of evidence, collect copies of evidence already used in the classroom, and/or take digital pictures of evidence that is too large for an 8-by-11 binder (e.g., large poster of classroom rules). Selecting evidence for a portfolio can span more than one school year, but if used as an assessment tool for a semester of student teaching, it may span only one semester or 4 months. See Table 8-3 for examples of evidence for the competency area of collaboration.

A certain degree of reflection is an essential component of effective teaching and thus should also be part of selecting your evidence for a teaching portfolio. Reflecting on the evidence collected will help you decide when you have enough evidence to support mastery of each of your selected competencies. During the reflection phase, you should articulate in writing your thoughts about each piece of evidence in your portfolio (Danielson & Abrutyn, 1997). You should indicate in your written reflections how the evidence was used in the classroom and what you would do differently with the evidence in the future in your classroom. Written reflection may be a new skill for you. See Table 8-4 for guidelines on how to write your reflections on the evidence that you want to include in your portfolio. See Box 8-2 for examples of reflection journal entries.

---

*TABLE 8-3*  *Examples of Evidence for Collaboration Competency*

---

To provide evidence of competency in the area of collaboration, a special education teacher might want to consider including the following in the portfolio:

Working with parents:
  Copies of parent contact log
  Copies of progress notes sent home
  Copies of telephone calls and e-mails with parents
  Copies of class newsletters/school letters
  Copies of IEP and documentation of progress
  Photos of parent conferences or back-to-school night

Working with school professionals:
  Copies of notes from meetings
  Copies of telephone calls and e-mails
  Copies of IEP team meetings
  Copies of accommodations and modifications for student

Working with Co-teachers:
  Copies of joint unit/lesson plans
  Copies of telephone calls and e-mails

---

*Note.* Student confidentiality should be maintained. Please block out any identifying information.

**TABLE 8-4** *Guidelines on Writing Reflections*

Reflections are key components in developing a portfolio. Writing reflections involves a process in which teachers develop their own voice in the evaluation of their professional practice. It is the glue that holds the portfolio together. When teachers first learn to reflect on their work, they tend to focus on superficial criteria, such as neatness, length, and mechanics. The reflection sections should be written in the first person and be honest and accurate.

Steps in the reflection process include the following:

- The first step in the process is that you need to describe the evidence in terms of the standard chosen; the clearer the description, the better.
- The second step is to analyze the evidence. Analysis may include the positives and negatives of the evidence and also how one might improve next time.
- The final step is the discussion of the future impact. How did the evidence impact you, and what changes would you make in the future on the basis of the evidence?

Prompts that facilitate writing reflections:

- Think about why you are doing what you are doing.
- Think about the outcomes.
- How can the information gained be used for improvement?
- "I chose this piece as an example because . . ."
- "One thing I improved on this semester in my daily co-teaching with the English teacher is . . ."

Important points to remember:

- Work with a buddy initially to generate and share ideas.
- Practice writing reflective comments and provide examples.
- Remember that no right or wrong exists in terms of the reflections.
- Avoid bias and insensitive language when writing reflections.

---

**BOX 8-2** *Examples of Reflection Journal Entries*

Thursday, October 15

I had a very busy day. I met with the fifth-grade team to discuss the upcoming unit in math, and we also talked about two of my students (F and L) who are falling behind in language arts. The team had some great ideas of ways to modify the math lessons, but we are having difficulty finding a way to work with F and L. F seems to be having a hard time with the transition to a new teacher and is generally disruptive. Since both F and L are in the inclusion class, I am going to spend some individual time with them during small-group reading. We'll keep data on when F is disruptive in class to see if a pattern exists. L may need some extra practice time with word sounds. We'll have to work on getting that in during small-group time.

I also had an IEP meeting for a newly diagnosed ADHD student (B) with reading problems. His parents seemed very overwhelmed at the meeting. I'll need to follow up with regular parent notes, and I'll probably give them a day or so, then telephone them. They were very positive about the IEP goals and services being provided, but I am not sure that they fully understood how B would be helped in the inclusion class.

While I felt very busy today, I also felt that some progress was being made on solving problems. I know it is hard for parents to come into the special education system, but these parents were really trying to do what is best for their son. It is also so great to work with such a supportive team in the fifth grade. Everyone was trying to come up with ideas that might work. I really appreciate how open to modifying lessons everyone was. I'm feeling more up to date with my paperwork, too.

Wednesday, February 20

I co-taught a lesson on world history. My co-teacher and I worked out the lesson with some really great activities. We had the students create a mosaic out of construction paper as an introduction to mosaic artwork in Constantinople. Both my co-teacher and I moved around the classroom working with students. Then I used some PowerPoint slides to provide key information (the special needs students were given the notes pages to help them).

## PACKAGING A PORTFOLIO

A portfolio can take on many different shapes and sizes. The quality is based on the depth of the evidence and reflection. As you begin to collect materials, you should review the legal parameters of copying student work or providing pictures of students in your classroom. The basic rule is to determine the audience. If the audience is someone besides you, such as your immediate supervisor or professor, then you should obtain a release form from the student's parents allowing their child's work to be included in the portfolio. In addition, you should black out all names, refer to students and other professionals anonymously in reflections, and try not to use pictures identifying students' faces.

As you begin the process of collecting evidence for the portfolio, you should save all evidence and materials in a box or a container in your classroom. You may want to purchase a three-ring binder and plastic sheets for the final product. Most teachers enjoy creating a cover with their name, level of teaching, and date of completion. Be sure to include sections for the opening teaching philosophy, each competency area with its own reflection piece, and a reflection journal section, including a final review of the process. Use Table 8-5 for guidance on how to package the sections in your portfolio. Table 8-6 provides an example of a teacher's written teaching philosophy section.

---

**TABLE 8-5** *Guidelines on Packaging the Portfolio*

1. Opening statement—teaching philosophy
   - Include your current teaching position
   - Discuss your educational philosophy
   - Provide an opening paragraph or two discussing why you selected each competency
   - Keep brief (two to three pages)
2. Each selected competency area
   - Write opening statement (one to two pages) introducing each competency using supportive research and theory
   - List evidence you will provide (list/table of contents)
   - Provide evidence/examples
     - Worksheets, photos, tests, student work
     - Need a variety of items
     - Need more than one piece of evidence per competency area
   - Write final statement (one to two pages) reflecting on what worked and what did not, your conclusions about your documentation/efficacy, and future impact
3. Reflection daily journal
   - Write reflections for approximately 50 days—one or two paragraphs each day
   - Reflect on your instruction, classroom performance, and other school issues
4. Overall summary/conclusion statement
   - Write final summary/conclusion (one to two pages)
   - "What I learned during the portfolio process"
   - "What I've learned about teaching"
5. General notes
   - Put in a three-ring binder
   - Purchase and use protective sleeves
   - Write short notes to provide on each page of evidence so that it is clear how evidence was used (may want to use small yellow sticky notes)

**TABLE 8-6**  *Example of a Teacher's Educational Philosophy Section of Portfolio*

My educational philosophy is a product of my experience as a student, my teacher education courses, and my experience as a new teacher. All these have influenced how I believe students learn and how I try to manage my instruction to facilitate their learning. As a student, I appreciated those teachers who were engaging and passionate about what they were teaching. While I may not have liked the subject (economics), I appreciated their enthusiasm for the material. I hope to convey a similar passion to my students. I have tried to distill my personal philosophy into the following tenets of good teaching: (a) know my learners, (b) create a positive classroom environment, and (c) maximize my instructional time.

*Know my learners:* I think it is important to know where my learners are academically and as individuals. Academically, I need to know their strengths and weaknesses so that I can plan effective instruction that will help them achieve to their potential. I need to determine their zones of proximal development (ZPDs) on a regular basis so that I can provide targeted instruction within their ZPDs. I incorporate informal checks for understanding in all my lessons and listen to their questions to measure their knowledge of what is being taught. I also spend time assessing their individual special needs to determine appropriate accommodations and modifications. This is time consuming, as I must regularly meet with general education teachers to gain insight into the general education curriculum's requirements. I must also spend time with each student to determine the effectiveness of individual accommodations and modifications. If something is not working, I feel that, together with the student and his general education teachers, we must find an alternative solution to try in the classroom. In addition, students should be seen as individuals with personalities. Each student has his or her own "story" that may influence how he or she performs in class. I try to get to know my students so that I have a sense of their humor, engagement, and learning difficulties.

*Create a positive classroom environment:* I think a positive classroom environment includes appropriate behavior limits (classroom rules), engaging instruction, sequencing activities to include movement, and reducing student frustration. To accomplish all these, I must always be prepared for my lessons, and I recognize that I may need to change a lesson midstream. At the beginning of the school year, I establish classroom rules and emphasize the importance of using manners. I think students should use the terms "Please" and "Thank you," so I role model using these phrases. I know that engaging instruction is my best behavior management tool; therefore, I carefully sequence my instruction to recognize when attention might become unfocused. I also try to incorporate movement into all my lessons. When reprimanding a student, I gently state the rule. I am careful to use a stern but not "mad voice." I have found that by targeting my instruction to the students' ZPDs, frustration with learning has been reduced. If I note a student becoming frustrated, I will attempt to provide other opportunities for the student to master the content or skill. Sometimes, this means that I reteach the entire lesson to a small group of students using different methods.

*Maximize my instructional time:* Special education students are behind in school and have learning difficulties, so it is important that I use all my instructional time wisely. To maximize my instructional time, I have a daily lesson plan with a detailed timed sequence of activities. In my methods classes, I was taught that some instructional methods were more effective than others. I try to use the most efficient and effective methods with my students. This can be challenging because I may need to locate specific resources (direct instruction) and materials (counting cubes) to design or modify one lesson. Because it is so important that my lessons are effective, I regularly collect data on how my individual students are doing. I have used stopwatches for reading fluency, tally sheets for mistakes, worksheets, and unit tests to determine how an individual student is doing in a particular area. I try to assess how a student is doing on a specific IEP goal regularly.

## CREATING DIGITAL PORTFOLIOS

The emergence of digital portfolios has been exciting (Kahn, 2003). The advantages of being able to present your evidence with a click of a button and without the bulk of a binder are numerous. Digital teaching portfolios, sometimes referred to as multimedia portfolios, electronic portfolios, e-folios, and Web folios, are electronically augmented portfolios containing the same materials that would be placed in the traditional paper portfolio (Milman, 2005). The materials in a digital portfolio are presented using a combination of digital media, such as audio recordings, hypermedia programs, spreadsheets, and word processing software.

How a digital portfolio is published depends on the following: the purpose, the student's experience with technology, the resources available, and the amount of time to complete it. Digital portfolios may demonstrate wider dimensions of learning, as their parts can be interconnected. In addition, they save space in comparison to more traditional paper-based portfolios. Evidence can be presented using animation, simulation, or video clips. Digital portfolios also foster confidence in teachers' professional and technology skills (Milman, 2005). Yet several disadvantages exist: (a) too much emphasis may be placed on the "bells and whistles" of the portfolio rather than on using technology to support the content of the portfolio and meeting the objectives, (b) the reviewers may need to be provided with appropriate hardware and software to access information on a disk or on the Internet, (c) portfolio readers and reviewers may need to be educated about the importance of reviewing diverse portfolio components, and (d) it may be inconvenient for the reviewers to access the electronic information presented (Kahn, 2003).

Despite the disadvantages, more and more teachers are developing digital portfolios. Ideally, you should have knowledge of the software and have access to the technology needed prior to beginning this process. Barrett (2000a) lists the following steps to create your digital portfolio:

**Stage 1:** Defining the Portfolio Goals and Context

1. Identify the purpose and audience for the portfolio (e.g., part of your student teaching requirements).
2. Identify the standards (i.e., competencies) that will be used as the organizing framework for your portfolio.
3. Identify the computer equipment and software available.
4. Identify the level of technology skills you will need.
5. Select the appropriate level of software and programming to begin electronic portfolio development (see Figure 8-1).
6. Set up electronic folders for each standard (i.e., competency) to organize the artifacts (i.e., evidence)

**Stage 2:** The Working Portfolio

1. Identify the portfolio artifacts (examples of your work) and/or identify experiences you have that demonstrate that you have met the competencies and put all into electronic formats. You may have evidence that demonstrates more than one indicator, and that is fine.
2. Collect and store the evidence in appropriate folders on your computer or server.
3. Interject personality into the portfolio design. Use some of the graphics capabilities of the software to add your own style and flair to your portfolio.
4. Use appropriate multimedia to add style and individuality to the portfolio.

**FIGURE 8-1**   *Portfolio Development and Software Needed.*

| Level 1 (Basic) | Level 2 (Advanced) | Level 3 (More Advanced) | Level 4 (Even More Advanced) | Level 5 (Most Advanced) |
|---|---|---|---|---|
| Software used to create word documents (e.g., Microsoft Word) | Database, PowerPoint, HyperStudio, programs (e.g., Microsoft Office) | Adobe Acrobat and PDF Writer software (e.g., digital picture software) | HTML using Netscape Composer (e.g., other HTML authoring programs) | Macromedia Director (e.g., other multimedia software) |

**Stage 3:** The Reflective Portfolio

1. Write general reflective statements on achieving each standard (i.e., competency).
2. Review the evidence that represents achievement of each of your competencies.
3. Write reflective statements for each piece of evidence, elaborating on why it was selected and its meaning and value in your portfolio.
4. From the reflections and feedback, set learning goals for your future.

**Stage 4:** The Connected Portfolio

1. Organize the digital files. Select software that allows the creation of hypermedia links between your files containing your goals, student work samples, rubrics, and/or your assessment protocols. Identify patterns through the "linking" process.
2. Convert word processing, database, or slide show documents into either PDF or HTML format.
3. Create hypertext links between goals, student work samples, rubrics, and assessment.
4. Insert multimedia evidence.

As portfolios move from paper-and-pencil collections to electronic digital platforms, we must focus on how the medium supports and influences the process of the portfolio (Barrett, 2000b). What technology is needed and how familiar teachers are in the field with this technology are important considerations. We need to continue to study the use of digital portfolios to support teachers' learning and self-reflection in their classrooms.

## SUMMARY

A teaching portfolio provides a record of your teaching activities. It documents both the complexity and the individuality of your teaching. The inclusion of evidence from a variety of resources allows for a selected set of competencies to be viewed. It allows you as a new teacher the flexibility to document and display your teaching in a way that stays connected to the particular situations in which your teaching occurred. The portfolio also provides the needed structure for your self-reflection on which areas of your teaching need improvement. It should not be considered an exhaustive compilation of all the documents and materials that bear on your teaching performance but rather a selective set of materials that provide solid evidence of your competency in self-selected areas of teaching.

## ACTIVITY QUESTIONS

1. Purchase a notebook that can be used for your reflective journal entries. Begin writing in it during the first week of school.

2. Try to find a teaching buddy who may want to work with you to put together a portfolio. If you are taking a class requiring a portfolio, work with one of your fellow classmates. It is always easier to work together and brainstorm ideas.

3. Discuss the portfolio project with your immediate supervisor, mentor, or principal to get advice. Ask if there are others who have put together portfolios that they can share with you.

4. Talk to any teachers you know who have completed their National Board Certification, as they were required to put together a teaching portfolio. See http://www.nbpts.org.

## SELECTED WEBSITES

http://electronicportfolios.com/portfolios/howto/index.html
*How to create your own electronic portfolio by Helen Barrett. This site offers great resources for those working on their teaching portfolios.*

http://www.teachnet.com/how-to/employment/portfolios/port002.html
*A site that provides useful tips on creating your teaching portfolio.*

http://www.aurbach.com
*An example of a private company's (Aurback & Associates, Inc.) Web page designed to help prepare a teaching portfolio.*

## REFLECTION JOURNAL ACTIVITIES

1. List the competencies you want to cover in your portfolio and discuss with other teachers what evidence might fit with each. Determine if your list of evidence matches their lists.

2. Try to keep a daily or weekly journal reflecting on how your days progress. You may find that some days go smoother than others. You may also see a pattern in the days that do not go well. You may find that by writing down your reflections with regular precision, your teaching improves.

3. What do you see as the major differences in the preparation of a digital portfolio versus a paper portfolio? Other than the need for technology, do you find the digital portfolio considerably more involved, and, if so, why?

## REFERENCES

Adams, T. L. (1995). A paradigm for portfolio assessment in teacher education. *Education, 115,* 528, 568–570.

Adams-Bullock, A., & Hawk, P. P. (2005). *Developing a teaching portfolio: A guide to preservice and practicing teachers* (2nd ed.). Upper Saddle River, NJ: Pearson/Merrill/Prentice Hall.

Barrett, H. C. (2000a). *How to create your own electronic portfolio.* Retrieved August 9, 2005, from http://electronicportfolios.org/portfolios/howto/index.html

Barrett, H. C. (2000b). *White paper: Researching electronic portfolios and learner engagement.* Retrieved August 9, 2005, from http://electronicportfolios.org/reflect/whitepaper.pdf

Campbell, D. M., Cignetti, P. B., Melenyzer, B. J., Nettles, D. H., & Wyman, R. M., Jr. (1997). *How to develop a professional portfolio.* Boston: Allyn & Bacon.

Council for Exceptional Children. (2005). *CEC performance-based standards.* Retrieved January 11, 2006, from http://www.cec.sped.org/ps/perf_based_stds/standards.html#standards

Danielson, C., & Abrutyn, L. (1997). *An introduction to using portfolios in the classroom.* Alexandria, VA: Association for Supervision and Curriculum Development.

Kahn, S. (2003). Making good work public through electronic teaching portfolios. In P. Seldin (Ed.), *The teaching portfolio: A practical guide to improve performance and promotion/tenure decisions* (3rd ed., pp. 36–50). Bolton, MA: Anker Publications.

Milman, N. B. (2005). Web-based digital teaching portfolios: Fostering reflection and technology competence in preservice teacher education students. *Journal of Technology and Teacher Education, 13,* 373–396.

Verkler, K. W. (2000). Let's reflect: The professional portfolio as a prerequisite for internship. *Action in Teacher Education, 22,* 116–121.

# CHAPTER *Nine*

## *Evaluating Your Initial Teaching Experiences*

**OBJECTIVES**

After reading this chapter, the reader will be able to:

- discuss the importance of beginning teachers' first-year experiences or college students' student teaching experiences, especially with recent emphasis on highly qualified teachers;
- discuss the importance of field or practicum experiences or student teaching on retaining good teachers;
- identify parts of the observation process used to view teachers in action in their classrooms;
- identify common objectives listed on tools used for evaluation of teachers' portfolios.

**INTRODUCTION**

This chapter provides a discussion of student teaching or beginning teaching experiences and the issues involved in observation and evaluation. A discussion of how observations are conducted in teachers' classrooms is provided. In addition, a discussion of the supervisor's written evaluation of beginning teachers is included. Examples of templates frequently used to evaluate and observe teachers in action are provided for preview. Advice also is given concerning the evaluation of teachers' initial teaching portfolios.

### *My Classroom*

Ms. Peattie is excited yet worried about her first observation as a teacher. Her supervisor is planning on visiting her class during her social studies period after lunch today. She sent the lesson plan to her supervisor yesterday, but is worried that the class might be somewhat crazier given the weather—it was forecasted to snow this afternoon. Most of the students are hoping for an early dismissal. In addition, she is nervous about her supervisor sitting in the back of the room. Ms. Peattie feels that she has over-planned, and is sure she has enough material. It will be interesting!

**FOCUS QUESTIONS**

1. What does the research say about the value of student teaching and field experiences in terms of retaining beginning teachers?
2. What are the parts of the observation process?
3. How do supervisors and mentors differ in their observations and guidance?
4. How are teaching portfolios evaluated?

## *EXPERIENCING THE FIRST YEARS OF TEACHING*

Learning to teach is complex. How does a teacher make all the daily decisions needed to be effective in the classroom? It is a daunting task for beginning special education teachers to work successfully in increasingly diverse and inclusive school settings. In addition, "a growing body of evidence suggests the teachers who lack adequate initial preparation are more likely to leave the profession" (Darling-Hammond, 2003a, p. 9). The student teaching experience, in particular, may influence a teacher's decision to remain in the field (Conderman, Morin, & Stephens, 2005). A National Center for Education Statistics report found that 29% of new teachers who had not had any student teaching experience left within 5 years compared with only 15% of those who had done student teaching as part of a teacher education program (Henke, Chen, Geis & Knepper, 2000).

The National Commission on Teaching and America's Future (2003) suggests that beginning teachers who receive training in curriculum, instruction, and child psychology; complete student teaching; and receive feedback on their teaching do not leave the profession at rates as high as those who do not have such experiences. The more preparation beginning teachers receive, the more likely they are to remain in the profession (Darling-Hammond, 2003a).

Student teaching experiences for traditionally trained teachers usually occur during their last semester of course work and may involve a 16-week full-time teaching opportunity. During the 16 weeks of teaching, student teachers learn to take full control of a classroom, put together a portfolio, and are observed frequently by their university supervisors. After completing such training successfully, they often seek employment in a school setting similar to their student teaching experience. Student teachers in traditional training programs are encouraged to work collaboratively with their peers to share what they learned and to reflect together on what makes for excellence in teaching (Pelletier, 2004). Many teachers rate student teaching as the most valuable experience of their preparation (Guyton & McIntyre, 1990).

In contrast, alternatively licensed special education teachers, after initially choosing another career path, enter the classroom after completing only a few education courses. They begin teaching while concurrently taking the remaining courses needed for their professional license. They may complete a supervised teaching experience during their last semester of course work, or they may complete the licensure course work with little supervision and feedback. If they are supervised, it is during this supervised experience that they are observed and evaluated formally by both university and school district supervisors. Often the alternatively licensed teachers are organized by university programs in cohorts for support, yet some have fulfilled the licensure requirements with little peer support (deBettencourt & Howard, 2004).

Both traditionally trained and alternatively licensed teachers need to learn to balance theory and practice. During their initial years of teaching, they need to learn to link what they gathered from their teacher preparation courses to their own practical classroom activities. For example, many teacher education courses introduce the theories of collaboration and inclusion. But beginning teachers need to know how to plan a lesson with a more experienced co-teacher using cooperative learning groups ensuring that all the students remain on task. Given the diversity of inclusive classes, the teacher also needs to make sure that students with disabilities are not overwhelmed by the tasks or that gifted students do not go unchallenged. It may take years to learn how to balance theory and practice effectively such that all students gain from each instructional lesson.

## GUIDING AND EVALUATING NEW TEACHERS

Guiding and evaluating teachers during their first years of teaching is critical. Such guidance is an integral part of many teacher education programs (Zeichner, 1996). Yet many first-year teachers are given few directions and feel they are lucky to stay one step ahead of their students. Zeichner (1996) referred to this approach as the "sink or swim" apprenticeship model. Willard-Holt and Bottomly (2000) suggest that, for guided experiences to have the greatest positive impact on teachers, the connection between education course work and classroom experience must be made explicit to the teachers. It is also critical that such connections be made during the first years of teaching careers. Many believe that quality teaching is directly related to the preparation teachers have received and the support they have found during their first years in the field (O'Shea, Hammitte, Mainzer, & Crutchfield, 2000). Carefully designed teaching experiences that allow new teachers to integrate information they acquired during their training will allow for more competency in beginning teachers than experiences that do not have this integration (Brownell, Ross, Colon, & McCallum, 2005).

All teachers are evaluated by others, and the measures chosen for evaluation are critical. Any measure of observing or evaluating the quality of beginning teachers must account for their abilities to (a) teach students with drastically different needs, (b) provide differentiated instruction across different content areas, and (c) engage in different collaborative roles to interact with students, administrators, and parents. Evaluation of teachers once they are hired by a school district is often infrequent, and when completed the methods used provide limited guidance. Many school districts are hesitant to lose needed special education teachers even if they are not the most effective. In addition, the time and the methods needed to assist new teachers in the field of special education are not always available to school district supervisors.

Beginning in 2000, colleges of education accredited by the National Council for Accreditation of Teacher Education had to provide multiple samples of reliable and valid evidence that their teacher candidates had mastery of content knowledge in their respective fields, that they had pedagogical knowledge, and that they illustrated positive effects of instruction on their students' learning. Teacher training programs are expected to set benchmarks for acceptable teacher performance (Roberson, Woolsey, Seabrooks, & Williams, 2004). Many colleges of education use student teaching for the assessment of teaching performance.

Once teachers are hired, they may be observed in their classrooms during their first year. These observations and the feedback given to teachers afterward are critical. Observing teachers while they are in their classrooms is especially critical in this age of highly qualified teachers. Highly qualified teachers must have content knowledge in the area they are responsible for as well as the pedagogical skills. See Table 9-1 for recent criteria discussed at the state level for a highly qualified teacher.

Classroom observations, whether completed during teachers' student teaching experiences or during their first years of teaching, must be coordinated with all involved, including beginning teachers, cooperating teacher-mentors, and university or administrative supervisors. The following section discusses how teachers are observed in action—both why it is important and what steps should be taken to make it beneficial for all.

## PREPARING FOR SUPERVISION AND OBSERVATION

Supervised teaching experiences provide many opportunities for you as a beginning teacher and for your mentors and supervisors to develop relationships that allow for the development of risk taking and exploration on your part.

*TABLE 9-1*   *Defining a Highly Qualified Teacher*

Highly qualified beginning teachers should be able to do the following:

1. Possess a deep knowledge of the core academic subjects they teach
2. Evidence a firm understanding of how students learn
3. Demonstrate the teaching skills necessary to help all students achieve to high standards
4. Create a positive learning environment and use a variety of assessment strategies to diagnose and respond to individual learning needs
5. Integrate modern technology into the curriculum to support student learning
6. Collaborate with colleagues, parents, community members, and other educators
7. Reflect on ones practices to improve teaching and student learning
8. Pursue professional growth in both content and pedagogy
9. Instill a passion for learning in students

*Source:* From National Commission on Teaching and America's Future (2003, p. 73). *No Dream Denied: A Pledge to America's Children.* Washington, DC: Author.

Everyone involved wants you to succeed. The experiences are the heart of any beginning teacher process and must assist you in your understanding of the complex conditions of schools and children. Supervisors tend to give different types of feedback to you than your mentors. Mentors tend to give specific advice about what will work in the immediate situation, while supervisors suggest more generic advice, including many alternatives that may or may not fit with the students you are working with. It is critical that you use both types of observations to benefit your growth as a teacher. See Box 9-1 for ideas on how to benefit from being observed.

Being observed is never easy, even after you have been teaching many years, but for a beginning teacher it can be even more difficult. At least four types of observation opportunities exist: (a) classroom observations by university supervisors (e.g., during your student teaching); (b) pre- and post-individual conferences with your university supervisor; (c) classroom observations by your mentor or administrative supervisor (during your first years of teaching); and (d) formal or informal conferences with your mentor or administrator. In some school districts, a surprise observation by your principal or assistant principal may also occur. Your principal or assistant principal may in some cases also serve as your immediate supervisor. Yet in some school districts, the immediate supervisor may be your department chair. See Box 9-2 for tips on how to prepare for an observation.

Your cooperating teacher should serve as a vital partner, role model, and mentor in your teaching experience (Conderman et al., 2005). Yet cooperating

---

*BOX 9-1*   *How to Benefit from Your Observation Experiences*

- Talk to student teachers who have just completed the experience and review their tips.
- Take some time to think about why you want to become a teacher.
- Free up your schedule and allow for some downtime.
- Take care of yourself to avoid the typical stresses of student teaching.
- Follow advice of cooperating teacher and university supervisor.
- Get regular exercise and sleep during your student teaching.

- Network and connect with colleagues—use them as support.
- Connect with professional resources—use them for guidance.
- Connect with resources in your school district, such as mentors and free classes or workshops—use them as support.
- Keep your humor—remember that not every observation will go smoothly.
- Your students will react to the observer, so prepare them for the visit.

---

**BOX 9-2**   *How to Prepare for Being Observed as a Beginning Teacher*

---

Think about how you like to receive feedback and note that you may not always receive it that way. Remind yourself not to be defensive! Supervisors want you to be the best possible teacher.

**Prior to Observation**

Prepare lesson—review how you will engage and assess the students' learning.

Ask your cooperating teacher for any last-minute advice.

Discuss how you will be observed.

Be prepared to be nervous or a little anxious—it is normal.

Remember that the observer is there to provide feedback.

**During the Observation**

Don't perform the lesson as theater—keep to your agenda without "grandstanding."

Focus on the students in your class—keep them on task.

Try to ignore the observer—your students will follow your lead.

Don't include the observer in the lesson by eliciting help from them.

**After the Observation**

Discuss how your expectations for the lesson compare to the reality of what occurred.

Discuss the information your supervisor collected.

Listen carefully and be willing to take advice.

Take notes

Ask questions to clarify what was said.

Repeat back what the supervisor said to get verification.

Set goals for next observation.

---

teachers are often chosen because they volunteer rather than being representative of the attitudes or beliefs or best practices associated with effective teacher education (Renzaglia, Hutchins, & Lee, 1997). In addition, many cooperating teachers have not received training in mentoring and are often very busy with other tasks. A number of studies have found that well-designed mentoring programs raise retention rates for beginning teachers by improving their attitudes, feelings of efficacy, and instructional skills (Darling-Hammond, 2003a). Mentoring programs will produce positive benefits only if they are well designed, supported, and attended. Mentors should be given release time by their school district and should be trained in positive and constructive mentoring procedures. Research suggests that the state induction programs that are tied to high-quality preparation hire beginning teachers and provide them with mentors who have received training in the state's teaching standards and its portfolio assessment system (Darling-Hammond, 2003b). It is hoped that you will be assigned a mentor who has been trained in special education and has the time to assist you. If not, check with your supervisor to determine if other special educators are available whom you can ask for support.

In any situation, a quality observation should consist of three parts: (a) a preobservation conference, (b) the observation itself, and (c) a postobservation conference. In pre- and postobservation conferences, you have the opportunity to explain your instructional decisions in light of your grasp of the subject matter, the principles of learning and teaching, and the individual backgrounds of your students (Sindelar, Daunic, & Rennells, 2004).

The preobservation conference may take place in person or by e-mail or phone. The purpose of the preconference is threefold: (a) to set dates and times for the observation and postobservation conference, (b) to determine where the observer is to sit in your class, and (c) to provide the lesson plan for the class that is to be observed. You and the observer may want to discuss prior to the observation one or two skills that the observer will watch for in the lesson and what kind of data they will be collecting. The observation itself should be done with as little interruption to the normal classroom routine as possible. Examples of templates that are often used by supervisors while observing a new teacher are given in Table 9-2. Ask your supervisor for a blank template prior to your observation.

Classroom observations are usually guided by the following questions:

1. How do you manage the classroom?
2. Which instructional strategies do you use during the lesson?
3. How do you have the classroom environment organized?
4. How is your lesson planned in terms of the larger curriculum unit or standards of learning?
5. How do you assess the learning of your students?
6. How do your students react to the lesson?

The postobservation conference should occur as soon after the observation as possible and often begins with the observer asking you, "What did you think? How did your feel the lesson went?" Through the conversation that ensues, you should be encouraged to articulate your intended goals, reflect on the design and implementation of your lesson, and consider the ways in which the lesson was successful and/or unsuccessful. If you cannot meet immediately after the observed class, you should ask to schedule a meeting for later the same day. Supervisors may often facilitate the process by posing a series of probing questions designed to scaffold your self-critique (Freidus, 2002). Ideally, your supervisor begins with something positive and then mentions the areas that need improvement and ends with another positive insight. In addition, you and your supervisor should set goals for the next observation.

In most situations, the two primary topics covered by supervisors and beginning teachers in the postobservation sessions are curriculum or instruction methods and classroom management techniques. In the former, supervisors may share materials and help teachers develop structured and innovative lesson plans. In the latter alternative, management techniques may be suggested. Although developing dynamic lesson plans and basic classroom management skills are important components of a beginning teacher's experiences, emotional support plays a key role for beginning teachers. Ideally, your supervisor and mentor have set a routine for meeting regularly with you to discuss how you are doing emotionally.

It is always a good idea to take notes during your meetings with your supervisors. At the conclusion of the meetings, review your notes together so that both of you are in agreement on what areas need improvement and what areas seem strong. If at a later date either of you disagrees about the areas of concern, you can refer back to your notes and discuss the issues again. In addition, it is always a good idea to keep any written observation notes in the same file as the notes taken at the meetings. By keeping everything together, you can use the file for support and for encouragement as you note the changes in your growth as a teacher.

You should also consider finding time to observe other teachers in your school to collect different ideas. Teachers benefit greatly from observing other teachers both in their schools and outside their schools. If you do not know how to find the time, check with your principal.

## PREPARING A TEACHING PORTFOLIO AS AN EVALUATION COMPONENT

In addition to being observed, a teacher is often asked to put together a teaching portfolio as part of his or her initial teaching evaluation. Teaching portfolios are required also as part of the process of becoming certified by the National Board. A teaching portfolio is a collection of sample work products that best represent the teacher's efforts. (See Chapter 8 for more details on preparing your teaching portfolio.) Campbell, Cignetti, Melenyzer, Nettles, and Wyman

*TABLE 9-2* Observation Template

Teacher: _____    Observer: _____    Date: _____    Time: _____    No. of students: _____

- ❑ Has all materials ready
- ❑ Conducts beginning review
- ❑ Provides guided practice

- ❑ Provides an advanced organizer
- ❑ Assesses background knowledge
- ❑ Provides for independent practice

- ❑ Begins instruction promptly
- ❑ Models instruction
- ❑ Conducts ending review (closure)

- ❑ Introduces future lessons

| Teacher Behaviors | Frequency | Frequency | Teacher Behaviors |
|---|---|---|---|
| Gains student attention | | | Does not gain student attention; continues during student talk |
| Asks factual questions, one at a time | | | Asks multiple questions as one |
| Asks questions requiring reasoning skills | | | Asks nonacademic questions |
| Recognizes student responses | | | Ignores students; misses student responses |
| Probes students for answers; provides scaffolding | | | Doesn't follow through on an incorrect student response |
| Gives specific academic praise; amplifies answers | | | Gives nonspecific academic praise |
| | | | Fails to praise |
| Expresses enthusiasm; shows interest (smiles and gestures) | | | Uses loud, monotone, or inaudible talk; is unenthusiastic |
| Orients students to academic task; refocuses unrelated talk | | | Allows unrelated talk or activity |
| Enforces classroom rules; reminds students of rules | | | Does not enforce classroom rules |
| Is consistent with consequences (follows through) | | | Misses opportunity to apply consequences |
| Gives specific directive (e.g., "Read page 4") | | | Asks student to do task (e.g., "Would you . . .") |
| Uses surface management techniques (proximity, redirect, "the look," calling student's name, and stating expected behavior) | | | Is punitive; uses sarcasm or harsh tones |
| | | | Allows misconduct to continue |
| Gives specific behavior praise | | | Does not give specific behavior praise |
| Circulates | | | Does not circulate |
| Other: | | | Other: |

(1997) state that a portfolio is an organized, goal-driven collection of evidence. For teachers, portfolios have become more common over the past 5 years. Portfolio building involves a process as much as a product since work samples should be collected and reviewed in a systematic way. The sampling can be completed across time to demonstrate professional development and can be used as a self-reflection device for formulating and monitoring future professional goals. As such, the process of creating and maintaining a teaching portfolio can play an important role in the initial years of teaching and may be more significant than the portfolio product itself (see Figure 9-1).

As many colleges are using portfolios to document teachers' content knowledge, teaching abilities, and reflective skills, it is critical for teachers to understand what evaluation procedures will be used to determine successful completion. Research on assessing portfolios is largely devoid of information detailing effective ways of examining the portfolio (Valencia, 1990). Prus and Johnson (1996) suggest that teachers submit portfolios as part of a course requirement, especially at the conclusion of a program, and have more than one rater for each portfolio.

Many supervisors provide descriptions of the necessary components of the portfolio and use a rubric to evaluate their teachers' portfolios. The most frequently used types of rubrics are the holistic and the analytical. The holistic rubric usually has competency labels associated with it (e.g., skillful, promising, and ineffective). Only one score is given. The analytical rubric usually uses the same set of competency labels for each category but is applied across different headings (e.g., instruction, motivation, and professional growth), and a rating is given for each heading (Linn & Gronlund, 1995). The holistic rubric tends to be used to assess portfolios completed as part of a licensing process. The analytical rubric often is used in providing diagnostic feedback, as it assesses across individual categories. See Box 9-3 for guidelines on how to prepare for evaluation of your portfolio.

Teachers should be given copies of the rubrics to be used at the beginning of the teaching experience. The example provided in Table 9-3 is a rubric

*FIGURE 9-1*    *The first portfolio.*

"I KEPT SAYING 'MAYBE WE SHOULD CLEAN OFF THE FRONT OF THE REFRIGERATOR'... BUT, NOOOO...."

appropriate for use with an electronic portfolio, and it uses a third column, "Right on Target!" as the standard. If the teacher goes beyond the standard, he or she can earn more points. An example of a blank holistic rubric with space for comments appropriate for a paper portfolio can be found in Table 9-4.

---

**BOX 9-3**  *Preparing for Evaluation of Portfolio*

Many teaching programs require a student teaching portfolio at the end of the experience. Use the following tips to make the task less overwhelming:

Get started early

Review the standards set by the university

Collect evidence (artifacts) throughout the time you are teaching

Document classroom organization (e.g., draw diagrams and take digital pictures)

Take pictures (make sure you have permission if you include your students)

Collect copies of lesson plans, student worksheets, and progress sheets

Keep a daily reflective journal

Complete a final self-assessment, including asking yourself the following: Does this portfolio represent my growth as a teacher? What do I like about my portfolio? What is missing? Ask a peer to review and give suggestions.

---

**TABLE 9-3**  *Electronic Portfolio Scoring Rubric*

|  | **Missed the Mark!** **(5 points)** | **Getting Close!** **(10 points)** | **Right On Target!** **(15 points)** | **Bull's Eye!** **(17 points)** |
|---|---|---|---|---|
| Title card | Design is inappropriate. | Design could be neater or might be inappropriate. | Design is attractive and colorful. | Design is attractive and colorful and shows creativity. |
| Mechanics | Spelling and punctuation errors are distracting. | Spelling and punctuation errors are evident. | Errors in spelling and punctuation are minor and few. | There are *no* errors in spelling or punctuation. |
| Buttons | The student project card contains four or fewer buttons that link to projects. | The student project card contains five or six buttons that link to projects. | The student project card contains seven buttons that link to projects. | The student project card contains eight buttons that link to projects. |
| Sounds | Many sounds are inappropriate and/or distract from the stack. | Some sounds are inappropriate and/or distract from the stack. | Sounds are of high quality and are appropriate. | The sounds enhance the quality of the stack. |
| Content of project reflections | Few reflections include the program used and the main skills learned. | Some reflections include the program used and the main skills learned. | All reflections include the program used and the main skills learned. | All reflections include the program used and a detailed account of all skills learned. |
| Personal reactions to projects | Few reflections include personal reactions. Reactions are vague or repetitive. | Some reflections include personal reactions. Reactions may be vague or repetitive. | Reflections include personal reaction that clearly reflect the student's feelings. | All reflections include personal reactions that are descriptive and insightful. |

*Source:* http://www.essdack.org/port/rubric.html (accessed 6/8/06).

*TABLE 9-4*  *Paper Portfolio Scoring Rubric*

| Standard Evaluated | 1 Missing Materials: Detracts From Overall Presentation | 2 Marginal: Does Not Greatly Add or Detract | 3 Effective: Helps Communicate Message | 4 Great Job! Enhances Information Presented |
|---|---|---|---|---|
| Introduction | | | | |
| Reflective journal | | | | |
| Competency 1: | | | | |
| Competency 2: | | | | |
| Competency 3: | | | | |
| Summary | | | | |
| General appearance | | | | |
| Organization | | | | |
| Reflection quality | | | | |

## EVALUATING TEACHERS: FUTURE ISSUES

Organizations that accredit, approve, or recognize teacher education programs are moving away from detailing field experiences and student teaching requirements (Prater & Sileo, 2004). Many colleges are developing 5-year teacher education programs that allow teachers to earn a bachelor's degree in a liberal arts content area and a master's degree in teaching. By completing a 4-year liberal arts degree in a particular content area (and passing state tests in that area), teachers meet the highly qualified state standards. In the field of special education, the field experience's standards are brief and do not focus on specific hours or weeks (Council for Exceptional Children [CEC], 2003). See Box 9-4 for the CEC's Field Experience Standards.

College supervisors continue to work to identify creative yet rigorous means to effectively evaluate teachers and to help new teachers make the adjustment from inexperienced to experienced teaching. Everyone would agree that meaningful and forthright feedback is critical in preparing quality

---

**BOX 9-4**  *Council for Exceptional Children's Standards on Field Experience*

"Special education candidates progress through a series of developmentally sequenced field experiences for the full range of ages, types and levels of abilities, and collaborative opportunities that are appropriate to the license or roles for which they are preparing. These field experiences are supervised by qualified professionals."

*Source:* From *What every special educator must know: Ethics, standards, and guidelines for special educators* (5th ed.) by The Council for Exceptional Children, p. 123. Copyright © 2003 by The Council for Exceptional Childern. Reprinted with permission.

---

**BOX 9-5** *How to Decide Whether Teaching Is Not for You*

---

If you are not happy in your teaching situation, ask yourself the following:

Do you enjoy the students but not the administration in your school? If so, can you change to another school?

Do you enjoy your professional colleagues but feel you do not have much time with them? Can you structure more time with them outside of school?

Do you work close to your home? If not, can you change to a closer location so that you do not spend as much time commuting?

Is your contract with the school district secure in terms of tenure? If not, what can you do to make it secure (e.g., take more classes)?

---

beginning teachers. Whatever evaluation system is used in your system, it should have clear and consistent expectations. A common concern cited by teachers is the lack of clarity regarding performance expectations.

Teachers need to be prepared to successfully meet the daily challenges they will face (e.g., identifying and implementing instructional accommodation and modification, implementing individualized education programs, and collaborating with parents and other key personnel). In order to meet these challenges, supervisors will need to focus on preparing teachers who are reflective problem solvers (Darling-Hammond, 1998). It is critical to guide teachers in making meaningful connections between the fragmented but critical pieces of course content by self-evaluating their actions and reflecting on the daily challenges that occur. If the student teaching experience is effective and quality feedback is provided, individuals who are not going to be successful as teachers are made aware of their deficiencies and are able to self-reflect on the decision to continue. Learning to teach is complex, and it is not for everyone. If you begin to question whether teaching is for you, look through the ideas in Box 9-5 for guidance prior to making your decision.

Many of us who have been teaching for years will tell you that teaching is the only profession to choose. Keep in mind that teacher preparation must be seen as a career-long continuum of development. Professional development does not end when you receive your basic license in special education. Ongoing professional development is essential for you to remain current in your teaching methods and confident in your teaching abilities. Always remember that teaching is a profession that shapes all other professions. Welcome—we wish you much success!

## SUMMARY

Supervisions and observations are always a part of your initial licensure teaching experiences, and they will continue throughout your professional career. The evaluations given to you should be both formative and summative. This means that you will be coached and supported in mastering the competencies of teaching. No one expects you to be the perfect teacher the first day. Find out early what support services are available to you (e.g., mentors, workshops, cohort support group meetings, friends, beginning teachers, and supervisors) and make use of them. Look on each observation and each visit as a guide in your development as an effective and competent teacher.

## ACTIVITY QUESTIONS

1. Why did your colleagues choose teaching? What are your first memories of thinking about becoming a teacher? Who were the people who affected your decision to become a teacher?

2. What is your mentor's view of the profession of teaching?

3. What are some of the special education buzzwords you need to know? What words do your colleagues think should be on your list?

4. What are three descriptive qualities of the neighborhood near your school? What resources are in your community?

5. How is your teaching improving? What parts do you need to improve on or get help with? Keep your ideas in a daily journal.

6. What are your district's requirements for being highly qualified?

## SELECTED WEBSITES

http://www.nctaf.org/home.php
*The National Commission on Teaching and America's Future is a nonprofit organization dedicated to providing every child with competent, caring, qualified teachers in schools organized for success. This site provides many reports, research, and resource links on teacher quality and improvement.*

http://www.teachers.net
*A great beginning teacher site with lesson plan ideas, teacher chat rooms, and resource links.*

http://electronicportfolios.com/portfolios/howto/ index.html
*How to create your own electronic portfolio by Helen Barrett. This site offers great resources for those working on their teaching portfolios.*

http://www.inspiringteachers.com
*This site provides a Beginning Teachers Tool Box to help empower new teachers. The information on the site supports not only beginning educators but also those training and working with first-time teachers.*

http://www.teachingld.org
*TeachingLD is a service of the Division for Learning Disabilities (DLD) of the Council for Exceptional Children. DLD is the largest international professional organization focused on learning disabilities. The purpose of TeachingLD is to provide trustworthy and up-to-date resources about teaching students with learning disabilities.*

## REFLECTION JOURNAL ACTIVITIES

1. As you prepare to be observed by your supervisor, ask yourself the following questions: How will I sequence the lesson activities and keep the learners engaged? How will I evaluate the success of the lesson? What materials will I need?

2. How did you feel after your first observation? How could you be better prepared in terms of both the lesson preparation and the emotional preparation?

3. Do you need to discuss other issues with your university supervisor other than the teaching that is observed? Do you feel that the development of your portfolio is moving along successfully?

4. Do you feel during your first years of teaching that what is expected of you is clearly explained? Are you evaluated by your supervisors in a way that is beneficial to your daily teaching responsibilities?

## REFERENCES

Adams-Bullock, A., & Hawk, P. P. (2005). *Developing a teaching portfolio: A guide for preservice and practice teachers* (2nd ed.). Upper Saddle River, NJ: Merrill/Prentice Hall.

Brownell, M. T., Ross, D. D., Colon, E. P., & McCallum, C. L. (2005). Critical features of special education teacher preparation: A comparison with general teacher education. *Journal of Special Education, 38,* 242–252.

Campbell, D. M., Cignetti, P. B., Melenyzer, B. J., Nettles, D. H., & Wyman, R. M., Jr. (1997). *How to develop a professional portfolio.* Boston: Allyn & Bacon.

Conderman, G., Morin, J., & Stephens, J. T. (2005). Special education student teaching practices. *Preventing School Failure, 49*(3), 5–10.

Council for Exceptional Children. (2003). *What every special educator must know: Ethics, standards, and guidelines for special educators* (5th ed.). Arlington, VA: Author.

Darling-Hammond, L. (1998). Teacher learning that supports student learning. *Educational Leadership, 55*, 6–11.

Darling-Hammond, L. (2003a). Keeping good teachers—Why it matters, what leaders can do. *Educational Leadership, 60*(8), 6–13.

Darling-Hammond, L. (2003b). Teachers: What leaders can do. *Educational Leadership, 60* (8), 7–13.

deBettencourt, L. U., & Howard, L. (2004). Alternatively licensing career changers to be teachers in the field of special education: Their first-year reflections. *Exceptionality, 12*, 225–238.

Freidus, H. (2002). Teacher education faculty as supervisors/advisors/facilitators: Playing multiple roles in the construction of field work experiences. *Teacher Education Quarterly, 29*, 65–76.

Guyton, E. M., & McIntyre, D. (1990). Student teaching and school experiences. In W. R. Houston (Ed.), *Handbook of research on teacher education* (pp. 514–534). New York: Macmillan.

Henke, R. R., Chen, X., Geis, S., & Knepper, P. (2000). *Progress through the teacher pipeline: 1992–93 college graduates and elementary/secondary school teaching as of 1997* (NCES 2000–152). Washington, DC: National Center for Education Statistics, U.S. Department of Education.

Linn, R. L., & Gronlund, N. E. (1995). *Measurement and assessment in teaching* (7th ed., pp. 249–257). Upper Saddle River, NJ: Merrill/Prentice Hall.

National Commission on Teaching and America's Future (2003). *No dream denied: A pledge to America's children.* Washington, DC: Author.

O'Shea, D., Hammitte, D., Mainzer, R., & Crutchfield, M. (2000). From teacher preparation to continuing professional development. *Teacher Education and Special Education, 17*, 170–180.

Pelletier, C. M. (2004). *Strategies for successful student teaching: A comprehensive guide.* Boston: Allyn & Bacon.

Prater, M. A., & Sileo, T. W. (2004). Fieldwork requirements in special education preparation: A national study. *Teacher Education and Special Education, 27*, 251–263.

Prus, J., & Johnson, R. (1996). *A critical review of student assessment outcomes.* Rock Hill, SC: Winthrop University.

Renzaglia, A., Hutchins, M., & Lee, S. (1997). The impact of teacher education on the beliefs, attitudes, and dispositions of preservice special educators. *Teacher Education and Special Education, 20*, 360–377.

Roberson, L., Woolsey, M. L., Seabrooks, J., & Williams, G. (2004). An ecobehavioral assessment of the teaching behaviors of teacher candidates during their special education internship experiences. *Teacher Education and Special Education, 27*, 264–275.

Sindelar, P. T., Daunic, A., & Rennells, M. S. (2004). Comparisons of traditionally and alternatively trained teachers. *Exceptionality, 12*, 209–223.

Valencia, S. (1990). A portfolio approach to classroom reading assessment: The whys, whats, and hows. *Reading Teacher, 43*, 338–340.

Willard-Holt, C., & Bottomly, D. (2000). Reflectivity and effectiveness of preservice teachers in a unique field experience. *Action in Teacher Education, 22*, 76–88.

Zeichner, K. (1996). Designing educative practicum experiences for prospective teachers. In K. Zeichner, S. Melnick, & M. L. Gomez (Eds.), *Currents of reform in preservice teacher education* (pp. 215–234). New York: Teachers College Press.

# SELECTED RESOURCES FOR BEGINNING TEACHERS

Burnette, J., & Peters-Johnson, C. (Eds.). (2004). *Thriving as a special educator: Balancing your practices and ideals.* Arlington, VA: Council for Exceptional Children.

*Cohen, M. K.*, Gale, M., & Meyer, J. M. (2004). Survival guide for first year special educator (Rev. ed.). Arlington, VA: Council for Exceptional Children.

Dover, W. (2000). *The classroom teacher's guide to working with paraeducators.* Port Chester, NY: National Professional Resources, Inc.

French, N.K. (2003). *Managing paraeducators in your school: How to hire, train, and supervise non-certified staff.* Thousand Oaks, CA: Corwin Press.

Murray, B. P. (2002). *The new teacher's complete sourcebook.* New York, NY: Scholastic Inc.

Rosenblum-Lowden, R. (2000). *You have to go to school. You're the teacher!: 250 classroom management strategies to make your job easier and more fun* (2nd ed.). Thousand Oaks, CA: Corwin Press.

Palmer, P. (1997). The *Courage to teach.* CA: Jossey-Bass, Inc.

Pelletier, C.M. (2004). *Strategies for successful student teaching: A comprehensive guide* (2nd ed.). Boston, MA: Allyn and Bacon.

Pullen, P. (2004). *Brighter beginnings for teachers.* Lanham, MD: Scarecrow Education.

Thompson, J.G. (2002). *First-year teacher's survival kit: Ready-to-use strategies, tools, and activities for meeting the challenges of each school day.* San Francisco, CA: John Willey & Sons.

Wiggins, G. & McTighe, J. (1998). *Understanding by design.* Alexandria, VA: Association for Supervision and Curriculum Development.

Wong, H. K., & Wong, R. T. (2001). *The first days of school: How to be an effective teacher* (Rev. ed.). H. K. Wong Publications.

# INDEX